The

PECULIAR CASE

of the

ELECTRIC CONSTABLE

The

PECULIAR CASE

of the

ELECTRIC CONSTABLE

A TRUE TALE OF PASSION, POISON & PURSUIT

Carol Baxter

ONEWORLD

A Oneworld Book

First published by Oneworld Publications 2013
Copyright © Carol Baxter 2013

ISBN: 978-1-78074-243-4
Ebook ISBN: 978-1-78074-244-1

Cover design by nathanburtondesign.com
Printed and bound by Page Bros Ltd.

Oneworld Publications
10 Bloomsbury Street, London WC1B 3SR

Stay up to date with the latest books,
special offers, and exclusive content from
Oneworld with our monthly newsletter

Sign up on our website
www.oneworld-publications.com

Really, sir, you cannot be serious in proposing to stop the escape of a thief or swindler by so small an electric spark acting on a needle. If you had talked of sending a thunderbolt or flash of lightning after him, I might have thought there was some feasibility in it.

Sceptic to would-be electric telegraph inventor
Edward Davy, 1830s, quoted in J.J. Fahie's *A
History of Electric Telegraphy* (1884)

CONTENTS

PROLOGUE

Of all the physical agents discovered by modern scientific research, the most fertile in its subserviency to the arts of life is incontestably electricity, and of all the applications of this subtle agent, that which is transcendently the most admirable in its effects, the most astonishing in its results, and the most important in its influence upon the social relations of mankind and upon the spread of civilisation and the diffusion of knowledge, is the Electric Telegraph.

Dr Lardner,
The Electric Telegraph (1867)

EVERY NIGHT, as the clock strikes midnight, a new date emerges from the wings, initially blind to the events that will transpire as the next twenty-four hours unfold, the events that will mark its place in history. Most days pass by unnoticed or are soon forgotten – in a particular locality, at least. Yet pluck any date from the historical calendar and somewhere on the world's stage something momentous happened. Perhaps it had long been marked for glory. Perhaps it exploded cataclysmically into view. Often, though, while seeming inconsequential at the time, its importance is recognised only when history's binoculars are refocused on that particular stage.

Tuesday, 25 July 1837 was a date that Britain's Professor Charles Wheatstone was hoping would in time be celebrated in the history books. It was late in the evening when he entered the carriage shed at Euston Station, the terminus of the London and Birmingham Railway then under construction. Hammering had ceased in time for the station's ceremonious opening five days earlier, an occasion already marked for posterity. Yet, despite the current lack of ceremony and the dingy surroundings, Wheatstone believed that this date would be of far greater importance – if all went according to plan.

Small and slight, curly-headed, bespectacled and excruciatingly shy: the mould of the eccentric scientist might have been fashioned with Wheatstone in mind. He had long been fascinated by the workings of musical instruments and by acoustics, optics and electricity, and his inquisitive mind had led him to experiment with the possibilities of a communication system driven by electricity – a so-called 'electric telegraph'.

By the flickering light of a tallow candle, Wheatstone could see his recently patented electric telegraph machine squatting on the table in front of him. The model had a simple four-needle display that allowed only twelve letters to be indicated. Its 'clock face' was a diamond-shaped grid, with lines heading north-east and north-west from each of the four needle bases that were positioned across a central horizontal axis. When two needles were simultaneously tilted towards each other at a forty-five degree angle from the vertical, they pointed along these lines towards a junction at which a letter was inscribed. To each needle was attached a single wire along which the electric current would pass. The wires trailed from the machine and became part of a thirteen-mile circuit wrapped around a frame sitting in the carriage shed, before heading out the door and disappearing into the shadows.

Wheatstone made a last-minute check – all the wires were securely fastened to needles, all the needles moving freely – like a teacher anxious for his prize student to shine. He then lifted his hands to the machine's controls and deflected the two needles that would signal the first letter. Obligingly, the machine began transmitting his message.

A mile-and-a-half away in the winding-engine house at Camden Town sat his partner, William Fothergill Cooke, facing an identical instrument. An impecunious ex-military officer, Cooke was desperate to make money – lots of money – and had seen the commercial potential of an electric telegraph machine. Energetic and resourceful, he had the personality necessary to attract business but lacked the scientific know-how to construct a telegraph efficient enough to appeal to customers. He had approached the celebrated Professor Wheatstone for assistance.

Cooke's passion and practicality galvanised Wheatstone. Although foresighted enough to have taken out patents for some of his inventions, Wheatstone had always prided himself on being a man of science rather than an entrepreneur – until this visionary Gilbert encountered his pragmatic Sullivan. The pair imagined wires crisscrossing the countryside, with vast distances conquered in a fraction of a second but, thus far, the electric telegraph had been dismissed as just another 'newfangled thing'. Cooke, however, had identified an ideal customer for their instrument: the railways. Not only would the telegraph allow speedy inter-station communication, it could be constructed to run beside the railway tracks – an exquisitely efficient coupling.

The railways were suffering their own teething problems. Railway mania had gripped the nation after the Liverpool and Manchester line opened in 1830, but serious safety issues had yet to be resolved. A speeding train had little warning of trouble ahead. Departures were scheduled using a simple time-interval system. Train drivers had to rely upon vigilance and the occasional railway policeman stationed along the route to run the tracks safely. Even greater vigilance was required when both the up-and-down trains used a single, meandering track. In darkness, storms or fog, the lack of an adequate warning system had proved deadly.

It was a business problem in need of an enterprising solution and Wheatstone and Cooke were keen to display their system. Cooke was not alone when he waited at Camden Town on the evening of 25 July. The Railway's chief engineers, Robert 'the Rocket' Stephenson and Charles Fox, were standing by his side. Stephenson was the son of George Stephenson, also known as the Father of the Railways, while Charles Fox would go on to construct the majestic Crystal Palace. They were accustomed to scrutinising rough prototypes and seeing the future in all its glory.

All of a sudden, two of the needles on Cooke's machine clicked and tilted. A message was coming through. Cooke read out the letter and an assistant jotted it down. Again the needles clicked and tilted, and again. When the message was completed, Cooke clicked out a reply which travelled back along the nineteen miles of wires to Euston where Wheatstone was awaiting his response.

Stephenson was delighted. 'Bravo!' he cried. 'Bravo!' He asked Cooke to send his message of exaltation down the wires – not once but twice. Backwards and forwards the messages zipped until Stephenson asked Cooke to invite his partner to join them at Camden Town.

'I will do myself the honor,' Wheatstone messaged back. Later he would write: 'Never did I feel such a tumultuous sensation before as when all alone in the still room I heard the needles click. As I spelled the words I felt all the magnitude of the invention now proved to be practicable beyond cavil or dispute.'

The world's first patented electric telegraph machine had just passed its first long-distance test. Not only had Wheatstone and Cooke proved that words could be communicated along a nineteen-mile stretch of wire at astounding speed, they had harnessed as their energy source the power of 'God's lightning', as 'electricity' was known in their day. In doing so, they had also proved that electricity could be mobilised at will and had a practical, commercial use. It was an historic moment.

But these four men were ahead of their time. Convincing the remaining London and Birmingham Railway directors would not prove so easy – indeed, the wires would later be abandoned because the directors deemed the system a flight of fancy and too costly to install across the entire network. Convincing the public would prove even harder. Until one fateful day seven-and-a-half years later ...

⁓

A steam-driven passenger train? An electric telegraph? Spare a moment to reflect upon these wonders of human achievement. With blithe smugness, we tend to dismiss the feats of the past. What's a track-hugging steam train when spacecraft blast through the universe? What's a mile-long stretch of telegraph wires when radio waves whisper to a billion computers around the globe and beyond?

Yet it wasn't so long ago that trains and telegraphs were themselves merely the dreams of glazed-eyed seers and woolly bearded prophets, as unrealistic as discovering the elixir of life. Of course, humans have long employed transportation of one form or another, and communication systems beyond the spoken word: drums that hypnotically enticed men into battle, fire and smoke signals that heralded danger, flashing shields and mirrors, coloured flags, simple pieces of inscribed parchment carried by the fleet of foot or by messengers on horseback. For millennia, however, little changed. No new pathways were forged.

The first inkling of progress came in the 1740s when, among others, the French *abbé* Jean-Antoine Nollet tested a recent invention known as the Leyden jar – a primitive condenser that stored static electricity, the type of electricity generated by scuffing feet along carpet. After positioning two hundred Carthusian monks in a huge circle and threading a mile-long piece of iron-wire between their outstretched hands, he discharged his Leyden jar into one end of the wire. As the monks grunted and jerked, their neat circle disintegrating, he proved that electricity could travel almost instantly along a lengthy wire. In 1753 a writer to the *Scots Magazine* proposed a communication system powered by such static electricity. Later that century, the French Chappe brothers built an experimental apparatus but found static electricity too volatile: like a deadly snake it was difficult to control and, when released, discharged its fury in one explosive surge. Instead, they introduced the word *telegraphe* or 'distant writer' into the lexicon through their invention of a semaphore – an optical telegraph. In a short while, it was adopted by British and European military forces, however, it too had significant limitations, particularly in darkness and inclement weather.

The problems inherent in the use of static electricity were solved around the turn of the century when Alessandro Volta invented the voltaic cell battery (similar to batteries still used today), which provided steady and controllable low voltage currents of electricity. In the decades that followed, scientists learnt more about electricity and then electro-magnetism. Each discovery pushed science along the inexorable path towards the invention of a practical and commercial use for electricity: an 'electric telegraph'.

With communication still limited by transportation systems, terrain, visibility and the weather, life had continued to amble along as it had for millennia. News travelled slowly; decisions were made leisurely. Patience was not only a virtue but a necessity. Then, in the 1830s, the world began beating to a different, faster drum.

Initially, the quickening was infinitesimally slow, frustratingly slow for those who foresaw social metamorphosis. Yet none could have imagined that the unexpected events of one day would prove pivotal in a paradigm shift, and that these events would kick-start what we now call the Communication Revolution.

The

PECULIAR CASE

of the

ELECTRIC CONSTABLE

Part 1

ALARM

Such a machine reveals a new power, whose stupendous effects upon society no effort of the most vigorous imagination can anticipate.

The Times
(25 November 1837)

Chapter 1

*A display of brilliant electric experiments ... never fails
to afford ample gratification.*

William Sturgeon,
Lectures on Electricity (1842)

PADDINGTON STATION was the usual whirl of noise and
activity on New Year's Day 1845 as travellers prepared to board
the Great Western Railway's steam trains, the iron horses that
thundered across the countryside westward to Bristol. Bells
pealed, passengers scrambled into carriages, porters stuffed cases
into luggage vans, doors clanged, flags flapped, the locomotive
chugged slowly from the station, the visitors hastened from
the platform, and for a moment, too short a moment, there
was blessed silence ... until it all began again – just another
day in one of London's modern transportation hubs, the vast
cathedrals paying homage to the newly exalted gods of science
and industry.

Perched atop the carriage sheds a short distance from the
busy passenger platforms were the railway offices, their doors
slammed shut against the insidious soot and distant noise. The
first door at the top of the stairs opened into the humble abode
of Thomas Home. It was a room bereft of the usual green-
visored clerks scratching away at ledgers or corpulent directors
breezing charm and schemes. Instead, Home stood in front of
a peculiar wire-trailing contraption, peering intently at some

dials. It was his job to monitor this clock-like object which had a face unlike anything most people had seen.

Thomas Home wasn't employed by the Great Western Railway although he practically lived at Paddington Station. Chest puffing with pride, the young entrepreneur would announce to anyone who asked – and those who didn't – that he was licensee of the world's first commercial electric telegraph, a new technology that allowed instantaneous communication across great distances. Admittedly, such communication was limited by the availability of the machines and their connecting wires. His own operation had only two machines: the one he manned at Paddington Station and another manned by his brother Richard at Slough Station, eighteen miles away. The machines themselves were connected by wires strung alongside the tracks of the Great Western Railway. Messages were infrequent; nevertheless, it was their job to be ready when they did come through – even on New Year's Day.

As the clock ticked off the evening's hours, the peal of the telegraph's alarm sounded. He signalled back that he was ready then picked up a pencil and began to jot down the letters.

'A murder has just been committed …'

In the now-eerie quietness, he read over the words. The needles kept lurching, one way then another. His brain decoded the letters while one hand flicked the necessary acknowledgements to the sender and the other raced across the page forming the new words.

'… at Salt Hill …'

The village of Salt Hill lay about a mile west of the railway station at Slough and was policed by the local parish constabulary. Why was he being informed?

'… and the suspected murderer was seen to take a first-class ticket for London by the train which left Slough at 7.42 p.m. …'

Murder?

Of course, Home had communicated important messages in the past. He had manned the Paddington office for twenty-three interminable days and nights prior to the birth of a royal prince at Windsor Castle five months previously – 'a prisoner during Her Majesty's pleasure,' he would later quip. He had even passed on a police message: that London's notorious pickpocket, Fiddler Dick, and his cohorts were on the train to Slough intending to ply their trade at the annual Montem Day celebrations held by exclusive Eton College. He relished the gleeful response: 'Several of the suspected persons are lurking about Slough uttering bitter invectives against the telegraph.' As a stepping stone in these communication streams, he felt strangely connected to the events and individuals, and rather proud and important – a pleasant change to the tedium of the daily message exchange. But to communicate information about a murder? Now that was disturbing, almost as if he carried the power of life and death in his own hands.

Like Professor Charles Wheatstone and William Fothergill Cooke, the inventors of his machine, Home had long realised that the electric telegraph's ability to send rapid messages could offer unprecedented power to those who used it and boundless wealth to those who controlled it. Unfortunately, the world at large hadn't quite grasped the electric telegraph's importance. Or forked out the money to use it. To most people, it was little more than an amusing novelty – like watching circus magicians pluck pigeons from hats! True, during his one-and-a-half-year tenure as licensee, he had promoted the telegraph's attractions as if they were worth seeing as well as using: eye-catching posters plastered to the walls of Great Western Railway stations and in the windows of tradesmen's shops; bold advertisements in London's newspapers. He'd even financed a regiment of sandwich men whose billboard-bedecked forms trudged London's streets thrusting leaflets into the hands of passers-by. For the 'low' cost of a shilling, the leaflets grandly proclaimed, they could visit the telegraph office at Paddington and see the amazing electric telegraph in action.

The curious had come knocking. He would take them outside and point up to the wires stretching into the distance, the arteries channelling the lifeblood of this new species of communication. Then he would usher them into his office and bustle over to a bench-mounted machine, about the size of a small china cabinet. Flexing his hands slightly – an artist about to paint, a surgeon to operate – he would grab hold of the two handles and twist his wrists, showing how the left handle deflected the left needle and the right handle the right needle, and that moving the two handles produced coded letters that formed words and sentences, even paragraphs.

He would then flip the butterfly switch on the side of the instrument, changing it from telegraph to alarm, and turn one of the handles. This alerted his brother at the Slough office that a message was about to zip down the wires. When a shrill ring erupted from his own machine a moment later, he would explain to his startled guests that the alarm was meant to wake a deeply slumbering operator – although, in this instance, it was signalling Slough's readiness to receive London's message. He would flip the switch back to telegraph mode. Glancing at the words on the page in front of him, he would begin twisting the handles. Eighteen miles away at Slough, a needle would tilt and a letter form. Communication was under way.

Some found the concept confusing. One man complained that his message mustn't have been sent because the telegraph operator was still holding the piece of paper. A woman grumbled because her bowl of special soup couldn't be sent down the wires to her sick friend.

Most of his visitors were intrigued. He'd had many proud moments as he explained its workings to inquisitive European kings and princes and to pompous British dukes and parliamentarians. The shillings had trickled in, but they were not enough, not when he was paying £170 annually for the licence to operate the telegraph. Another £170 would soon be due – a hefty investment that hadn't yet made his fortune. It would need more than the birth of a Royal babe or a few felons warned off by the Peelers before the world would truly appreciate the value of his wondrous machine. These 'singing wires' were not just a siren's lure but the future whispering its secrets. What would it take to convince everyone of its worth?

He and his governors had overcome many challenges in the seven years since the directors of the London and Birmingham Railway had spurned their system. Ever the entrepreneur, Cooke had not only approached Stephenson and Fox, he had also met with Isambard Kingdom Brunel, Chief Engineer of the Great Western Railway. At a Directors' Board Meeting, Cooke extolled the virtues of the electric telegraph, explaining how the manager of the Paddington office would be 'like a spider, live along the line'. While some of the directors laughed at the simile, the Napoleon of Engineers applauded. Brunel agreed to trial an electric telegraph along the thirteen miles of track between Paddington and West Drayton stations.

Cooke and his team of workmen pushed the insulated rope of copper wires through small-bore iron pipes and secured them to rails sitting six inches above the ground, parallel to the railway tracks. When the line was activated in July 1839, it became the world's first operational electric telegraph – God's lightning permanently tapped and now in the hands of mere mortals.

While the railway authorities found it useful, its short distance limited its potential. Gradually, as the rubber insulation decayed and the wires shorted, the telegraph stopped working. The costs outweighed the benefits of fixing it.

In 1842, Cooke suggested extending the telegraph line to Slough, five miles further along the track from West Drayton, as Slough was a more commercially viable location because of its proximity to Windsor Castle. The Great Western Railway directors were reluctant to agree until Cooke offered to take responsibility for the telegraph's operations: he would carry railway messages for free and charge a fee to the public. Cooke reduced costs by replacing the old system with a two-needle cipher-based instrument. He pushed galvanised iron wires through glazed pottery insulators and suspended them from iron posts rammed into the ground alongside the railway tracks. He also built a telegraph cottage on a mound near the almost-completed Slough railway station. The new Paddington-to-Slough electric telegraph commenced operations in May 1843, with Thomas Home as licensee.

Although the partners had installed telegraphs along other railway lines in the intervening years, most were signalling systems that rang a warning bell or used a small vocabulary of codes; they were unable to communicate random messages. The government had at last recognised the benefits of a 'speaking' electric telegraph for military purposes and in August 1844, in partnership with the London and South Western Railway Company, contracted Cooke and Wheatstone to string a private telegraph line from the Admiralty Office in Whitehall to the naval headquarters in Portsmouth. The pair were also promoting and patenting the electric telegraph in Europe and planning to test a submarine cable in Swansea Bay, Wales.

Over in America, their arch rival, Samuel Morse, had constructed an experimental telegraph line between Washington, DC, and Baltimore. He successfully sent his first message – 'What God hath wrought' – in May 1844, and other messages on special occasions in the months that followed. Many would later honour Morse as the Father of the Electric Telegraph, conveniently ignoring the fact that Wheatstone and Cooke had the first electric telegraph patent as well as years of commercial operations before Morse's evocative yet tardy message was sent. When the new year dawned on 1 January 1845, the eighteen-mile stretch between Paddington and Slough still remained the world's only 'speaking' electric telegraph in regular use, the only 'wires' that at a moment's notice were capable of sending a detailed message of warning that could outpace a train and outrace a fugitive.

Thomas Home glanced at a nearby clock. The second hand jerked inexorably onwards. The telegraph message had said that the murder suspect's train left Slough at 7.42 p.m. It would reach Paddington in less than half an hour.

The message hadn't finished. '… He is in the garb of a kwaker,' it continued, the left needle moving once to the right to indicate that the word was completed.

Home hesitated then flicked the left needle twice to the right, twice to the left. 'No,' he was telling his brother in Slough. 'I don't understand the word.'

'k-w-a-k-e-r,' his brother signalled back.

'Kwaker?' Home mouthed. Of course. The two-needle telegraph didn't include all twenty-six letters of the English alphabet, and contained no code for the letter 'q' despite the fact that their ruler was a queen. His brother was reporting that the suspect was dressed in the distinctive, old-fashioned attire of the supremely respectable and conservative Quaker religious movement. Home deflected the needle twice to the left, twice to the right to acknowledge that he understood. The needles continued to click as more details came through.

⌐◦

Home dashed out of his room and into the office of Deputy Superintendent De May, the man in charge of Paddington railway station that evening. De May read Home's scrawl then sent for Sergeant William Williams of the Great Western Railway Police.

The 7.42 from Slough was due at 8.20. They had little time. They had to make plans. The message didn't order them to apprehend the 'kwaker'. That was understandable. The man was not suspected of committing a crime against railway staff or passengers. Nor had the message been dispatched by the Slough police, as far as they could tell. It simply alerted them to a suspect's presence in the train's first-class compartments and provided a description to help identify him. So that's what they would do.

Still, they mustn't risk alarming the man by showing their interest. De May and Williams were familiar faces at the railway station, and Williams was dressed in the Great Western Railway Police uniform: trousers, boots, dress coat and varnished leather top-hat modelled on the outfit worn by the London Metropolitan Police. If they were seen hovering around the first-class carriages, the suspect might notice and bolt. Thomas Home, however, was largely unknown, as he spent most of his working day closeted in his office above the carriage sheds. He would serve as lookout.

The three men hastened to the platform where a familiar rumble alerted them to the imminent arrival of the up-train from Bristol. The superintendent and sergeant found a protected spot near the station entrance. The first-class carriages were tucked behind the engine so these choice customers had the shortest distance to walk along the platform and under the arches to reach the horse and carriage-filled square. There would be little time to find their man before he blended in with the crowds entering and exiting the station. Thomas Home eased his way through the eager throng to stand right beside the tracks. The train chugged into the station and, with a final demonic scream, ground to a halt.

Home had worked at the station long enough to know the drill. The Great Western Railways' large, lofty first-class carriages were designed to resemble stagecoach compartments in order to ease the adoption of railway travel. Each carriage contained a set of isolated compartments, with two rows of seats that faced each other and doors granting its inhabitants immediate access to the platform. Home walked towards the last compartment of the second first-class carriage, where the suspect was reportedly ensconced, and opened the door as though he were an usher. Would the suspect still be on the train? There were three stations between Slough and Paddington. If the man had alighted at any of those stations …

And disturbing his concentration was the biggest question of all. What dreadful happenings at Slough had prompted the telegraph message to be sent in the first place?

CHAPTER 2

The life of the dead is placed in the memory of the living.

Marcus Tulius Cicero,
Philippica IX

THE LONG straggling town of Slough had once been a hamlet far from the madding crowd – indeed, containing the very churchyard that had inspired Thomas Gray's 'Elegy', or so some declared. It couldn't escape the crowds, however, when it became a staging post on the route between London and the fashionable watering hole of Bath. Eighty stagecoaches had barrelled into town every day, with horns blaring and horses foaming. Each had stopped at one of the many inns fronting the main road where weary passengers could alight for refreshments and ostlers change the spent teams.

As the railways began to replace the stagecoaches, a new breed of person stepped from the cheaper carriages at Slough – and onto the railway tracks themselves for a time as the town lacked a station for the first few years of operations. When the Great Western Railway Bill had come before Parliament, the headmaster of Eton College had wielded his money-backed power to prevent a station from being erected at Slough, arguing that it would interfere with the boys' 'discipline' (trains being more exciting than lessons). The railway authorities managed to evade the letter of this law – signalling issues invariably held up trains as they passed through the town – though it was years before the Etonians accepted that they should abandon the battle in favour of modernity. A proper station opened in 1843, around the time that the electric telegraph office was constructed.

A mile or so west of the station lay the village of Salt Hill, where the reported death had just occurred. Any stranger wishing to visit Salt Hill could read in Robson's *Commercial Directory* of its exquisite surroundings and numerous coaching inns, among them the charming and commodious Windmill and the less salubrious Three Tuns. Salt Hill's public houses had thrived until the iron horses outpaced their four-legged rivals. Although many travellers remained wary of these new beasts and preferred the old ways, their numbers were dwindling. Salt Hill was a place uncertain of its future, yet it remained friendly, one might even say happy, and not the sort of place where serious crimes were perpetrated. Pickpocketing, burglary, shoplifting, highway robbery, drunkenness, pranks by the Eton schoolboys – undoubtedly. But murder?

The report of a suspicious death in their sleepy neighbourhood had roused the local police. The Slough officers dispatched a message to Constable Thomas Hollman of Farnham Royal, the parish in which the death had occurred. He was ordered to take charge of the body and question any witnesses.

Hollman made his way along Bath Road to Bath Place, a recently built row of four terraces, each with two bedrooms upstairs and a living room and kitchen downstairs. There he found Mrs Mary Ann Ashlee in the second cottage from the east. He asked her what had happened.

~

Mrs Ashlee had been working at the table in her sitting room, a candle carefully positioned in front of her to illuminate her work area. Sewing, knitting, darning: she always had chores to do. A retired couple needed to stretch every penny, especially in the hard days of winter. The crackling fire nearby helped to soothe her usual daily anxieties, but something else was niggling at her.

A grumble of voices penetrated the thin wall separating her own cottage from that of her neighbour, Sarah Hart. Sarah was a lovely person, kind and pretty, a modestly dressed, respectable woman with a quiet, unassuming nature who was well-liked in their small community. And her young children: what a delight! The girl, Sarah, was little more than a toddler. Her older brother, Alfred, was small for his age but fine-looking and intelligent, quiet and well behaved. Their mother was teaching them well, instructing them in general knowledge as well as manners and religious observances. The boy scrupulously said his prayers morning and night as well as grace before and after his meals. He was a credit to his devoted mother, and a worthy son who would make any father proud.

But Alfred's father was overseas and had not seen what a fine boy his namesake was growing up to be. 'My husband, Alfred Hart, has gone abroad for five years,' Sarah had explained when she moved into the cottage some eighteen months before. She also mentioned that she had once lived in service with the family who employed him and that her old Quaker master, Mr Talbot, would regularly visit to deliver her allowance – as proved to be the case. Yet Mrs Ashlee had noticed that occasionally, confusingly, Sarah and her children would refer to the old gentleman as 'Mr Tall' – when he wasn't tall at all.

The rumble of voices continued. Mrs Ashlee knew that Sarah had a visitor. She had seen him arrive around 5 p.m. His long brown coat and broad-brimmed hat announced his Quaker affiliation. It must be Sarah's old master bringing the money from her husband. Sarah had mentioned him just that afternoon when Mrs Ashlee dropped in for a chat. Arms deep in the washing, Sarah had said that he was expected to visit that week and would bring her quarter's allowance.

Mrs Ashlee knew it would be a welcome relief. Sarah had mentioned money worries of late, and that the old gentleman had been niggardly with her allowance. The bills were piling up. The previous quarter's rent was unpaid, the next now overdue. 'I have been advised to put the children out to be taken care of,' Sarah mentioned fretfully. She didn't say if the suggestion had come from the old gentleman himself, merely that money was always discussed these days when he called.

The two women had talked companionably for about twenty minutes, the remarks about the Quaker gentleman gliding into a discussion of religion. Sarah was not overtly religious but she opened up for a moment, offering an insight into her spirituality. 'If I join any sect,' she told her neighbour, 'it should be that of the Quakers.'

Although the Quaker gentleman was a regular visitor, Mrs Ashlee had not been officially introduced. She had often heard Sarah talking to him, though. The thin walls allowed few secrets. Not the words, of course, just the murmur of a man's deeper voice mingling with Sarah's brighter timbre. The thin walls did allow some secrets.

This was different, however. Not an argument exactly, just Sarah's voice talking loudly, nearing but not reaching hysteria. Yet Sarah wasn't one for passionate remonstrances. What could be going on? The back and forth continued for a short time, then childish piping tones and feet clumping up the stairs hinted at bedtime. Silence followed.

Mrs Ashlee continued to work quietly, her thoughts drifting onto other subjects. Presently, a murmur surfaced from next door, the background hum she'd grown used to.

Then an eerie howl pierced the walls – a moan, or perhaps a stifled scream. She tried to ignore it, to allow her good neighbour some privacy. The cry came again and again, hauntingly, pleadingly. She could ignore it no longer.

Lifting the candle, she moved to her front door and opened it, peering out into the evening gloom. The air was still. Her candle flickered only slightly as she headed towards her front gate, a dozen or so paces down her path. The moans continued, louder perhaps. They were definitely coming from Sarah's house.

A door closed. She turned and looked towards Sarah's front door. She saw a man hurrying down Sarah's front path, a mere six or seven yards away.

'What is the matter with Mrs Hart?' she called to him. 'I am afraid she is ill!'

The man didn't reply. He didn't even turn towards her. It was as if he hadn't heard her. Yet it was a still night and she had spoken loudly – at least loudly enough for him to hear. She said nothing more, just continued along her own path as he hastened along his parallel course.

Reaching her wicket gate, she opened it and advanced towards Sarah's gate. The man was standing on the other side, fumbling with the latch. She lifted her candle over the gate to see why the latch wouldn't open. Then she glanced up. The soft light from her candle illuminated his features and clothes, the distinctive long brown coat and broad-brimmed hat. It was the Quaker gentleman who had arrived earlier. He was agitated, his trembling hands unable to unfasten the latch.

'There's a little button, sir,' she said to him. 'Allow me to open it.'

He didn't reply. He merely stared at her. Then the moans breached the night again.

She dropped her gaze to the latch and twisted her fingers, opening the gate. The man pushed through without thanking her, then crossed to the other side of the road and began walking towards Slough.

She hurried down Sarah's path. Reaching the front door, she glanced back towards the road. In the faint evening luminescence – or perhaps the glow of her own imagination – she saw the man turn and glare at her. With a shiver of fright, she opened the door and slipped through, locking it firmly behind her.

~

Sarah was sprawled on her back with her head near the door and her legs towards the fire. Her cap lay about a foot away and a tangle of unruly hair framed her face. Her gown was ripped, its left sleeve drooping. Her skirts and petticoats were tossed above her knees, exposing her stockinged legs. One stocking was torn and had slipped down almost to her ankle, while her left shoe lay discarded on the floor nearby. 'Oh! Oh! Oh!' she continued to moan.

Mrs Ashlee dropped down beside her and looked into her eyes. Sarah's gaze was fixed and unseeing and her lips weren't moving. The cries weren't really words, just strange noises expelled with each panting breath. Grasping Sarah's hands, she cried, 'Oh Mrs Hart, what is the matter?' There was no verbal reply – just the slightest of squeezes on her hand, not enough to be certain if she had felt it at all. She cradled Sarah's head and raised it from the floor. Froth seeped from her mouth. Whatever dreadful thing had happened, she knew that Sarah was extremely ill, probably dying.

Easing Sarah's head down to the rug, she picked up her candle and headed out the back door – as was their custom. She sped down the longer back path and through the gate, then continued past the empty cottage on Sarah's left until she reached the back gate of the westernmost cottage. Opening the gate, she ran up to the back door of their landlady Mrs Wjverd. She pounded on the door and cried out for help.

Mrs Wjverd's widowed daughter, Margaret Jane Burrett, raced back with her. Sarah was still alive but a haunting vision. Little Alfred and Sarah remained upstairs, asleep.

The women pulled a cushion from one of the children's chairs and gently placed it under Sarah's head. Mrs Ashlee bathed her face and temples with vinegar and cold water. Mrs Burrett went into the kitchen and brought out a large yellow jug of water. She set it on the table in front of the middling fire. Several other items were present. An open and partly empty black porter bottle with a Guinness label stood on the table between two glass tumblers. The tumbler near the chair closest to the kitchen – the visitor's chair – was half-filled with a liquid that appeared to be porter diluted with water. An empty tumbler and a partly eaten piece of plum cake were sitting near Sarah's usual chair, not far from her body. Her tumbler appeared to have contained porter, but only a trace of froth remained at the bottom. A similar puddle of froth had been spilled on the table.

Mrs Burrett picked up Sarah's empty glass and poured in some water, swishing it around before tossing the frothy mixture into the fireplace. Then she filled it again with clean water. Mrs Ashlee understood her intention and lifted Sarah's head so that Mrs Burrett could tip some water into her mouth. The water dribbled from her lips along with some more foam, similar to the patch on the table.

'She cannot swallow!' cried Mrs Ashlee. 'Don't give her any more! It will choke her.'

The pragmatic Mrs Burrett instead threw the water in Sarah's face. It failed to revive her.

'Send one of your apprentices for the doctor,' Mrs Ashlee urged. She knew that Sarah usually tried to manage without the surgeon's services because she could not afford them. This time, however, it was clear that his services were needed, desperately – and possibly for the last time.

Chapter 3

Is there anything of which one can say, 'Look! This is something new?'

Ecclesiastes 1:10

THE REVEREND Edward Thomas Champnes and his surgeon cousin Henry Montague Champnes were enjoying their evening meal when the gate bell rang at about 6.55 p.m. Their living arrangement was felicitous, with one cousin meeting the community's physical needs, the other its spiritual. Experience had taught that urgent door-bell peals generally indicated a need for medical rather than religious services, so Surgeon Champnes rose and went to the door.

A young woman was standing on the doorstep. 'Will you come immediately?' she begged. 'A woman has fallen down in a fit.'

'Where is she?' he demanded.

'In Bath Place. I am afraid she is dying.'

The twenty-six-year-old doctor grabbed his medical bag and ran the two hundred yards to Bath Place. Mrs Ashlee had been watching out for him and let him in. He found Mrs Hart lying flat on her back, her arms by her sides, her head upon a pillow. He noticed that her clothing was in disarray and a stocking torn. Worryingly, her eyes were fixed and unseeing.

Kneeling beside her, he picked up her wrist and felt for her pulse. Was that a beat? Another? No – nothing more. Then her tongue and jaw moved slightly, just the once, seemingly in the final death throes. He slipped his hand inside her bodice but couldn't feel a heartbeat. 'She is dead,' he announced.

He decided to bleed her, so he asked Mrs Ashlee to find a basin. He didn't expect to bring her back to life; he just hoped that the state of her blood might suggest a cause of death. Mrs Ashlee brought a basin from the kitchen and held it beneath the woman's right wrist. He nicked a vein. About an ounce of blood poured out. Its free-flowing nature suggested that the woman was still alive, yet he was sure there was no heartbeat and that Mrs Hart was dead. Looking closely at the blood, he noticed nothing else unusual – no strange colour or odour. He was none the wiser as to the woman's cause of death.

Mrs Burrett had just returned to the cottage so he asked her to send another messenger to his house, this time to inform his cousin of Mrs Hart's death. The vicar arrived a few minutes later. As they all stood looking down at her body, the surgeon reported that he thought her death seemed suspicious. The ugly word 'murder' hovered in the air … unspoken, but silently acknowledged.

Then Mrs Ashlee told them what she had seen.

~

The Quaker's strange departure from Mrs Hart's house added to their concerns about the scene that lay before them. Reverend Champnes offered a suggestion. He could go to Slough station to see if the Quaker gentleman was waiting for the next London train. Even if the man hadn't caused Mrs Hart's death, he was still a critical witness. And while the man had a head start, more than twenty minutes, he was travelling by foot in the dark. With the grace of the good Lord, they might be able to find him before a train carried him into oblivion.

Reverend Champnes ran back to his house and harnessed his pony-trap, then steered it onto the road and turned towards Slough. He urged his pony faster. As they galloped along the road, he peered from side to side. There were few people about on this cold winter's evening, and none wore the distinctive habiliments of the Quakers.

Arriving at the station, he hopped down and tied his reins to a post. He hurried inside and stared around the waiting rooms. No sign of the Quaker. He asked about the up-trains and learnt that the next train to London left at 7.42 p.m. That meant he had twenty minutes or so to spare. It was only a mile back to Bath Place. He would return there and consult with his cousin.

⁓

Although Reverend Champnes had missed seeing the Quaker, others had noticed him. Salt Hill's post-boy, George Lewis, was standing in the doorway of the Windmill Inn around 7 p.m. when he spotted a man jogging towards Slough. In the light of the house lamp, Lewis recognised the runner's attire. 'How are you, sir?' he called out, having frequently encountered the Quaker during the man's journeys from Slough station to Bath Place and back.

The man turned his head, allowing Lewis to see his face clearly. It was the Quaker gentleman to be sure. Yet he made no reply. Perhaps he was puffed and in too much of a hurry. But the station was only a quarter of a mile away and the next train to London didn't leave for some time. It was a bitterly cold night – maybe he was running to keep warm.

⁓

Robert Roberts, the owner of Eton's George Inn, was on the last leg of his journey home. Having spent the day in London, he had caught the 6.30 p.m. down-train which had arrived at Slough Station just a few minutes earlier. After exiting the station, he had climbed into Mr Dyson's Windsor omnibus and was patiently waiting for it to depart when he saw a man approach the driver.

'Are you going to Eton?' the man asked.

Receiving an affirmative reply, the man climbed into the omnibus and sat down beside Roberts. The man appeared to be a Quaker.

The driver called out, 'Where shall I put you down, sir?'

'At the house where Sir John Herschel lived,' the Quaker replied. Herschel was a world-famous astronomer – as was his father William, who had discovered the planet Uranus in 1781 – and their Slough home had been a tourist attraction for fifty years until Sir John dismantled his father's iconic 'forty-foot telescope' in 1840.

'But that is a long way this side of Eton, sir,' said the surprised driver.

'Ay, so it is, friend, but that's where I want to be set down.'

As the innkeeper and Quaker sat quietly, without speaking, the omnibus travelled along the Bath Road towards Bath Place. Before reaching the cottages, however, the driver steered left into Windsor Road. He drove for a further two hundred yards, then stopped.

A railway guard heading home to Eton was standing on the omnibus's back step acting as conductor. He shone his lamp into the carriage and called out, 'Is there anyone here for Herschel House?' No one answered. He called out again and flashed his light around the carriage.

The Quaker started. 'I get down here,' he said. He climbed out and paid the guard his fare, then stood there uncertainly.

'That is Herschel House, sir,' the guard told him, and motioned towards the nearby building.

Roberts saw the Quaker take a couple of tentative steps towards Herschel House, then the driver cracked his whip and the omnibus trundled off. The man was soon lost to sight. A moment later, they passed another omnibus travelling towards Slough. It carried passengers to catch the 7.42 train to London.

$\backsim$

Ephraim Weymouth was standing on the steps of Herschel House as the Windsor omnibus approached. The London plasterer was visiting the butler there and had just rung the doorbell when the omnibus driver eased his horses to a halt. As Weymouth idly watched, he heard the conductor calling out to the passengers once … twice … before flashing his light into the carriage. Then he saw a man dressed in a long coat climb through the door and step down from the omnibus.

Weymouth rang the doorbell again and looked back at the omnibus passenger. The man did not move. Weymouth rang the bell a third time, then saw the man turn and follow the omnibus towards Eton. A moment later, he disappeared into the darkness.

$\backsim$

Back at Bath Place, Surgeon Champnes was looking around Mrs Hart's front room, trying to ascertain what might have killed her. He guessed it was poison, perhaps administered in a liquid. The Guinness bottle was partly filled with a brown liquid, while a nearby tumbler contained a paler fluid – more the colour of ale. The relics of a bun were suspect too. Picking up these items, he carried them over to the fireplace and placed them in an adjacent recess. 'Let no one touch them,' he ordered Mrs Ashlee.

Outside, Reverend Champnes was slowing his pony-trap. He called out that he hadn't seen the Quaker, but they had enough time to get back to the station before the London train departed. Could the surgeon join him?

As the cousins drove off towards Slough, the two women began searching the house. They had been instructed to look for a phial or medicine bottle. Nothing obvious caught their eye. Mrs Ashlee noticed the froth on the table and leant over to smell it but couldn't detect any particular odour.

With their search a failure, Mrs Burrett headed to one of Sarah's cupboards and pulled out a black portfolio, mentioning that Sarah had advised her to look there for an address if it ever proved necessary. The two women turned over the sheets of paper. They could find no address for Sarah's husband nor her Quaker visitor, only that of a London friend, one Mrs Moss.

Nor could they find any sign of Sarah's quarterly allowance, the reason for the Quaker's visit that day. The only money in the house was a shilling, a sixpence, two pennies, three ha'pennies and a miserable farthing. No wonder Sarah was distressed about money.

The children had remained asleep throughout the moaning and ensuing disturbances. It was time to remove them in case they ventured downstairs and stumbled across their mother's body. Mrs Ashlee nudged them awake and led them out the back door and through the back gardens to her own cottage. As she tucked them into bed, she asked little Alfred if the Quaker gentlemen had given his mother any money.

He had seen no money, the boy told her, but he had heard his mother say to the old man, 'You are a very naughty man, and very cruel.' The man had replied, 'I will never come to visit you again.'

The Champnes cousins leapt from the pony-trap and raced into the station. The 7.42 train to London was due to depart in a few minutes. They quickly found Superintendent Henry Howell and explained the situation. Howell said that a Quaker had just asked him the way to the train.

The three men searched among the people thronging the platform: the whiskered gentlemen in 'chimney pot' hats and dress coats and their bell-skirted ladies; the scruffy labourers and neat maid-servants. They couldn't see the suspect. Their hunt became increasingly frantic as a whistle pierced the hullaballoo. 'Stand back! Stand back!' it demanded. 'The train is about to depart!'

Then they spotted the Quaker. He was outside the waiting room. He crossed the platform and climbed into one of the first-class carriages. For a moment, they simply stood there, watching. 'From his manner,' murmured Reverend Champnes, 'I do not think he could be a guilty man.'

Of course, the man of the cloth's concerns weren't prompted by the suspect's manner but by his clothing, and what it signified. A Quaker committing murder? It was unprecedented. The Quakers were peacemakers, opposed to war, to slavery, to executions, even to field sports and hunts. Their very garb served as a testament to their values and virtues. Could this man have committed a murder? Or was it all a horrible mistake?

As the three men dithered, the train snorted and glided from the station. The murder suspect was gone.

They watched the departing train, aghast. They had no idea who he was. Mrs Ashlee had called him Mr Talbot, or something like that, but she had also said that she knew nothing else about him. Just because he came on the London train didn't mean that he lived there; London was the nexus for trains coming from every corner of the country. How would anyone find him again? As they watched the train pick up speed, their eyes were drawn to the posts running alongside the tracks and to the wires suspended between them. The electric telegraph!

The men hurried through the station exit and headed west towards the telegraph house, which was perched on the summit of a man-made mound near the railway bridge. They burst in on the telegraph operator to explain their idea. There they drafted their message:

> *A murder has just been committed at Salt Hill, and the suspected murderer was seen to take a first-class ticket for London by the train which left Slough at 7h. 42m. p.m. He is in the garb of a kwaker with a brown great coat on which reaches nearly down to his feet. He is in the last compartment of the second first-class carriage.*

They handed the text to Richard Home, who switched the telegraph to alarm mode to alert his brother in London of an incoming message. Then he deflected the needles, forming one letter at a time.

Half an hour had passed since the message had been telegraphed to Paddington. During that time, the Champnes cousins had reported the suspected murder to the Slough police, then returned to the telegraph office to await a reply. The train was due to arrive in London at 8.20 p.m. They should hear something soon afterwards.

Every so often, the railway superintendent would break the tense silence by stating where the train would be: West

Drayton ... Southall ... Hanwell ... There was always the chance that the suspect would alight at one of these stops. If he did, they would lose him, since only the stations at Slough and Paddington had electric telegraph machines.

The minute hand inched to 8.25, then to 8.26.

Chapter 4

Steam bears him off more rapidly than the winds of heaven; but the electric current is his pursuer.

Pictorial Times
(11 January 1845)

❧

AT PADDINGTON, Thomas Home stood on the platform next to the first-class compartment. The passengers inside were gathering their handbags and hat-boxes, umbrellas and newspapers. Which one was he after? He looked away, attempting to mimic the blank face of an invisible factotum. Then he surreptitiously peeked into the carriage again. That's when he saw it: the distinctive flat hat bobbing towards him. A moment later, a man dressed as a Quaker stepped through the carriage door.

He was a slender, middle-aged man of smallish stature dressed neatly and expensively in the Quaker 'uniform' of dark trousers, long dark coat and broad-brimmed hat. Pale-faced and whiskerless, he had an intelligent countenance and the mien of sober respectability that typified members of his sect. With umbrella in hand, he passed within inches of Home and headed off towards the platform exit without turning back.

Home hurried over to the railway officers. Deputy Superintendent De May and Sergeant Williams had stepped from their nook and were watching the suspect walk away. 'It's a mare's nest,' muttered De May as Home reached him. 'He has no more committed murder than you.'

The men hesitated, unsure what to do. Their eyes followed the suspect as he made his way across the station. Perhaps it would be best if they didn't lose sight of him. De May grabbed a coat and handed it to Williams, who pulled it over his Great Western Railway livery and hurried after the Quaker, through the exit and out into the square. De May and Home followed at a discreet distance. There, the usual cacophony of London street noises greeted them, punctuated by the shouts of omnibus conductors announcing their routes. Passengers' cries for assistance were followed by resounding thumps as heavy trunks were tossed on top of carriages.

'Princes Street and the Bank,' called one omnibus conductor from his elevated perch on the back step of a carriage. The Quaker walked towards the Princes Street omnibus and spoke to the conductor, who opened the back door allowing him to step inside.

Sergeant Williams bounded towards the omnibus, beckoning to the conductor who came to meet him. They spoke for a moment. Instead of returning to his previous vantage point, the conductor walked to the front of the carriage and climbed up beside the driver, while Williams took the conductor's place on the back step. Moments later, the omnibus lurched off, heading towards Edgware Road and the city.

The superintendent and telegraph operator stood in Paddington Square and watched the omnibus until it passed out of their sight. It was time to return to the telegraph office. They needed to draft a message for the authorities at Slough.

~

A trill rent the silence, startling the waiting men. A message was coming down the wires from Paddington. Richard Home picked up his pencil:

> *The up-train has arrived; and a person answering*
> *in every respect the description given by telegraph*
> *came out of the compartment mentioned. I pointed*
> *the man out to Sergeant Williams. The man got*
> *into a New-road omnibus, and Sergeant Williams*
> *into the same.*

With a last awed look at the newfangled instrument, the railway superintendent, the vicar and the surgeon left the telegraph office. There was no point in lingering. It might be hours before any further news came through. Superintendent Howell resumed his duties at Slough station, while the Champnes climbed into their pony-trap and took the dark road back to Salt Hill.

~~~~~~

For three-quarters of an hour, the omnibus followed the same routine. The driver pulled on his reins, the carriage slowed and stopped, the conductor cried out the location and Williams opened the back door to allow passengers to alight. He could see the Quaker sitting on one of the benches running along the side of the carriage, but the man seemed unaware of the eyes watching him.

Around 9.15 p.m., the driver again called 'Whoa!' and the conductor announced that they had reached the Princes Street junction. This time the Quaker made a move. He pushed past knees and bags then stepped through the open rear door. As he did so, Williams swung the lantern towards him, trying to get a clear view of his face for identification purposes. He noticed with surprise that the man had a cast in his left eye, that his pupil drifted towards his nose. The telegraph message had not mentioned such a distinctive feature.

The Quaker handed over his sixpence fare then stepped down onto Princes Street. London's financial centre was quiet by this time of night. Most of the self-important gentlemen were gone, although some weary stragglers could still be seen, coats clutched around them as they hurried home after a trying day. The bawdy street sellers had also disappeared, replaced by night-dwellers who had seeped from the city's pores as the sun faded.

As the Quaker headed towards the statue of the Duke of Wellington in front of the Royal Exchange, Williams handed the sixpence to the conductor and quietly advised that he could resume his duties. He then slipped into the shadows and watched as the Quaker stopped near the statue and glanced up at the bronze figure of the duke on horseback, erected only the previous year. The man looked around cautiously, then crossed over to Cornhill and walked east, pausing at number fifteen, the famed dining house and confectioners known as Birch's. But he didn't open the door.

Williams ducked behind Wellington's statue, keeping himself out of the suspect's view. In the light of London's plentiful gas lamps, he could clearly see the Quaker, so there was a danger that the man might see his pursuer if he glanced over his shoulder. The suspect began walking again, beside Cornhill's elegant frontages as he headed further east. Williams kept to the shadows as the man turned right into Birchin Lane. Peering around the corner, Williams saw that the man had stopped at the first premises on the right and was rapping on the door. As it opened, light and an enticing aroma of coffee and spices spilled out. The Quaker had called at the Jerusalem Coffee House – though it was closed for the evening.

A conversation ensued. The man in the coffee-house doorway stepped back for a moment then reappeared with a greatcoat and parcel, which he handed to the Quaker. The

Quaker gave him his umbrella in exchange, then turned to leave. Williams withdrew into an alcove, careful to keep out of sight in case the suspect retraced his footsteps. Some lengthy seconds later, having heard no footsteps, he peeped out. The Quaker had vanished.

Frantically, Sergeant Williams looked right and left, then raced down Birchin Lane towards Lombard Street. The man might have entered one of the houses bordering the lane. He might have turned into an alley or court and entered a house there, or passed through to a nearby street. Wherever he had gone, Williams knew that his chances of finding the man again were slim.

Then he spotted the Quaker's distinctive form turning left into Lombard Street. He hurried after him. They walked east along Lombard Street then turned right into Gracechurch Street, a busier area populated by many Quakers because of their importance in the financial industry. He hoped he would not lose his Quaker among others dressed similarly.

The Quaker continued south towards London Bridge – a still-busier area. Williams and his prey joined the richly decorated carriages with paired horses and liveried footmen, the elongated omnibuses and sprightly gigs, the trotting horse-riders and trudging pedestrians, the wheel-barrow and pram pushers, the cows and pigs and other livestock, all travelling from the city proper to Southwark via a bridge that had neither lanes nor even an unwritten rule as to which side of the road to travel upon. Although navigating through the crowd was a nightmare, the thoroughfare's busyness allowed the sergeant to close in on the suspect.

Reaching the south bank of the Thames, the pair traipsed down Wellington Street (now part of Borough High Street) until the Quaker veered towards a door. From the number of

people entering and exiting the building, as well as the intoxicating aroma, it was evidently another coffee house – this time
one that was open.

Williams ducked into another alcove and waited. Five minutes passed ... ten. He crept over and read the sign – the Leopard
Coffee House – then returned to his hiding place. Fifteen minutes ... twenty ... Eventually, the door opened and the Quaker
came out.

They began retracing their steps, crossing over London
Bridge again. This time, instead of returning north along
Gracechurch Street, the suspect turned west into Cannon Street.
As he tramped down the road, he reached into his pocket and
pulled out a piece of paper, stopping under a gas-lamp to read
it. Before long, he turned left into Bush Lane then right into
Scott's Yard and knocked on a door. When it was unbolted, he
stepped through.

Williams stole over to read the sign. The Quaker had entered
an accommodation house situated at 7 Scott's Yard. The sergeant found another suitable vantage point and settled there
to watch. Three-quarters of an hour passed, and the suspect
didn't reappear. He must have settled in for the night. Williams
decided to return to Paddington Station to report his evening's
perambulations and provide a physical description of the man
along with details of his current location. Perhaps, in the intervening period, Superintendent De May had received orders to
apprehend the Quaker and charge him with murder.

Yet, considering the man's religious affiliation and his innocent behaviour in the hours in which he had been unwittingly
pursued, it seemed more likely that the telegraph's finger had
pointed towards the wrong man.

Chapter 5

Always suspect everybody!

Charles Dickens,
The Old Curiosity Shop (1841)

SURGEON CHAMPNES returned to Bath Place around 9 p.m. to continue his investigation. Kneeling beside Sarah's corpse, he sniffed at her gaping mouth. Nothing. No offensive odour, anyway. He examined her face but couldn't see any foam around her mouth. In fact, he couldn't see anything that was unexpected or noteworthy. He collected the beer bottle, tumblers and bun from the recess and told Mrs Ashlee that he was taking them home and would lock them in his cellaret. They would need to be tested for poison.

A short time later, the parish constable, Thomas Hollman, arrived at Bath Place and announced that he was taking charge of the corpse and the premises. He then asked Mrs Ashlee to describe the events of the evening. After she had finished, she handed over Sarah's portfolio, explaining, as Mrs Burrett had done earlier, that he should contact the person listed inside.

Hollman immediately wrote to Mrs Moss. Gingerly, he began his letter by mentioning that her friend was very ill. He ended with the details of her death and a request that she come to Salt Hill the following day to attend an inquest. The constable knew she would receive the shocking news that same evening or early the following morning, in time for her to catch a train to Slough. London received ten mail deliveries per day so, even without the services of an electric telegraph, some news travelled surprisingly swiftly.

Constable William Hill of Slough appeared at Bath Place around 10 p.m. He had seen the Quaker gentleman at Slough Station earlier that evening. After being informed of Mrs Hart's suspicious death, he had decided to conduct his own investigation. If the woman had been poisoned, he might be able to find a bottle or other receptacle that had contained the toxin.

Slowly he moved from one room to another until he had searched the entire house. It didn't take long. The cottage was not only small, it was simply furnished – decently furnished – and was extremely clean and tidy, a lovely home for Mrs Hart and her young children. Like Surgeon Champnes, he couldn't see anything obviously suspicious, although he did find a small phial tucked away in a cupboard. A large plum cake, presumably the source of the partly eaten bun that the doctor had collected from the table, was stored nearby. He also counted nine or ten apples in a box that appeared once to have been full.

Scanning the front room again, he tried to think how a murderer might act. Table … chairs … shelves … the fireplace! A murderer might toss a bottle into the fire hoping the heat would melt it. Grabbing the poker, he prodded the wood and embers until the fire went out, then he raked through the cinders. Again, nothing.

~

As the news swept through the community, shock and sadness followed – then outrage. Everyone knew Sarah Hart. This wasn't a distant happening, faceless and impersonal. This wasn't even a local blackguard long overdue such a reprisal. This was one of their neighbours, one of their friends.

Many had seen the Quaker gentleman walking to or from Slough Station during his regular visits. In the aftermath of Mrs Hart's death, rumours about him spread like wildfire. He had, reportedly, come from London to pay her some money. After taking the receipt, he had barbarously killed her and fled with the cash. The alarm had been raised and the suspect traced to Slough Station where he boarded a train for the city. The electric telegraph had forwarded his details to Paddington Station so he could be captured, but in the confusing aftermath the man had escaped.

~⁓~

Sergeant Williams was frustrated. He faced the predicament all the railway policemen faced: their powers were restricted to their railway company's premises and property.

After returning to Paddington Station the previous evening, he had prepared a report of his activities and forwarded it to Slough. No response came. It was nearing midnight by then, so presumably it was too late to reach the superintendent. But important decisions needed to be made.

It was now after 9 a.m. on Thursday morning. A short time before, the telegraph operator had passed him a message saying that instructions were being dispatched by the first up-train from Slough. He hastened down to the platform and waited for the train to arrive. One of his subordinates stepped from a carriage and approached him, handing over an envelope.

Williams opened it and skimmed through the letter. It advised that he was to apprehend the suspect and bring him to Slough to attend a coronial inquest. He flipped over the page and saw an attachment: a letter from the surgeon who had attended the woman in her death throes. The doctor reported that one of the woman's neighbours had seen an agitated

Quaker gentleman leaving the property – the suspect mentioned
in the telegraph message – and that the neighbour and another
local had said that the man's name was Tarbot or Herbert or
something similar. Scrawled across the bottom of the doctor's
letter, in a different handwriting, were the words: 'Act upon this
as you think advisable.'

Williams knew that the only way he could act upon this
information was by visiting the nearby Paddington Police Station
and asking for the assistance of the London Metropolitan Police.
The delay could prove costly. Too many hours had already
passed since he had left the Quaker in the lodging house without
anyone watching to make sure the man didn't leave. If they lost
track of him, they might never find him again.

⟳

The weak sun was still climbing when the time Sergeant
Williams and his companion, Inspector William Wiggins of
Paddington Police Station, approached 7 Scott's Yard. Both
had covered their uniforms with overcoats so that the suspect
would not be instantly alerted to their identities. They hammered on the door.

To their disbelief, the person who opened the door was
dressed like the suspect – but he wasn't their man. The lodging
house was run by Quakers. The policemen asked the landlord
about his previous night's guest, a Mr Tarbot or Herbert. No
guest by that name had stayed the night, they were told.

The officers looked at each other, nonplussed. Thus far, the
Quaker's uniform had distinguished him, a raven among peacocks,
but he was now nesting with his own. They needed another
means of identification. Williams mentioned the suspect's cast
eye. The landlord immediately knew who they were looking
for. 'His name is Tawell and he is a gentleman and a merchant.'

The officers asked to speak with the fellow. He had already left, they were told. Where had he gone? The landlord shrugged his apology.

Dispirited, the policemen turned from the door. With no other lead at their disposal, Williams suggested trying the Jerusalem Coffee House where the suspect had stopped the night before and handed off the umbrella for no apparent reason. It was only a ten-minute walk away. The pair marched along the lanes and alleyways, crossing King William Street and Lombard Street until they reached Birchin Lane.

The coffee house was humming. Ship's captains and merchants congregated there, along with anyone else interested in trade to the East Indies and the Pacific. Some men were studying the papers, either the London or international newspapers, or lists of shipping and stock prices. Others conversed earnestly, as though the Empire's fate depended on winning or losing a debate; still others, old or new friends alike, joked and laughed. Waiters wove between them carrying trays filled with steaming cups of coffee and other delicacies.

The policemen signalled one of the waiters and asked if Mr Tawell was present. Earlier, they were told, but he had since left. Did anyone know where he might have gone? Try the Hall of Commerce.

The two officers crossed over Cornhill and headed up Finch Lane to Threadneedle Street, beetling towards the Hall of Commerce as if the police commissioner was snapping at their heels. As they stepped through the hall's imposing door, they passed under a bas-relief of figures personifying such virtues as peace, liberty, civilisation and education. It seemed a far cry from murder – the last place where a killer might be found.

Mr Tawell was certainly a member, they were advised. In fact, he had visited that very morning. However, he had left a short time before with no indication as to where he was heading.

The policemen wandered through the financial district for the next hour, constantly spotting the distinctive Quaker dress. Unfortunately the raven was still flocking with his own. The Quakers, with their reputation for honesty and integrity, were the guardians of much of England's gold, having founded many of the great banks, Lloyds and Barclays on Lombard Street among them. Over time, Lombard Street had become the golden heart of London, so Quaker attire surrounded them.

Around midday, they decided to revisit the Jerusalem Coffee House on the off-chance that their Quaker might have returned. With little hope, they enquired after their prey.

He was there.

CHAPTER 6

What's done can't be undone.

William Shakespeare,
Macbeth

※

SURGEON CHAMPNES was not alone when he opened Sarah
Hart's front gate on the morning after her death. He was accompanied by an older and more experienced doctor, Mr Edward
Weston Nordblad of Slough. They informed the officer on
sentry duty outside the front door that they were under Coroner
John Charsley's orders to examine the corpse and determine
the cause of death.

Sarah's unearthly moans had long ceased but the sight of
her body remained as disturbing. The dishevelled clothing suggested violence, even the unmentionable.

Downing their bags, the two men began to undress the
corpse, slipping off her stockings and remaining shoe, unbuttoning the dress and underclothes and tugging them down.
They carefully examined the naked torso and limbs but could
find no blood, bruises or broken bones, no knife or needle
wounds, no bullet holes or garrotte marks, no evidence at all
to suggest a physical cause. Nor did the body reveal external
signs of possible poisoning. There was no blackness or lividity to the skin, no swelling or offensive odour. The doctors
surveyed her mouth, nose, eyes and ears and found nothing
out of the ordinary. All was as one would expect from a death

beyond suspicion. Yet, like Champnes, Nordblad saw the signs of a rapid end. He too presumed that the woman had been killed by poisoning.

The surgeons reported their findings to Coroner Charsley. Earlier that morning, Charsley had appropriated a room at the Three Tuns tavern on the junction of Farnham and Bath Roads, a few hundred yards from Bath Place. Men were gathering at the tavern, among them the local yeomen and merchants called to serve as jury members for the inquest into Mrs Hart's death. Charsley explained that he would swear in the men then take them to view the body. Afterwards, the doctors were to dissect the body.

Death lurked around every corner for those living in nineteenth-century Britain. Dead bodies were a familiar sight. Murder, however, was different. As the jurymen traipsed down Bath Road, they were as curious as the local gossips to see the suspected crime scene and the hapless corpse.

Word of the suspicious death had circulated through neighbouring villages and parishes. Ghouls were flocking. Smocked agricultural labourers tramped down Bath Road in ones and twos, clamouring to be allowed in to view Sarah Hart's home – and the dead body lying on the sitting-room floor. They were not alone. Pinafored matrons had made the pilgrimage with children in tow. Even some besuited gentlemen had driven their pony-traps and carriages to Bath Place in the hope of seeing the room in which Mrs Hart had been 'murdered'. The stolid constable on guard at the front door refused all their entreaties. 'I am under instructions from the coroner not to suffer anyone to enter the premises,' he intoned over and over. Only the coroner, jurymen and surgeons were to be allowed inside. Still the voices wheedled, until their owners moved off, to be replaced by newcomers determined to try their own luck.

Coroner Charsley knew that country medical practitioners often lacked pathology skills, particularly those required to undertake a comprehensive post-mortem. If the woman had been murdered, it was essential that the surgeons were thorough. Although Surgeon Nordblad had practised medicine for ten years, Charsley thought it prudent to seek the assistance of a surgeon with more experience in conducting this crucial examination.

Dr William Bolton Pickering arrived from London around noon. Soon afterwards, the surgeons returned to Bath Place to continue their examination. They pushed aside the furniture and spread a covering over the floor, carefully positioning the corpse before pulling medical instruments from their bags. At 1 p.m., eighteen hours after the woman's death, they made the first incision. The skull was sawn open, the brain carefully inspected, removed and dissected – they found nothing odd. Then the torso: slashed open from the neck to the groin. The heart and valves were examined and deemed to be healthy. There were no foreign objects lodged in the trachea or oesophagus, so the woman had not choked. The gall bladder was a natural colour. The bowels and intestines appeared healthy, and the abdominal viscera, though rather fat, was otherwise healthy-looking too. The lungs: aha! They could see a large lesion on the left lobe of her right lung. But it was old, very old; it couldn't have caused death even if she had been extremely distressed. Otherwise her lungs were fine.

So far they could find nothing to account for Mrs Hart's death. They weren't ready to say that she had died naturally, however. Poisons often left few traces. Sometimes the stomach provided clues. They had left that examination until last.

Champnes pulled the woman's stomach out from under her ribs and laid it on the table, then picked up his scalpel and sliced it open. The acrid smell of beer and partly digested food slapped them. One man hurried into the kitchen and brought back a clean dry basin. Champnes poured in the stomach contents. First, the surgeons examined the stomach itself, noticing that its internal surface was covered with more mucus than normal. Did that suggest poison? They decided not. Otherwise, the tissue seemed normal.

Turning back to the basin, they scooped through the pulpy mass that had been the woman's last meal. Nothing visually suspicious. No smell other than beer and digestive juices, as foul as they might be. Whatever poison had killed her – if a poison had indeed killed her – it had left no obvious traces. They would need the services of an analytical chemist to investigate further.

Champnes asked the attending constable to locate a glass bottle that could be sealed and carried away. The officer returned with a broad-mouthed pickle bottle. Would it do? Champnes smelt it and held it up to the light, remarking that the glass was clean and odour-free. He poured in the contents of Mrs Hart's stomach then sealed it, tying a string around the neck for added security. The other surgeons helped secure the stomach itself by trussing its ends with another piece of string. Then Champnes stowed the bottle and stomach in his medicine bag and carried them home to his cellaret to join the other items from Mrs Hart's house. He locked the cellaret door and pocketed both keys. This was one pickle bottle he didn't want the cook to mistake for a preserve.

⌒

The doctors' conclusion that a poison had probably killed Sarah Hart led Slough's Constable Hill to search her cottage again that afternoon. Concentrating on the fireplace, he swept the cinders through the grate and left them lying underneath, then he removed the grate and grubbed through the ash and cinders with his fingers. Again he found nothing out of the ordinary.

Superintendent John Larkin of the Stoke and Burnham police division joined him there. The investigation was now a three-pronged affair, a collaboration between Larkin, who was responsible for the district in which Sarah's body lay, Inspector Wiggins of the London Metropolitan Police, and Eton's police superintendent, Samuel Perkins. Despite the numerous previous searches, Larkin began his own inspection of the premises. He found two phials tucked inside a jug in a cupboard, apparently undisturbed for some time. One was empty. The other smelled of hartshorn, the acrid smelling salts used to revive the unconscious. Larkin took both bottles away with him.

Meanwhile Constable Hill asked Sarah's neighbours and friends about the plum cake and box of apples. He learned that the apples were a present, and that the box had originally contained a peck, or a quarter of a bushel, although less than two-dozen remained when Mrs Ashlee first saw them shortly before Christmas. Sarah had kindly given her a few. The plum cake was supplied by Sarah's laundress, Kezia Harding, and had been purchased from a cake-maker in Brentford. 'I had some myself,' Mrs Harding told the constable, 'and I suffered no inconvenience from eating it. It was a good cake.'

⁓

Anticipation brightened the eyes of those hanging around the Three Tuns that afternoon. The coronial inquest into the death of Sarah Hart was about to begin.

Coroner Charsley called his first witness, Mrs Mary Ann Ashlee, and asked her to describe the events of the previous evening. Everyone listened intently as she spoke of the strange moans piercing the walls, the agitated Quaker at Mrs Hart's gate, the ghastly sight of her friend sprawled across the floor, the shocking death a few minutes later. The coroner then called Mrs Burrett, who described her own involvement in the drama. Mrs Kezia Harding was the next to testify.

'I have washed for Mrs Hart since she lived at Slough,' the laundress told the jury, 'and I have often seen a Quaker gentleman at her house.' She talked further about his visits, reporting that he was due to bring Sarah's quarterly allowance that very week. She was in a position to know.

⁓

Kezia was working in Mrs Hart's front room around 6 p.m. on the eve of Christmas Eve when someone knocked on the door. A familiar figure stood on the doorstep – the old gentleman, Mrs Hart's Quaker visitor. Kezia had sometimes seen the man at Mrs Hart's home, or walking to or from the railway station, but she had never spoken to him. He always wore his traditional garb and always visited during daylight – on previous occasions, that is. Mrs Hart hadn't mentioned why he visited or where he came from. All she had said was that he never came on a Wednesday, as that was his Quaker meeting day.

'You are late, sir, tonight,' Mrs Hart said with surprise. She welcomed him into her home, then turned to Kezia and said quietly, 'Go out the back way.'

Kezia retreated into the kitchen, heading for the back door. 'Is she a lodger?' she heard the Quaker ask.

'I have no room for lodgers,' Mrs Hart replied.

Returning ninety minutes later, Kezia slipped through the back door just as the Quaker gentleman was leaving. She heard him say, 'Shall you be alone when I come again? I shall be down on Tuesday or Thursday week.'

Mrs Hart remained silent.

He again asked: 'Shall you be alone when I come on Tuesday or Thursday week?'

'Very well,' Mrs Hart agreed, then farewelled him.

Kezia rejoined Mrs Hart after the door closed behind him. 'He only gave me one sovereign instead of thirteen,' her employer complained, the first explanation she had offered for the man's visits. 'But it does not signify as I will wait until next week when he will bring me the remainder of the money.'

The following Monday, after Kezia delivered some clean linen, Mrs Hart said to her, 'Don't call again until Wednesday or Thursday as I expect the old gentleman to come to bring me some money.'

That was the last time she had seen Mrs Hart, Kezia told the coroner. She hadn't gone to her house the previous day, a Wednesday – not until the police contacted her.

'But had you seen this Quaker gentleman before?' the coroner attempted to clarify.

'I have frequently seen him at Mrs Hart's. I never spoke to him but I should know him again.'

Coroner Charsley looked over towards a policeman waiting solemnly at the back of the room. 'Bring the person in custody into the room,' he ordered.

Chapter 7

A change in motion is proportional to the motive force impressed and takes place along the straight line in which that force is impressed.

Sir Isaac Newton,
The Principia (1687)

WHAT SHOULD be done?

The two policemen standing outside the Jerusalem Coffee House moved away from the door to discuss their options quietly. The staff reported that the man they wanted had returned, but what if it was the wrong man? And if it was indeed the suspect, what if he guessed who they were and managed to escape before they reached him? They decided that Sergeant Williams should remain outside just in case the suspect recognised him from the previous evening, and that Inspector Wiggins would go inside and draw the suspect out. They could then question him in private – and easily control him if necessary.

With his uniform still hidden by his coat, Wiggins walked into the coffee shop and approached the gentleman pointed out to him. The man was dressed as a Quaker and sat alone at a table.

'How do you do, Mr Tawell?' Wiggins asked. 'I believe your name is Tawell?'

The gentleman looked up and acknowledged politely that his name was Mr Tawell. 'Where have I seen thee before?' he asked curiously.

Ignoring the question, Wiggins asked him to step outside. He ushered the puzzled Quaker through the coffee shop's door, where they were joined by the disguised sergeant.

'I believe you came last night from Slough by the Great Western Railway,' Wiggins continued.

'No, I did not,' Tawell replied firmly. 'I did not leave town all day yesterday.'

The inspector opened his coat to reveal his uniform. 'I want you to come with me to Slough. There was a woman found dead there and you are supposed to be the last person who was seen with her alive.'

'No, I was not there,' the Quaker assured him. 'I do not know anyone there.'

'Yes, you were, sir,' Sergeant Williams interjected. 'You got out of the train and got into an omnibus and gave me sixpence.'

'Thee must be mistaken in the identity,' the Quaker announced with gentle dignity. 'My station in society places me beyond suspicion.'

Inspector Wiggins and Sergeant Williams had heard it all before. Protests of innocence from the outwardly respectable were no proof of righteousness, no matter how vehemently professed. Admittedly, the only criminal Quaker in the history of that righteous sect – the only one that readily came to mind, anyway – was a certain forger named Joseph Hunton, once a resident of Great Yarmouth, who had been executed a couple of decades previously. After the Crown had terminated that threat to the nation's financial security, the term 'Quaker' had come to epitomise honesty and respectability again. The suspect was correct in declaring that his station in society placed him above suspicion – almost. Arresting a Quaker for murder? Their case needed to be solid.

The officers continued to question Mr John Tawell – as he stated his name to be – asking about his activities on New Year's Day. He repeatedly denied having been to Slough, repeatedly disclaimed any knowledge of the dead woman, repeatedly demanded to be allowed to return to his home in Berkhampstead. The indomitable Inspector Wiggins was not swayed. 'You are charged on suspicion of having administered poison to the dead woman at Slough,' he finally declared, and took Tawell into custody.

The Quaker didn't resist. He said nothing more, though he continued to maintain his air of respectability.

Wiggins and Williams escorted him to Paddington railway station. There the inspector forwarded a message to his superintendent saying that they were taking the suspect to Slough as requested. The trio boarded the train and began the eighteen-mile journey west.

All was quiet as they travelled past the glittering temple of Kensal Green cemetery, with mourners flocking like subdued witches; past cavalry officers, vivid with colour and energy as they exercised at Wormwood Scrubs; past the ugly brick Lunatic Asylum, which seemed to frown upon them; past lofty church spires that poked up through trees or behind hedgerows; and on towards the imperious towers of Windsor Castle. Finally, Tawell broke his silence. Looking up at the inspector, he said: 'I took thee for a gentleman I knew once.'

Surprised, Wiggins replied: 'I told you I was an officer.'

'Yes, but that was afterwards,' Tawell said bitterly. He mused for a bit longer then added, 'Mind, I have disclosed nothing.'

It was an odd remark from a pious Quaker. Indeed, it was the type of self-protective comment usually made by those with first-hand experience of the law. Who was this strange man?

When Coroner Charsley demanded the suspect's attendance, the message was sent to the Three Tuns' back parlour. There, Tawell had been closeted since his arrival at Slough earlier that afternoon. As he stepped through the door into Charsley's makeshift courtroom, all eyes turned towards him. He appeared taken aback, disturbed by so much attention, but he soon regained his composure. Forsaking Quaker custom, he whipped off his broad-brimmed hat and clutched it in front of him.

A murderer? Surely not. The jury saw a small, slender, exceedingly respectable gentleman dressed in a white cravat and black waistcoat, with dark olive-green trousers and a loose brown greatcoat. Age: between fifty and sixty. Face: narrow and clean shaven, with a slightly sallow complexion, somewhat lined as if he had frowned a great deal or lived a troubled life. Hair: short and swept back from his forehead, light coloured, perhaps greyish. And a discernible cast in his left eye. The superstitious looked pointedly at each other, wondering if it was an omen.

'I will desire you to put your hat back on,' Coroner Charsley requested. He was not acting out of religious deference; rather, he was forsaking courtroom custom to assist Mrs Harding in her identification.

At first confused, Tawell accepted the invitation and said politely, 'I am obliged,' as he donned his hat.

For a moment everyone continued to stare at the suspect. Then Kezia Harding's firm voice broke the silence. 'I have not the least doubt that the prisoner is the person I have seen several times at Mrs Hart's!' she announced.

A satisfied murmur rumbled through the courtroom.

'Search him!' ordered the coroner. 'Detain any papers or other property you might find upon him.'

As the policemen escorted Tawell into the back parlour, Charsley called his next witness, Mrs Mary Ann Moss, and asked her to explain how she knew Sarah Hart.

~⁓~

Mary Ann had been living with her husband and four children on the first floor of fruiterer William Byfield's house at 93 Crawford Street, Marylebone, when Sarah and her infant son moved into the second floor. It was the year 1840 and both women were pregnant. They felt an instant affinity and soon became friends.

Sarah was sorely in need of a friend. She rarely had visitors. She explained to Mary Ann: 'I left home at ill-friends with my relations and have never seen them again.' Her only regular visitor was a man who appeared during the daytime every six weeks or so. 'He brings money from my husband who is abroad,' she told Mary Ann. 'I became acquainted with his son and married him and both my children are by him but his father disapproved of the match.'

Yet in the twelve months that Sarah lived above the Mosses, and in the following years of their friendship, she never explained why she rarely wore a wedding ring, or why her husband never visited, or why her surname was different to that of her father-in-law – whom she called 'Mr Toll' or 'Mr Tall', and whom she said had once been her employer. She never explained why he visited so regularly to deliver an allowance when he supposedly disapproved of the match.

The Quaker first appeared about a month after Sarah settled into Crawford Street. He knocked on Mary Ann's door and asked, 'Does Mrs Hart live here?'

Sarah's voice sang out from the upper floor, 'Here I am. It is all right.' She invited him up to her rooms.

He was a regular visitor thereafter, bringing Sarah's £13 allowance every quarter, sometimes providing other gifts as well. One day a parcel of blankets was delivered for Sarah and, when he next visited, Mary Ann heard him asking anxiously if they were all right. He gave Sarah a five-pound note soon after she settled there to help furnish her home. He gave her another after her second baby was born a few months later.

Mary Ann assisted with Sarah's second confinement, when her daughter Sarah was born on 6 March 1841. When the Quaker visited immediately afterwards, Mary Ann left him alone in Sarah's room. She never sensed anything improper between them, either then or during any of his visits to Crawford Street in the months to come.

Mary Ann knew that Sarah was happy at Crawford Street so she was surprised when her friend announced that she was leaving after only a year. When she asked why, Sarah said that it was to gain greater privacy. 'It is at the desire of my old master,' she added. 'He thinks this is such a public street.'

Soon afterwards, Sarah moved to 62 Harrow Road, Paddington Green, a small house two doors down from the King and Queen pub. Fortunately, it wasn't far from Crawford Street. For nearly eighteen months the two women visited each other, while their children played together. Then in the winter of 1842–43, Sarah told Mary Ann that her father-in-law was moving her again, this time out of London to Slough. She was to reside with a family near the Dolphin inn, which was situated at the junction of Langley and Bath roads, on the outskirts of town. As it turned out, she resided there for only a few months. When Mary Ann asked why she was moving yet again, Sarah said: 'The old gentleman does not like being obliged to go through the sitting room occupied by the family to my rooms.' He was bringing her allowance, after all, and his sense of decorum should be accorded due respect.

In April 1843 Sarah moved to her Bath Place cottage at Salt Hill. The two women maintained their friendship so Mary Ann knew that Sarah had made a cheery home there, and was well-liked by her neighbours. She always paid her bills on time, so the locals were willing to provide services. She employed baker John Hawker to deliver her bread and laundress Kezia Harding to assist with the washing and running errands. And the Quaker gentleman regularly took the train out to Slough, carrying her allowance with him.

As time passed, however, Sarah began to mention financial difficulties. Her allowance was not enough to support them. A mother with young children had few income-generating options – respectable ones, that is. She could put Alfred and Sarah into care and become a house-servant again, knowing that there was little chance they would be raised and educated adequately, let alone loved and nurtured. She could take in piece-work and be paid a pittance for long, arduous hours with a needle. Or there was one other option.

Charlotte Howard was her name. Sarah's lodger arrived at Bath Place late in 1843, a heavily pregnant, unmarried maid-servant who stayed for four months. When she returned to work, she left her infant son, Charles, in Sarah's care. Charlotte spent a further two weeks at Bath Place late in September 1844. The visit proved timely as Sarah became violently ill while she was there, leaving Charlotte to care for all the children and to stow away the £13 allowance the Quaker visitor had left on the table. Then Charlotte took her baby away, and the trifle she had paid Sarah was gone.

The Quaker's September allowance should have covered the rent to Christmas 1844, but Sarah had other expenses to meet and delayed paying the landlady. She pawned some of her possessions to pay old bills, yet more bills were due, and another quarter's rent loomed. She had already written to the Quaker gentleman asking for more money – without success. She, who had always prided herself on paying bills promptly, was falling further and further behind.

Mary Ann was concerned for her friend but there was little she could do to help. Her husband's income was not large – he was a clerk – and they had a growing family to support. All she could provide was heartfelt sympathy and a ready ear.

And then a letter arrived from Slough saying that Sarah was dead.

Mary Ann finished her testimony to the coroner, having clarified that the Quaker gentleman was not simply Sarah's old master, as Mrs Ashlee had reported, but her father-in-law. 'I am glad he is found,' she said with relief, 'because of the children as nobody knew where to find him.' Then she faltered before adding with a note of confusion, 'I had no suspicion that he would do Mrs Hart an injury.'

She had just expressed the puzzlement felt by the district's perspicacious residents. If this expensively dressed, exceedingly respectable-looking Quaker had murdered the kindly Mrs Hart, why would he have done so? To save himself £50 a year? Who now would care for her children? The allowance he paid Mrs Hart was not intended simply for her own support, but to provide for her two young children – his own grandchildren, if Mrs Hart's admission to Mary Ann Moss was to be believed. It was perplexing.

After Mary Ann Moss stepped down, more witnesses were called to testify. Reverend Champnes, Superintendent Howell,

Sergeant Williams and Inspector Wiggins each described their roles in apprehending the suspect. Surgeon Champnes was then called. 'Neither I nor my coadjutor can arrive at any satisfactory conclusion as to the cause of death without further examination of the contents of the deceased's stomach by means of a chemical analysis,' he announced.

'Make such an examination, then,' Coroner Charsley ordered, adding that the doctor should take Mr Nordblad to London with him.

Before adjourning the day's business, Charsley ordered the officers in the back parlour to return their prisoner to his courtroom. When the Quaker arrived, he demanded that the man identify himself.

'My name is John Tawell.'

'From the nature of the evidence brought before the jury, I have to inform you that you must be kept in custody until Saturday morning when these proceedings will be resumed.'

'It would not, perhaps, be considered reasonable that I should hear the evidence read which has been brought forward?' the Quaker asked.

'Certainly not,' said the coroner. 'That cannot be done.'

'May I be permitted to go home?'

'You must remain in custody.'

'The fact is, I fill a public situation in society and my being kept here is a serious interruption to me. I am the town surveyor at Berkhampstead, and I pledge my word to attend on that day. Can I be permitted to go if I give ample security?'

'There is evidence to show that you were the last person seen in the house of the deceased and you must remain in custody,' Charsley declared with finality. 'If I were to release you, the county police would immediately apprehend you.'

The eyes flicking between the coroner and prisoner saw

Tawell accept the decree with surprising composure, the same equanimity he had shown earlier – after his initial agitation. But then, they hadn't seen him when Mrs Ashlee escorted young Alfred Hart into the Three Tuns' back parlour a short time before. At the sight of the lad, the Quaker had turned his head away, evidently distressed. The boy had already recognised him, however. 'That is the man,' he told the officers.

Coroner Charsley adjourned the inquest at 7.30 p.m., ordering Eton's police superintendent, Samuel Perkins, to take charge of Tawell and to return him to the Three Tuns at 10 a.m. on Saturday. 'Afford the prisoner every comfort compatible with his situation and standing in society,' he added. The Quaker gentleman was to be treated better than the run-of-the-mill criminal.

Superintendent Perkins took Tawell to Eton but didn't lock him up at the police station there. Instead, he escorted him through the door of the adjoining house, his own home, and settled him in for the night.

Inspector Wiggins had left Tawell with nothing but the clothes on his back. From the man's pockets, he had pulled out £12 10s. in gold, £1 1s. 6d. in silver and 2½d. in copper, as well as a valuable gold watch and guard, two pairs of spectacles, a pocketbook, a pencil case and penknife, a few silk and cambric handkerchiefs, some papers and blank cheques, and an opened envelope containing a letter.

He slid the letter from its envelope and began to read it. Written by Tawell's wife the previous day, the day of Sarah Hart's death, the chatty letter mainly described the day's activities at their home in Berkhampstead. It ended with a statement of blissful optimism. 'The year has opened with a lovely day,' she wrote. 'I hope it is an omen of the future which awaits us.'

Part 2

OBSESSION

The recollection of former days ought to induce John Tawell to endeavour to remain in as blessed state of obscurity as can well be imagined.

Miles's Boy,
Bucks Gazette (26 October 1844)

Chapter 8

He is quite a good fellow – nobody's enemy but his own.

Charles Dickens,
David Copperfield (1850)

NESTLING IN the valley of the River Bulbourne in Hertfordshire, Berkhampstead was a charming town with coaching inns sprinkled between its shops, houses, Norman church and nearby ruined castle. The town had a proud history. Once it was the principal residence of the kings of Mercia and the locale where the triumphant Guillaume de Normandie transformed himself into William the Conqueror. It was also a favourite home of later Norman and Plantagenet monarchs, and of Thomas Becket before Henry II uttered his immortal words, 'Will no-one rid me of this troublesome priest?' An historian writing in ages past even claimed that St Paul had visited Berkhampstead and driven away the serpents and thunderstorms for ever although, as one writer dryly observed, 'Nature felt disinclined to obey this apostolic injunction, for the thunderstorms, if not the serpents, have returned'. Some saw the returning serpents in the fiery dragons that swept into town from 1837 onwards along the newly built railway tracks, others in the passengers alighting from the beasts – particularly those who might settle and besmirch its illustrious pedigree with their own infamy.

Many of the alighting passengers were visitors to the town, content to stroll along its quaint streets enjoying the views and ambience. Some stopped to admire the Bishop of Lincoln's thirteenth-century church on the High Street, with its lofty nave and clerestory. As they looked around the vicinity, they couldn't help but notice the Red House, as it was customarily known, situated almost opposite the church. A splendid mansion, indeed the best house in Berkhampstead, it had a double frontage to High Street and extensive grounds behind. It was the home of wealthy Quakers John Tawell and his wife Sarah.

The Tawells were worthies in the local community, committed to philanthropy and the town's well-being. Only recently, Mr Tawell had been instrumental in plans to found a Mechanic's Institute, an educational establishment for adult men aimed at providing a more useful pastime than drinking or gambling. 'I am proud of the honour of residing in the ancient town of Berkhampstead,' Tawell told his fellow committee members at their inaugural meeting, 'and I have the indescribable pleasure of spending the proceeds of a life of honest industry among a population in every way qualified and disposed to appreciate my patronage and support.' While patronising – charity so often was – his speech was also a reminder that his wealth and success came from hard work, and that his story was one of triumph over adversity, a suitable role model for others.

Most in the town appreciated the couple's endeavours. Mrs Tawell was especially admired. Attitudes towards her husband, though, were ambivalent. Some viewed him as kindness and benevolence personified. Others found him rather haughty and arrogant. Most couldn't help but pity him, however, for lately being the butt of Miles's Boy's poisonous pen. This Quaker-hater enjoyed writing malicious letters to the *Bucks Gazette* about the 'unbaptised, buttonless blackguards', and John Tawell was his primary target.

At least the couple themselves were happy. They were clearly devoted to each other and to their children: Mrs Tawell's sixteen-year-old daughter Eliza and their son Henry Augustus, aged sixteen months. Even when Tawell went on one of his regular trips to London, generally only for a day or two, his wife could be seen walking to the postbox with a letter addressed to him. She usually received one in return, particularly when he was gone for more than a day. But this occasion appeared to be different.

～〜

Sarah Tawell grabbed the mail as soon as it arrived on Friday morning, 3 January, and riffled through the bundle. No word from John. She'd heard nothing the previous day nor had he returned home that evening as expected. Disquiet gnawed at her.

He had left home on the morning of New Year's Day. As the family sat down to breakfast, they knew they had no time to leisurely welcome 1845. Not that John was in any mood for celebration. He was catching the early train to London, hoping that a £700 remittance from Sydney had arrived. The money was badly needed.

The Tawell coffers were empty, worse than empty. Keen to increase his fortunes in England, John had decided to invest in four Berkhampstead cottages, agreeing to pay the owner £610 and handing over a deposit cheque for £100. As his funds hadn't arrived, his account was now overdrawn by £56. It was a small sum for a man of means, but a large sum – a year's wages – for many. If not covered soon, the bank's directors would start asking pointed questions.

John gathered enough cash to pay the expenses of his journey, leaving only a sovereign or two and some silver and copper coins for his wife's use. Sarah could see that his spirits were bleak as he headed off to Berkhampstead railway station.

Later that day, she sat down and wrote him a letter. 'My only loved one,' she began. 'My thoughts have been with thee throughout the day and I can't but hope thou art feeling better than when thou left us. Do, my endeared one, endeavour to keep up thy spirits for my sake.'

She mentioned the day's visitors, reporting that Eliza, soon to turn seventeen, had received an invitation to a dinner party. Some young gentlemen were to attend, she told her husband coyly, adding with a trace of disappointment that Eliza had declined the invitation. And darling Harry: he had been particularly delightful that morning, very merry and so sweet.

Her concerns for her husband's happiness soon pushed aside these trivialities. 'Oh, how I long to hear what the Sydney papers say of the state of things there. My poor mind rises and falls as I see how these vicissitudes affect thee. I think I could bear up better if the whole burden was on me alone; but that is impossible. I do hope, my dear husband, you will bear up.' Then she dashed off her final, hopefully uplifting, sentences and dispatched a servant to post the letter. John should receive it the following morning, Thursday, before he left London to return home later in the day.

But he hadn't come home, nor had a letter arrived on Thursday or with Friday's morning mail to explain his delay. It was most unusual. Worrying.

Sarah tried to pass the hours by opening that day's London newspaper. Skipping over the advertisements, she turned to the reports. Her eyes settled on the dramatic heading, 'Suspected Murder at Salt Hill'.

It wasn't John's intention that she should discover the news in such a distressing way, although he had delayed sending a letter via special messenger until Friday morning, despite Superintendent Perkins's advice. How does one break such dreadful news to a beloved wife?

When the special messenger arrived at the Tawell's residence later on Friday, he was told that Mrs Tawell had gone to London, though her daughter could perhaps provide the sovereign he demanded in return for handing over the letter. Recognising her stepfather's handwriting, Eliza took charge of the letter and read it. Her mother had not explained why she was unexpectedly travelling to the city, so Eliza was unprepared for the news it contained. Shocked and confused, she blurted out that she could scarcely believe that her father was in custody upon suspicion of some offence, let alone one committed at Salt Hill. 'My papa never knew any such person, either here or at Slough,' the bewildered lass said. 'There must be some mistake.'

The man wasn't interested. He just wanted his sovereign.

Eliza went to find some money but returned empty-handed. To add to her distress, she had to explain to the angry messenger that she had no money to pay him. Clearly, her mother had taken all their cash with her to London – or to wherever she had actually gone.

Could her mother have discovered the horrible news before the messenger arrived? While Slough was less than twenty miles south of Berkhampstead, she wouldn't have driven the carriage there. She would have taken the train from Berkhampstead to London, and another from there to Slough. She would indeed have been 'going to London' even if, from there, she journeyed elsewhere.

As the train crossed the English countryside on its way to London, Sarah was blind to the scenic panorama visible through its plate-glass windows, seeing only a kaleidoscope of thoughts and memories. She had been warned not to marry John, advised by her Quaker brethren that if she chose to do so then she – a birthright Quaker – would be guilty of 'marrying out'. She had first met him in 1839 while running a girls' school based at the Red House. Establishing the school had been the culmination of years of effort – and years of struggle that followed her marriage in 1825 to Quaker William Cutforth, a partner in a silk warehouse in Goldsmith Street. The difficulties began when his business went into bankruptcy only two months after their wedding. He wasn't to blame, concluded the Bankruptcy Commissioners, who refrained from gaoling him, and the Quakers, who refrained from disowning him for financial mismanagement. The consequences were devastating, nonetheless. They had to leave their Finsbury home and move to the seedier Whitechapel area where William began working as a tea and grocery dealer. The strain took its toll. He died in September 1827, leaving her five months pregnant and in dire financial straits. Their daughter Eliza Sarah was born on 21 January 1828.

Late in 1829, she decided to leave London and settle in Hemel Hempstead, Hertfordshire, a thriving market town on the busy coaching route between London and Birmingham. Five years later she relocated to nearby Berkhampstead. In each town she actively participated in local Quaker affairs, proving herself able and willing. Late in the 1830s, with the help of her fellow Quakers, she leased the Red House and established her school.

While small and catering mainly for the daughters of Quakers, the school offered a sound education with a particular focus on English and French studies. As time passed, it developed an enviable reputation, enough for a wealthy man like John Tawell to bring his niece to visit the school. She felt an immediate bond with this kind, intelligent, philanthropic businessman when he told her about his own educational endeavours, in particular his interest in female education. In the months that followed, their bond grew stronger.

She had not remarried in the years following her husband's death. The marriage pool had become too shallow – a serious and worsening problem among the Quakers. Whenever Friends married out, they were disowned by their brethren. This punishment lost to the society not only once-valued members but the birthright membership of their progeny, shrinking the next generation's marriage pool even further. Once sixty thousand strong, England's Quakers numbered less than fourteen thousand by the time Sarah's gaze fell upon John.

And therein lay the problem. John wasn't a Quaker – not according to the Society's strict definition of the term. He had fallen from grace.

CHAPTER 9

I had forsaken the priests ... for I saw there was none
among them all that could speak to my condition. And
when all my hopes in them and in all men were gone
... then, oh, then, I heard a voice which said, 'There is
one, even Christ Jesus, that can speak to thy condition';
and when I heard it my heart did leap for joy.

George Fox,
Journal (1647)

YOUNG JOHN TAWELL couldn't help but notice them. They
were a conspicuous lot, particularly among the Regency bucks
and belles who minced along the streets of Great Yarmouth
as the new century dawned. Yet their conspicuousness lay not
in their ostentation but in the plainness and simplicity of their
dress and customs. Indeed, 'plainness' was their mantra.

Dress, behaviour, religious beliefs: the world of the
Yarmouth Quakers was remarkably different to that of his home
parish of Aldeby, even though that drowsy riverside village was
only sixteen miles away. There in March 1783, just a few days
after his birth, his parents had him baptised, never expecting
that his views on the Anglican baptism ceremony, in fact his
views on Anglicanism generally, would change so dramatically
in the decades that followed.

The foundations for his interest in the Quakers could be
traced to his childhood in Aldeby. It had not been easy. His

father, Thomas, was a vain, pretentious man, as the excessive flourishes in his signature revealed even to those who had never met him. Boastful too. The whole parish had heard the tales of his wealthy, distinguished forebears: a mayor and a sheriff during the time when their home-town, Norwich, was second only to London in size and significance. However, his father had been unable to live up to his ancestors' glory. He was just a shopkeeper in a small, inconsequential village, a man struggling to support a large family – and a bastard daughter as well. He wasn't an inspirational father whose achievements motivated his offspring to strive to fill such distinguished shoes. Far from it. The only inspiration lay in their consequent determination to achieve more than rural ignominy.

John worked diligently during his years in the local village school, hunched over a slate, scratching away at his sums and his writing. His teacher provided him with a basic grounding in the humanities and sciences – as much as the man's limited training and the other students' limited interest would allow. John lapped it up. He was not only skilled at the physical sciences and fascinated by the natural sciences, he thirsted for knowledge generally. For a few short hours each school day, he was in his element.

Outside the classroom, however, everything was different. He was pale and scrawny, unlike the tough farmers' sons who were put to the plough at an early age, and was unforgivably quick-witted in an environment where brawn was valued over brain. He was also a carrot top, his hair of such a burning hue that other boys would jeer 'mind you don't get a haystack on fire'. Most difficult of all, he had a 'squint', his left eye drifting disconcertingly towards his nose. The kindly would try not to stare; the superstitious would shy away as if from evil. Misery, indignation, frustration, resentment, contempt, a simmering rage: all roiled inside him fighting for supremacy. What triumphed was a determination to prove himself to them all, to find a place where his abilities were valued, where he felt like he truly belonged.

Out of school hours, he worked in the family store, where his talents became obvious. His father decided to send him to work as an apprentice shop assistant in Great Yarmouth, the seaside town crouched crab-like on sand bars driven ashore by the tempestuous North Sea. Once merely a safe seaport, Yarmouth had recently come into vogue as a holiday resort. Those eager to enjoy its seaside delights swept into town in ornate carriages, alighting with the assistance of liveried footmen. Sweeping furs across their shoulders, they strode into the town's hotels, expecting to be pandered.

Many locals who watched the summer influx craved wealth's ostentatious trappings for themselves. John, however, was different. In the half-dozen years he lived in Yarmouth, he came to crave the wealth but disdain the trappings.

John's Yarmouth years proved a turbulent time, with the war-torn continent almost on his doorstep. The fall of the Bastille a decade earlier had echoed across Europe with symbolic significance. Across all classes, questions were being asked about man's place in the world: in society and politics and religion. Norwich, only a short distance away, was the 'Athens of England', a lively intellectual hub whose streetfronts were filled with French émigrés, talented artists, witty scholars and people of various religious persuasions – Anglicans and Roman Catholics, Quakers and Unitarians. Yarmouth, for all that its summer focus was on pleasuring the rich, was not immune to these influences. Nor was it immune to the fear of a French invasion that pervaded the countryside for much of the period.

Fear or thanksgiving, the need for a strong father figure to comfort or guide, the desire to have life's inscrutabilities explained or a structured framework to live within, or perhaps simple curiosity: John walked across a walled garden in Howard Street, through a doorway, down a stepladder and into an ancient sunken room. Once part of an Augustinian priory, the building now served the small Yarmouth community of the Religious Society of Friends – the Quakers.

There he learnt that the sect had emerged from the turbulence of the English Civil War of the mid-1600s, when revolutionary ideals and religious dissent marched hand-in-hand. The Friends were among the theists who came to believe that the established church and its 'hireling priests' had long manipulated religion for personal gain and class interests, and had smothered it with superstition and mystery to convince the masses that the priesthood alone could offer the pathway to salvation. The Friends wanted to return religion to its primitive, divine origins, allowing seekers after the truth to find salvation through personal experience. They received their then-derogatory nickname, the 'Quakers', when they heeded God's word. 'To this man will I look,' said the Lord in Isaiah, 'even to him that is poor and of a contrite spirit, and trembleth at my word.' So they quaked and trembled when God's light infused their being. Naturally, their beliefs were considered heretical and, in time-honoured custom, they were persecuted. As sometimes happens, however, persecution unified them into a movement.

That was in the 1600s. By John's day, Quakerism had fossilised. This once free-thinking sect was so obsessed with rigid conformity to the past and to the outward trappings of their religion that its followers had lost sight of the individuality and non-conformity that lay at its core. Their preoccupation with old-fashioned customs, their desire to maintain their purity and exclusivity by shunning the outside world, their willingness to disown anyone who breached their rigid rules, and their lack of concern at their rapidly dwindling numbers had spawned a new derogatory label: 'the peculiar people' – another nickname the Quakers adopted with pride. They knew the passage from Deuteronomy: 'For thou art an holy people unto the Lord thy God, and the Lord hath chosen thee to be a peculiar people unto Himself, above all the nations that are upon the Earth.'

The Quakers had little time or respect for finery or courtly fanfare, or for the obsequious bowing and scraping that ordinary mortals had to offer their betters. Their sect appealed mainly to the middle class, as the newer religions mostly did – the rich often too busy enjoying their present life to worry about the afterlife, and the poor too busy trying to have any life at all. It particularly appealed to those with middle-class business aspirations – people like John.

He soon learnt that the Quakers' connection with commerce was largely a by-product of their beliefs. Unwilling to pay tithes to the Anglican church to fund those 'hireling priests', as most landholders and tenants were obliged to do, many Quakers turned to entrepreneurial activities. With new trading prospects opening around the globe and their strong kinship and friendship ties, Quaker businessmen thrived. Honest and trustworthy, they became custodians of others' money, establishing many of the great British banks. As middle-men in the textile trade, and as shippers, brewers, millers and ironmasters, they were also a driving force behind the Industrial Revolution. Some of these early Quaker businesses still exist today, Cadbury and Rowntree among them. Yet while their business opportunities expanded, their social world shrank. Many common activities

were frowned upon because they breached strict Quaker regulations or were thought to distract members from more spiritual
pursuits. As time passed, business pursuits became one of the
few acceptable avenues towards which Quakers could direct
their energies. Wealth became the ladder to Quaker prestige,
'a gift and a blessing from God'.

With all the fervour of a new disciple, John became the plain-
est of the plain. He dressed himself in the dark, loose-fitting coat
and broad-rimmed hat that might once have reflected a desire
to serve God without wasting time and money on fashion and
frippery, but had long since become a uniform modelled on a
bygone age. He adopted the Quakers' speech idiosyncrasies,
the 'thee's and 'thou's that had once intimated equality rather
than the more deferential 'you', but now marked them as out-
siders. He refused to bow or to doff his hat, and abandoned
all honorary forms of address like Sir and Mr because these
tokens of civility and respect were deemed servile flattery. He
dutifully used 'first day' and 'second month' instead of the
customary names for days and months as the latter suggested
homage to ancient Gods – Janus first of all. He refused to swear
oaths, because all words must be spoken in truth. He abided
by the puritanical rules condemning the pleasures of painting,
singing and dancing, of learning or even listening to music, of
attending the theatre, of reading novels or other imaginative
literature, as these were all distractions from the search for
salvation. They poisoned the mind. They led to vanity and
vice. He abjured drinking, card games, gambling, blood sports
and field sports – 'vain sports', the Friends called them. And
he attended the interminable religious meetings where no one
spoke unless compelled by the prompting of the spirit, where
even the Quaker youths chafed at their tedious inactivity. In
so doing, he became – to the community at large – a man of

honesty, integrity, industry and piety, with wealth and success at his fingertips.

~~~

By early 1804, John was feeling the constraints of living in a small, seasonal town. Armed with letters of introduction from his Quaker friends, he left Yarmouth to seek his fortune in the western world's largest metropolis.

London was a seething mass of 860,000 souls, a city of polished manners yet crude morals, of refined sensibilities but brutal inhumanities – an unforgiving city in an uncaring age. While William Wilberforce and his humanitarian comrades strove for the abolition of the slave trade, many of Britain's workers remained enslaved. The Industrial Revolution had ushered in an era of exploitation, with long working hours and low working wages, a wretched existence lived in vermin-ridden hovels reeking of sewage and despair. Yet the new age had also ushered in the makings of the first consumer society and had led to a burgeoning, increasingly affluent middle class. There were opportunities aplenty for those with brains and ability, those like John who were keen and conscientious, although they were surrounded by the failures and an ever-present fear of joining them.

John found work at 142 Whitechapel, the linen-drapery and manufactory business called John Janson & Co. Initially employed as a porter, he soon impressed its Quaker proprietors with his intelligence, willing nature and courteous disposition. Before long, he was promoted to more responsible, well-paid positions.

As his status in the community increased, so did his religious zeal. He became an 'habitual attender' at Devonshire House, the Westminster Abbey of the Quaker 'meeting houses', as their places of worship were known. Those habitual attenders who adopted the Quaker uniform and customs also cloaked themselves in the sect's ready-made reputation for uprightness, as the public at large saw no difference between the anointed and the aspiring. Among the Quakers themselves, however, they remained second-class citizens. Accordingly, John was not permitted to attend the Friends' business meetings, such as the Monthly, Quarterly or Yearly Meetings, or the social functions associated with them, nor could he hold official roles or contribute to fund-raising efforts. He was forbidden from marrying a member. He was even gently reproved if he referred to himself as a Quaker. Most importantly, for a bright lad desiring commercial success, he didn't benefit from the Quakers' wealth-generating network of business connections.

Yet it was extremely difficult to become a member unless one was born to a Quaker family. Although they had once accepted all believers, embracing newcomers and nurturing their desire for the 'true' spirituality, by the late 1700s wariness had replaced welcome. 'Lay hands on no man suddenly, nor speedily admit any into membership,' decreed the elders. 'Let the innocence of their lives and conversation first be manifested and a deputation of judicious friends be made to inquire into the sincerity of their convincement.'

In July 1807, John decided it was time. He applied to Devonshire House for permission to enter the inner sanctum.

At that month's meeting, the Friends briefly discussed his character and respectability, his occupation and prospects. Quakers financially supported their own, so they preferred not to admit those who were likely to drain their coffers. They decided that John's application was worthy of consideration and appointed two members to visit him at his home and confer with him on his 'convincement' – his conviction of the truth of their religious principles.

John endured a few interrogations from the two men, answering questions about the Friends' distinctive teachings. He had to justify his desire for admission in the appropriate terms: purity of worship and so on. Naturally, 'wealth-creation possibilities' and 'respectable status in society' were not considered suitable reasons, for all that – to some extent, at least – they underpinned his decision to apply for admission to the sect. He had to wait a worryingly long five months before he received a response.

Devotedly attending meetings for year after year and following Quaker customs didn't ensure a smooth passage. The Friends had no formal admission guidelines and applicants could be rejected on spiritual, doctrinal or political grounds, or merely for reasons that reflected the austere sect's exclusivity and suspicion of strangers. One frustrated applicant quipped that it would be far easier to enter the Kingdom of Heaven.

Despite the Quakers' extreme reluctance to accept new members, John was found to be worthy. On 8 December 1807, at the age of twenty-four, he joined the ranks of the Peculiar People.

The rigid control necessary to become a Quaker had taken its toll, however. Having been accepted into their fold, John relaxed. Like his father before him, his eyes began to rove.

~~~~~

It was almost a truism among the Quakers that those recently admitted were those most frequently expelled. On 8 November 1808 an overseer reported to the Devonshire House Monthly Meeting that John was considering marrying a non-Quaker. Second Corinthians said that believers should not be 'unequally yoked together with non-believers' – which, in the rigid interpretation of the Quakers, meant anyone who wasn't a Friend.

To marry out to a non-Quaker in those days also required the services of a 'hireling priest'. Sacrilege indeed.

Two Friends were ordered to visit John and try to dissuade him from taking such a rash step, but they were too late. On 9 November, John had married twenty-one-year-old Mary Freeman in an Anglican ceremony performed at St James', Piccadilly.

John's interlocutors advised the December meeting that they had left his home without receiving any 'satisfaction' – that is, that he hadn't shown enough remorse and humility for such a serious breach of their rules. The clerk ordered that a 'testimony of denial' be prepared. This document would expel John from their religious community.

Then another rumour surfaced. 'We have recently been informed,' announced a grim overseer at the January meeting, 'that John Tawell has been of very disorderly conduct.' When the grave-faced gentlemen again appeared on his doorstep, John admitted to having been unchaste, but again he refused to offer his visitors any 'satisfaction'.

In February, the committee read out the testimony of denial to the entire meeting – to John's friends, workmates and business acquaintances, indeed to every Quaker attending this meeting of the largest branch of the British Quakers, everyone John was striving to impress. 'We therefore disown John Tawell as a member of our religious society,' the implacable statement concluded, 'nevertheless we wish he may sincerely repent of his evil and deceitful conduct and by a close attention to the principle of truth in his own mind, find forgiveness from the great author of all good.' It was a scathing denunciation from a community that prided itself on being understated – in every sphere of life. Word of John's misbehaviour was soon known throughout the small, select, narrow-minded sect.

But what did disownment truly mean to John? He could no longer attend official meetings, or hold any official roles, or contribute to Quaker funds. Still, he could attend worship meetings, register his children's births, and be buried in a Quaker burial ground. He had been rebuked, that was all, primarily so that the Friends could primly proclaim, 'He is not a Quaker.' It allowed them to step away from the shadow cast by any wrong-doer, particularly if the miscreant was later guilty of a serious crime. Of course, serious criminality was rarely a problem among the Quakers, and John was not criminally minded. He had simply fallen in love.

Many of the disowned stalked off or slinked away, perhaps joining a different church, or renouncing religious beliefs altogether. Some waited for memory and their own mortification to fade, then returned to the Friends' meetings, hoping that in time they would be quietly readmitted. Returning to the fold wasn't quite as difficult for those expelled for regulatory breaches like marrying out or bankruptcy. Sexual misconduct? It took strength of character and an unwavering determination for such an offender to walk back into a Quaker meeting. Yet John did so.

It wasn't Devonshire House, however.

John and Mary took lodgings in Camden Place, Islington, among the other aspiring middle-class residents who flocked to the freshly built terraces lining the borough's streets. John was working as an accountant when his eldest child, John Downing Tawell, was born on 6 September 1809, ten months after their marriage. They registered the child's birth at their local Quaker meeting house. Penned across the bottom of the registration was the dismissive notation 'not entitled to membership'.

Not long afterwards, the Tawells moved to 23 Craven Street (now Corsham Street), Shoreditch. They returned to Devonshire

House to register the birth of their second son, William Henry, born 3 November 1811. Again the child's birth registration dismissed the family as 'non-members'.

By this time, John had a new career as a 'commercial traveller', a sales representative engaged by Cheapside perfumer John Thomas Rigge, Southwark comb-maker John Paine, and the wholesale drug and patent-medicine business Spyring & Marsden. His Quaker garb immediately granted him the advantages of the public attitudes towards his sect – most especially, trustworthiness, reliability and good sense. He was a skilful salesman, too, and was soon showered with accolades from customer and employer alike. The 'Quaker traveller' – as he was nicknamed – was welcomed everywhere, in metropolitan stores as well as those in regional districts.

His career was progressing well: satisfactory to his employers, advantageous to himself. Nonetheless, financial difficulties beset him. Maintaining a home and family wasn't easy. Despite his continued piety, he still hadn't acquired the riches he desired. God hadn't seen fit to bless him.

Meanwhile, the wound from the Quaker's disownment continued to throb, a painful reminder of the snub he had received from those whose acceptance he desperately craved. Everyone else might call him the 'Quaker' traveller, but the Quakers still obdurately refused to accept him as one of their own.

CHAPTER 10

'Tis one thing to be tempted … another thing to fall.

William Shakespeare,
Measure for Measure

FOR A WHILE, Peter Bedford had sensed that something lurked beneath John Tawell's righteous cloak. He had befriended the lad some years previously and had witnessed his zealous religious observance. He knew that such devotion had helped John regain the Friends' esteem and confidence in the years since his disownment. Yet he found himself doubting John's sincerity, his very piety. Recently, his doubts had intensified. They kept intruding into his mind, clinging there limpet-like, refusing to be banished. Then a sense of foreboding enveloped him, coalescing into a dark vision: John was set to commit a crime serious enough to send him to the gallows.

He must talk to his friend, Bedford decided, so these doubts would no longer torment him. But what if he was wrong … what would John say … what might others think if they learned that he, a leading Quaker, was having such evil thoughts about one of their own? The struggle raged in his mind until he felt impelled to confront John.

From his own residence in Steward Street, Spitalfields, it was only a short distance to John and Mary's home in Shoreditch. As he trudged north along City Road and through the side gate next to St Luke's turnpike, his footsteps, at first decisive, slowed, then at last stopped. He could not do it. He turned and retraced his steps, reaching the turnpike again before the uneasiness he'd been defiantly ignoring halted him in his tracks. This time, when he swivelled and headed north, his footsteps carried him all the way to the Tawells' threshold.

There his fortitude deserted him again. Backwards and forwards he paced, remonstrating with himself, urging himself onwards, until finally he raised his fist and hammered on the door. Mrs Tawell received him gladly, as if he were on a friendly call. She ushered him into her husband's presence and chatted for a while until he indicated that he wished to speak privately with his host.

'John Tawell,' said Bedford when they were alone, 'I have come to tell thee that I believe thou art on the eve of committing a crime which will bring thee to the gallows.' Then he tensed, waiting for the outraged response.

A startled looked crossed John's face. Bewilderment followed, then horror. He buried his face in his hands and burst into tears, each sob an anguished testament to three decades of frustration and failure. After a while, he composed himself. Opening a desk drawer, he pulled out a wad of papers and held it up. He admitted that Bedford's charge was true, that he was holding forged money he'd been planning to cash. Then, watched by his astonished accuser, he ripped the forged notes into shreds.

Bedford headed home soon afterwards. He felt awed and humbled by God's majesty, honoured that he'd been chosen as the Lord's messenger.

John was left alone to ponder the day's happenings. If he had ever doubted the truth of God's presence, the magnitude of His power, he would never do so again. Nonetheless, his financial problems remained and his means of solving them lined his waste-paper bin.

~

It was an unusually severe winter, that winter of 1813–14. On the eve of Epiphany – 6 January – the thermometer plummeted. The Thames froze over, making it a skater's paradise. Heavy snowfalls tumbled from the sky, blocking roads and engulfing houses, hardening into rock-hard, dangerously slippery ice accumulations that were two feet thick. Those reliant upon clear roads or waterways found themselves unable to earn an income at the worst possible time in an exceptionally bad year.

Not long afterwards, a whip-carrying Quaker, booted and spurred, trod carefully along the icy streets of London's business district to 49 Cheapside, the premises of engraver and printer Edward Anthony Thorowgood. He introduced himself as Mr Smith, one of the partners of the Quaker-owned Uxbridge Bank. Pulling out a piece of paper, he offered it to the engraver for his perusal.

Thorowgood saw a blank one-pound note inscribed with the names of the bank and its partners, one of whom was named Smith. Curiously, the note lacked the customary date and signature.

'My bank is determined to have a new plate engraved,' Smith continued. He asked Thorowgood if he would be willing to engrave a facsimile of the specimen note and strike five hundred copies from it on paper already stamped with the duty. 'If the note when finished does not correspond in every particular with the copy note,' he warned, 'it will be of no use and will therefore not be taken.'

Thorowgood had received many strange requests in his time, although this one was not as odd as it might have seemed. The government didn't issue its own banknotes. While the Bank of England was the government's banker – established, in fact, to serve such an end – it didn't control banknote production. Each of the dozens of privately owned banks produced their own notes, which varied in reliability based on the stability and trustworthiness of the issuing institution. The Quaker banks, the Uxbridge Bank among them, were generally solid and wealthy. So, despite his slight qualm, Thorowgood agreed to execute the order. He took the wad of blank paper from the Quaker and told him to return in a few days' time.

With banknote in hand, Thorowgood chose a suitable copper plate and set it down on his workstation. Carefully, he measured the banknote's letters and plotted their positions – backwards, of course, as copper-plate printing required a reverse image – then lightly marked them on the plate. He picked up his trusted burin (a hardened steel tool with a sharp point) and laid it over the plate. Then, with a firm hand, he began the painstaking intaglio engraving of the plate, scoring lines over the fine markings. This produced the necessary grooves by removing some of the metal itself.

After completing the design he compared it with the original banknote. Close enough. Obviously, as it was a reverse image, he would need to print a note to make sure. He carried the plate over to another workstation where he poured ink into a tray, then he dipped a dabber into it and passed it over the plate, forcing ink into the new grooves. After cleaning off the excess ink with a piece of soft muslin, he laid a sheet of paper over the plate and slid the paper and copper onto a rolling press. He carefully checked the sample note against the original. As a master engraver, he knew that it was almost impossible to duplicate exactly a work of detailed engraving. However, the Uxbridge Bank's note was simple, without too much detail, like many other banknotes in production. He was satisfied. He laid out the sample to dry.

Smith returned as scheduled and asked to see the sample banknote. He placed it near a light and carefully examined it, comparing it with the original. 'There is a variance,' he announced grimly, 'and it is fatal to my object.' He asked the engraver to produce another plate.

As the door shut behind the Quaker, Thorowgood's original misgivings turned to dread. If Mr Smith required an identical banknote, why hadn't he appealed to the original engraver? Looking again at the banknote, Thorowgood saw that it listed the Uxbridge Bank's town agents, Messrs Masterman, Peters, Mildred, Masterman & Co. He decided to pay them a visit.

There, in the agents' offices, he described his assignment. The response was one of bewilderment. The Uxbridge Bank usually employed Messrs Masterman & Co. to fill such orders. What did the Quaker look like? A troubled frown followed when the agent realised that none of the Uxbridge Bank's partners resembled Thorowgood's 'Mr Smith'. The agent asked Thorowgood to take great care of the notes and plate, and to await further instructions.

'A fraud and forgery must be contemplated by the party who has given the order!' exclaimed the horrified Uxbridge bankers upon hearing the news. They appealed to the engraver to prepare the new plate – as 'Mr Smith' had requested – and to await the man's return.

This time 'Mr Smith' approved Thorowgood's workmanship and asked when the five hundred banknotes would be ready. Friday, 28 January, he was told.

⌒

Early that Friday morning, a policeman found a suitable hiding place in Thorowgood's workshop. After each ring of the door-bell, he listened anxiously for the prearranged signal. At last he heard Thorowgood loudly greet 'Mr Smith' and report that the notes were ready. A rustle of papers, a satisfied murmur, a jingle of coins cascading into the cash drawer, some words of farewell … then the plod of receding footsteps. His moment had come.

Hurtling from his hiding spot, the policeman seized upon the customer and announced that he was taking him into custody. He riffled through the Quaker's clothing and found some Bank of England notes. Flipping through them, he discovered that one of the notes had been cut – the first stage in preparing a counterfeit. He peered at the other notes. One of the two-pound notes had already been altered to represent a ten-pound note.

As the policeman knew, many Londoners unwittingly carried forged bank notes, a consequence of the monetary supply problems of the day. In 1797, in desperate need of gold coin for the war effort, Parliament had passed legislation allowing banknotes as low as one and two pounds to be printed. The Restriction Period, as it came to be known, brought paper currency into the pocketbooks of the labouring classes, many of whom lacked the literacy skills to distinguish the forged from the genuine. To make matters worse, the banks continued to print notes that were easily reproduced. Professional forgers rubbed their ink-smirched hands with glee. By the time the policeman was foraging through 'Mr Smith's' pockets, forged one-pound notes comprised nearly half the notes in circulation in some districts.

Most recipients could prove they had been duped. The Quaker's possession of a cut note, however, indicated malintent rather than misfortune. Even so, it showed the hand of a journeyman forger – small-scale, labour intensive. Faking a plate? That was master forgery, a colossal threat to the nation's currency and the security of her financial institutions. There would be no mercy offered this foolhardy Quaker. He would swing, for sure.

~

The Quakers of the Uxbridge Bank were keen to have a quiet, dignified hearing rather than the clamour of a public hearing, so 'Mr Smith' was escorted to the imposing Mansion House at the Bank – which served as the official residence of London's lord mayor, the city's chief magistrate. The blackguard's entry caused a mild disturbance among the Uxbridge partners. This forger wasn't impersonating a Quaker to rob a Quaker. He was a man they recognised: the respected commercial traveller, John Tawell.

As the bankers went through the formalities of signing the magistrate's paperwork, they began to think about the consequences of their anger over the attempted theft. They were about to kill a man. And worse – if that was possible – someone they knew. What's more, his death would not only be on their consciences, it would taint the Friends' reputation as a whole. They had always been vocal in their condemnation of the Bloody Code and its crop of gallows-fodder. A Quaker sending a Quaker to the gallows? It was unthinkable.

One of the shrewd bankers then realised that the forged note in Tawell's pocket might offer them an escape route. The exponential increase in forgeries over the past two decades had created huge problems for the English authorities, particularly in commerce and the banking industry. The Bank of England had taken up the cudgels, establishing a division devoted to prosecuting forgeries. It had achieved a remarkably high conviction and execution rate – until the broader community rebelled. Juries began taking the law into their own hands, acquitting those charged merely with having forged notes in their possession.

Death seemed too high a price for a crime that could easily have been an accident of fate.

This was not the message of deterrence the imperious Old Lady of Threadneedle Street demanded of the nation. The Bank of England's directors inveigled Parliament into enacting new legislation allowing a lighter punishment for minor offenders, so that all who broke the law would pay. If the Bank considered a miscreant worthy enough, it would offer the equivalent of a pre-trial plea bargain – the option of pleading guilty to the 'lesser count'. Its solicitors had sorted out a discreet arrangement with the Old Bailey officials, ensuring that the favoured would escape the gallows and instead be banished to the Antipodes. It was a once-only offer, however. Felons who disdained the offer and were later convicted could expect no mercy.

Would the Bank of England allow John Tawell this option, minor offender though he was not? The Uxbridge bankers approached the Bank of England's solicitors and appealed for their assistance. After some grumbling, the Bank's solicitors agreed to help.

John grasped the lifeline. He would plead guilty to knowingly having a forged Bank of England note in his possession. In return, both banks would drop their forgery charges. Accordingly, on 22 February 1814, he was sentenced to fourteen years' transportation, the mandatory sentence for those pleading guilty to the lesser charge.

Others sentenced on the same day were not so lucky. Fifteen were ordered to the gallows. If it wasn't for the Quakers' efforts – magnanimous yet self-serving – John would have joined them.

CHAPTER 11

If you imprison at home, the criminal is soon thrown
back upon you hardened in guilt. If you transport, you
corrupt infant societies and sow the seeds of atrocious
crimes over the habitable globe. There is no regenerating
a felon in this life. For his own sake, as well as for the
sake of Society, I think it better to hang.

Judge Heath, as quoted in Jeremy Bentham,
The Rationale of Punishment (1830)

THE QUAKER community was unable to forget John's crime,
for reasons that went far beyond his perfidy. They saw his actions
as a betrayal not only of his family and friends but of the Quaker
community as a whole. There was more at stake here than one
man's name and one man's neck.

Although regulations decreed that John was not – officially –
a member of the Society of Friends, his dress and behaviour
marked him as a Quaker. The Friends' reputation as men of
integrity and discretion in business dealings had made them a
steadying influence on the volatile financial world, and indis-
pensable actors in it. What might have happened if the news
had spread that a Quaker was counterfeiting currency? This
particular counterfeiting operation had been foiled, but others
could well succeed. The ripples from John's money-making
enterprise had the potential to crash down on the larger financial markets.

Thus they had shown their forgiveness by granting him life rather than death then casting him into oblivion. Many years would pass before they learnt the legacy of their actions.

⌒

Late in January 1815 John climbed up the ladder and stepped onto the *Marquis of Wellington*'s wooden deck. Sydney welcomed him with a typical summer's day: harsh sunlight bouncing off the water, smothering heat and humidity. And the noise: the incessant, mind-numbing drone of cicadas, and the raucous shriek of galahs and cockatoos.

Sydney was the third port of call on his Grand Tour after leaving his less than salubrious accommodations back home. His six weeks in Newgate Gaol hadn't proved too incommodious, not after someone paid the weekly half-crowns that funded his transfer from the Common Side to the more agreeable environs of the Master's Side. Privileged treatment for the monied? Absolutely! Admittedly, it wasn't merely a form of legalised bribery. Ever pragmatic, the gaol's governors had long realised that such indulgences reduced the costs of administering the gaol, even if they advantaged the already-favoured villains like John Tawell.

Those luxuries had ended on 12 March 1814 when he was rowed out to the *Retribution,* a filthy, vermin-infested prison hulk moored at Woolwich. There the guards forced him to bathe in the same tub of water used to wash the other convicts. These were men with little concern for cleanliness, let alone godliness. Afterwards, John pulled on the standard-issue slop clothing – his new habiliments of shame – then watched as the guards locked iron shackles around his ankles. Once all the convicts were dressed and ironed, the guards snapped out their marching orders. Shuffling and clanking, John took one heavy step after another down to the convicts' quarters. There were hundreds of prisoners in the wretched hulk awaiting transportation, although more than a quarter would never see freedom again, breathing their last in that squalid air.

The following morning, after a breakfast of almost inedible swill, his suffering worsened. He and the other convicts were rowed ashore to labour on the nearby docks from 7 a.m. until dusk, at the mercy of guards who turned cruelty into an art. The guards especially relished taunting the 'Specials', the educated convicts who had once enjoyed a better life. A Quaker in their midst was a delight. Satan revelled most in tormenting the fallen saints.

As summer faded, he was ferried out to the *Marquis of Wellington* – no aristocrat's floating palace but a humble merchant ship contracted to carry a human cargo of convicts. He and his fellow transportees climbed down the ladder to the between-decks, their accommodation for twenty hours a day for the next five months. The transport sailed on 1 September 1814, stopping first at the lush Portuguese island of Madeira, before hopping across the Atlantic to Rio de Janeiro where it anchored for three weeks. Finally, 148 days after leaving England, John caught a first glimpse of his new home.

Sydney was a town struggling to find its character. No longer was it just a garbage pit for Britain's refuse. Under Governor Lachlan Macquarie's visionary rule, it was fertile soil nurturing a sprouting seed. The lumpish St Philip's squatting on the York Street ridge and the nearby hotch-potch of military huts reflected the town's crude origins, the wrath of the Lord and the law that had banished so many to this distant ignominy. Yet the hammering that echoed across town and the handsome edifices rising brick by brick, row by row, represented its potential, a phoenix rising from the ashes of past sins, reinvigorated, ever hopeful.

The colonial muster clerks came on board, and John and his companions lined up before them. The clerks began gathering personal details – age, birthplace, occupation – while making their own pen-portrait descriptions: height, hair colour, eye colour, complexion. They were collecting useful occupational information as well as identification aids in case a convict later absconded. Most of the convicts answered with a shrug of indifference, choosing to tell the truth or to lie with little thought for the consequences. John was different. When asked the most critical question of them all – 'Occupation?' – he answered carefully and deliberately. He lied.

His five-month voyage to the colonies had proven surprisingly educational. Some of his fellow lags had communicated with earlier transportees and knew how the colonial penal system worked. John listened and he learnt. He discovered that the unskilled convicts were generally assigned to farmers to hack at rock-hard trees or snake-filled undergrowth to help clear the ground. Some with trade skills worked in government jobs – at the lumberyard or dockyard or in shoemaking or slopmaking shops. Educated middle-class convicts like himself usually received special treatment; the penal system, a huge bureaucracy, required an abundance of clerks. Ever the strategist, he considered what occupation he should ascribe to himself: shopman, draper, accountant, commercial traveller? Then he had a thought.

Back in England, as a commercial traveller, he had been most successful in selling Spyring & Marsden's drugs and patent medicines. His formidable memory and scientific aptitude meant that he offered more than the usual glib salesman's patter. He genuinely understood what he was selling. In fact, so rapidly had he grasped the uses of these medicines as well as the skills needed for their preparation that, within a few years, he could have found work as an apothecary's assistant. So when the muster clerks asked for his occupation, he answered simply and clearly: 'Druggist.'

His strategy worked. The convict transports rarely offloaded men with medical experience. He was assigned to the dilapidated General Hospital at Dawes Point to the choice post of working in the government dispensary.

Employment at the hospital provided opportunities for those keen to better their condition, although these opportunities were not what Governor Macquarie had envisaged when he lectured the convicts upon their arrival. Macquarie had advised that these shores offered boundless opportunities for those who used their servitude as a chance for redemption. Clergymen visiting the convicts declared the same, while offering homilies to help them return to the path of righteousness. But the system itself forced them to practise vices many had never previously employed: lying, cheating, thieving and worse – indeed, whatever it took to survive. John was persuaded that the only person truly concerned about the righteousness of his path was himself.

One day later that year, John and a hospital clerk were spotted slipping out of the hospital store with bundles they had no reason to be carrying. They were confronted. When opened, the bundles were found to contain towels and children's bed linen, both purloined from the store. John's punishment was a year at Coal River, the Newcastle penal settlement half a day's boat ride north of Sydney. By order of the magistrates he was 'to be employed in the public service in the usual way' which generally meant being assigned to one of the back-breaking, skin-corroding, soul-destroying jobs of mining, salt-panning, oyster-collecting or lime-burning. But John was not a 'usual' convict. His skills were always in demand.

Upon his return to Sydney, he was assigned to Mary Sims who had once served as the hospital midwife. A year later he was reassigned to Isaac Wood, schoolmaster of the Sydney Academy in Phillip Street. Wood assured prospective parents in an advertisement published late in 1817 that his new assistant was 'perfectly competent', but John didn't remain there for long. His health failed – probably as a consequence of consumption, the largest-ever killer of mankind and a common complaint at the time. In mid-1818 he was admitted as a patient to Governor Macquarie's new Sydney Hospital in Macquarie Street, where he remained for five months.

'Beware all ye who enter here' should have been the motto for Sydney's hospital, indeed for any hospital of the period. They were deadly places, plagued by unsanitary conditions, limited treatment, and inadequate and incorrectly administered medicines. The unskilled nursing staff were frequently intoxicated and always unreliable, their superintendence minimal during the day and non-existent at night. The wards were overcrowded and not segregated by disease, allowing highly contagious patients to mingle with those admitted for minor ailments. As for separation by gender, more patients returned home infected with venereal diseases than were admitted.

While convicts, soldiers and orphans had no choice but to endure these dreadful conditions, free people, particularly women, found them intolerable. As the population and economy grew, Dr William Redfern saw the growing need for an alternative to government-supplied hospital care, and began to offer his services privately. Still, medical supplies for patients came from the only available source, the poorly stocked government dispensary.

During his lengthy hospitalisation, John watched and listened and ruminated about the situation. He recognised that an opportunity existed for someone with his particular skills, one that could make him rich – if he survived his term in hospital. First, though, he would need his freedom: a ticket-of-leave, the colonial version of a parole pass. This would allow him to earn an income – so long as he remained within his specified district and attended a weekly muster. He knew that some convicts were lucky enough to receive such an indulgence after serving only a couple of years in the colony. Governor Macquarie had made it clear that he valued hard-working convicts and would reward them handsomely.

⤳

'Nearly five years of my sentence has expired,' John wrote to the governor in December 1818 when he was about to leave the hospital, 'and I humbly solicit the indulgence of a ticket-of-leave.' He mentioned his assignments to Mary Sims and Isaac Wood and his recent confinement in the General Hospital, but he thought it best to omit any reference to his sojourn at Newcastle. 'I humbly hope,' he added, 'that the liberal education I have received will secure me a respectable and comfortable maintenance, united with such conduct as hereto will ever meet His Excellency's approbation.'

Appropriately obsequious as his application might have been, it failed to include the necessary recommendation from a man of the cloth. Instead of receiving his freedom, he found himself tutoring the progeny of the indefatigable Deputy Surveyor General James Meehan.

John mulled over his error, soon recognising that piety, particularly of the Anglican variety, served a useful purpose in the penal settlements as well. After a timely interval, he solicited a recommendation from a 'hireling priest', the Reverend William Cowper, who was the incumbent of St

Philip's Church of England. In 1819 he was successful in his bid.

With his ticket-of-leave tucked in his pocket and his hazel eyes focused on his goalposts, John left Meehan's household. He found work as a clerk with Richard Brooks, a wealthy merchant and shipping agent who was one of the 'exclusives', the colony's gentry. Governor Macquarie had once remarked that colonial society comprised two classes: those sent out here and those who should have been. No doubt Brooks was in his mind when he caustically dismissed the virtues of Sydney's worthies. As captain of the ill-fated *Atlas* transport in 1802, Brooks's negligence and greed resulted in the deaths of a third of the convicts locked in his extremely cramped hold, the remaining space being filled with Brooks's personal cargo, which he traded for profit on his arrival. Censured, but never prosecuted (and even allowed to command another convict transport), he was among the pillars of rectitude now looking down their pinched noses at the convict scum, who had mostly been banished for such heinous deeds as poaching, thieving, forging and receiving. As the convicts sentenced to the penal settlements well knew, wealth dictated its own laws.

In January 1820, when John was ready to take the next step – applying for a conditional pardon – Brooks was among those who provided a character reference. Isaac Wood added his own kind words, extolling John's virtues and reporting that he owed the fellow a considerable debt of gratitude: 'Through his skill and attention, I have been restored to my health and through gratitude am prompted to make this application in his behalf.' Governor Macquarie heard their praise and signed his approval.

With his conditional pardon in hand, John could work and reside wherever he chose within the colonial boundaries until his fourteen-year sentence expired. If he broke the conditions of his pardon and returned to England, he would face the legislated punishment of death.

Appealing to the gruff Scotsman for a conditional pardon at this time was another of John's fortuitous decisions. Unknown to most in the colony, the tide had begun to turn. Commissioner John Thomas Bigge had recently arrived in Sydney and was prowling the countryside. Officially, his role was that of a public investigator, responsible for evaluating the effectiveness of transportation as a deterrent to crime. On the quiet, he was also a private inquisitor, briefed by his superiors in London to seek evidence of Macquarie's 'ill-considered compassion for convicts'. Transportation, they claimed, should be an object of real terror. Bigge would report back that, under the governorship of Lachlan Macquarie, it was not.

Never again would convicts like John have the same opportunities to reap the rewards of their own industry and intelligence, to kick away the shackles of their past in this land of second chances.

CHAPTER 12

The whole population, rich and poor, are bent on acquiring wealth ... I am not aware that the tone of New South Wales Society has yet assumed any peculiar character; but with such habits and without intellectual pursuits, it can hardly fail to deteriorate (and become like that of the people of the United States).

Charles Darwin,
Diary of the Voyage of H.M.S. Beagle (1836)

AS HIS petition for a conditional pardon sat in the governor's in-tray, John went down to Sydney Cove to watch his aspirations take root. The *Regalia* from London had dropped anchor and was beginning to offload its cargo of general merchandise. Among the boxes and casks and kegs winched from the hold were medicines addressed to John Tawell. He had been ordering stock to fill the shelves of a retail pharmacy, the first to be opened in Australia.

Sydney was desperately in need of a private apothecary, as John had realised during his stay in hospital. He had totted up his skills: his knowledge of medical preparations, honed by his time in the Sydney hospital dispensary; his contacts from his days as a commercial traveller in London, who could source medical preparations; his gifts as a salesman, accountant and shopman; his willingness to work hard. Through his mind's eye, he could already see God's golden blessings falling from heaven into his ready hands.

A small advertisement on the third page of the *Sydney Gazette* advised the colonists that their health was about to take a turn for the better. John announced that he had received a shipment of high-quality medicines and would accurately prepare physicians' and family medicines – a relief to those who knew how error-ridden the hospital's efforts were, as much because of supply shortages (exacerbated by constant purloining) as of deficiencies in skill. He concluded with a coy remark: 'The Advertiser takes this opportunity to state that his qualifications are neither unprofessional or irregular.'

Professional? Regular? John had many things to recommend him, but accredited qualifications were not among them. Likely, his boxes of supplies included texts on how to prepare many medicines, solutions that with one grain too many could transform from curative to killer.

The Quakers loathed this type of word-twisting. 'Let our yeas be yeas and our nays be nays', they sternly admonished the flock, priding themselves on their reputation for honesty and integrity in all affairs. Of course, John had barely reached the dizzying heights of Quaker sanctity before sliding back down again. How wicked was a subtle double-negative to a man already convicted of forgery?

On 1 March 1820, John took one last look around his shop at 6 Hunter Street, Sydney. Apothecary scales rested on a counter. Shelves of oddly shaped pots and jars wallpapered the sides of the room – carboys for holding corrosive liquids, gallipots for storing ointments, containers of roots and leaves and barks, specie jars and pillboxes. Barrels of oil sat on the floor nearby. He was ready. And the customers came.

They stepped from gigs and carts or panted up the meandering hill from the Pitt Street gully, eager to venture inside the town's latest Aladdin's cave. John measured, pounded, boiled and dried, producing potions, powders, ointments, infusions and tinctures. Notes and coins piled up in his cash drawer.

Within a short time, he knew that his business success was assured. His expertise had been validated by a board investigating colonial medical conditions. 'We have examined all the Empirics [medical quacks or charlatans] who have come within our knowledge at Sydney,' the naval and military surgeons reported to the governor, 'and found them totally ignorant of every branch of the medical profession with the exception of John Tawell who is qualified to act as an apothecary.' John had convinced them through knowledge alone – unless, that is, he had returned to his old criminal ways.

John purchased larger premises at 18 Pitt Street, a few doors north of the King Street intersection. The move allowed him to broaden his product range. He displayed drugs and chemicals in one section of his shop, with grocery goods and cleaning products lined up in another. Shrewdly recognising the benefits of stocking confectionery and delicacies that appealed to the refined tastebuds and bulging pocketbooks of Sydney's wealthier citizens, he added to his order. The following February the *Midas* brought seeds and spices, fish sauces, French capers, Spanish liquorice and sugar candy.

John began to channel some of his profits into philanthropy, which was considered an obligation for the wealthy and respectable even in colonial society. His charities also reflected his spiritual beliefs and growing evangelism: the Good Samaritan offering a helping hand to the needy, the believer perhaps fearful of God's wrath if he didn't spread God's blessings. His benevolence would increase in later years, after his family's arrival in Sydney.

For seven long years his wife Mary had suffered back in England, shocked by John's criminality and humiliated by his treachery. While John had cast off his fetters soon after arriving in the colony, she had remained shackled to his infamy. Divorce was not an option. It required an Act of Parliament – that is, political connections and plenty of money – neither of which she enjoyed. So she gathered herself together and found work and a new home for herself and her children. Then she received word that John had asked the government to pay their passages to Sydney so he could be reunited with his family.

With their arrival in February 1823, John became the committed Quaker family man again. He sent his boys to Laurence Halloran's Grammar School and supported Halloran's plans to establish a Free Grammar School, even signalling his interest in becoming one of its governors. Supreme Court Justice John Stephen and members of the Macarthur dynasty also joined the board. John was mingling with a new elite – the colonial nobility.

John's philanthropy became more ecumenical. By 1824 he was on the board of the Wesleyan Auxiliary Missionary Society of Sydney, again with Justice John Stephen and also a wealthy ex-convict, Samuel Terry, who would later gain the nickname the 'Botany Bay Rothschild'. John donated money towards the building of a Roman Catholic Chapel and some secular endeavours too, including provision for a 'School of Industry' for the colony's lasses and a dispensary for the poor. He found time for intellectual pursuits, purchasing the works of budding colonial literati as well as history, biography, poetry, classics and French titles. Yet he didn't neglect his business interests, and was among those who joined Sydney's newly established Chamber of Commerce.

These were long-desired openings – shaking hands over common business interests or joining hands in spreading God's word and rewards. But outside the halls of commerce and religion and social work, John's proffered hand was disdained. It wasn't long before he and his fellow ex-convict nabobs grasped that no matter how law-abiding they were, how wealthy and intellectual, how pious and benevolent, how supremely *respectable* they had become, the gentry would always see a broad arrow tattooed indelibly across their palms.

This time, he didn't let his frustration get the better of him. Instead he redirected his energies towards his business dealings, becoming even wealthier as he invested in land, houses, pubs and farms. With the income from these other sources, his apothecary shop was no longer the prow of his freewheeling business empire, but a golden fetter shackling him to colonial shores. He attempted to sell the business. He also petitioned for an absolute pardon, the ultimate accolade the penal system could grant a convict. Both attempts failed. So he returned to broadening his product range – adding perfumery, fancy snuffs and snuff boxes, fire boxes, and oil and watercolour paints to his wares – and started to export soap and whalebone to England.

From early on, the shop had carried veterinary goods, bird seed as well as medicines for sheep, cattle and horses, the first to do so in New South Wales. In this line of business, he wasn't only a retailer. One day in 1827 the Honourable Captain Henry John Rous sought help for a sick horse. John mentioned that he owned the chaise waiting at his shop's door and volunteered to drive the captain back to his stable and administer it personally. Although largely self-taught he was, as always, supremely capable. The horse survived. The captain would remember such unsolicited kindness when John's name was later splashed across the newspapers.

Early in 1828, he had a double celebration. No longer was he a convict or even a tradesman – as shopkeepers were considered – but a landed gentleman worth nearly ten thousand pounds in property alone. A year later, he and his wife and youngest son stepped onto the deck of the beautiful, teak-built *Henry Wellesley* and began their three-month journey home to England.

~

London was the same yet also vastly different. The meandering River Thames, the approaching metropolis, were so familiar, as if he'd been gone for just a moment. But here, the huge new dockland area near the Tower ... and there, in the distance, could that be *two* London Bridges? ... and even further in the distance *another* bridge across the Thames to Southwark. Seedy lanes and alleys had become handsome streets; foul swamps were now breathtaking squares and circuses; gas lights flickered and glowed. The greatest city in the world was somehow grander than ever, magnificent in its modernness. John had come home.

The changes were more than cosmetic. A new king had been crowned, although he would die within the year. The long shadow of the war with France had at last receded, leaving more parochial issues in the spotlight. Some of the exposed evils were splintering the once war-united nation into bickering factions. They squabbled over political and penal reforms, over religious dissent and Catholic emancipation. And while the England of the previous century had willingly bowed down before the rule of the aristocracy, modern Britain remained defiantly head-high, with its men demanding a greater voice in their own governance.

John settled his family in Great Prescott Street, Whitechapel, and financed a medical apprenticeship for his elder son. He ventured into Cheapside and across the Thames to the Borough, visiting old friends and employers, and repaying his debts in coin and contrition. Eventually, he marched up to the Quakers' front door. Society had forgiven him by handing him his certificate of freedom after fourteen years of enforced banishment. God had anointed him with riches. It was now the Quakers' turn to welcome back the prodigal son.

The Quakers had also changed in the time he had been away – remarkably so. The sect that had long slammed its doors to the outside world, even latched its shutters against philan-thropy because it exposed them to other denominations and distracted them from nurturing God's fire in their own hearths, had stepped out again. The Quakers' profoundly humanitarian principles had eased open the shutters. They had spurred the fight for the abolition of the slave trade in the 1780s, and this had brought them into contact with like-minded evangelicals from other denominations – particularly Anglicans who, unlike the Quakers, could at that time sit in Parliament. These reli-gious crusaders believed that true converts donned the mantle of Christ, that one sign of sanctification was the desire to do good works and convert sinners.

The evangelical concept appealed to John. If a sanctified soul was reflected in the desire to do good, then surely the doing of good must reveal a genuine convert. In truth, the paradox of evangelism was that it did not work both ways. The more introspective among the believers recognised this, developing a strongly marked fear of death as a result. Only when one met one's maker could the truth of a conversion experience, the sufficiency of a person's faith, be truly judged. But there was another side to evangelism that interested John. The great evangelicals were venerated by the whole community, revered for their godliness and acclaimed for their benevolence. He had another noble ladder to climb.

John's repentance and righteousness impressed his family, friends and business associates as well as the Quakers generally. They all conceded that his sins did appear to have been expiated on the cross of banishment. The Quakers welcomed him back, albeit a touch warily. He resettled his family at 10 Trinity Street, a short distance south-east of Borough High Street, one of the splendid houses recently erected for the burgeoning middle class. With everyone content, he purchased a passage on one of the fastest vessels out of London, sailing for Sydney in March 1830, in order to wind up his affairs.

Advertisements appeared in the newspapers soon after his return to New South Wales, announcing that he was retiring to Europe and that his pubs, houses, business blocks and farms were to go under the hammer. Some of these holdings proved nicely profitable; however, three years of severe drought had halved the value of his farms. He turned some of his profits into mortgages, charging the going rate of ten and fifteen percent. The landed gentry – those who continued to spurn his hand of friendship – were in particular need of the money spilling from his pockets.

Late in 1831, twenty ex-convict nabobs attended a farewell dinner for him at Hart's Tavern. It was a night John would always remember, a night when he felt accepted and appreciated, when he knew he belonged. After the toasts, he stood up and graciously thanked them all for their well wishes. 'Whether I should again return to the colony or remain in England,' he assured them, 'the recollections of thy kindness will ever be to me one of the greatest pleasures of my life.' Afterwards, he carefully packed into his trunk the newspaper report of the dinner, a treasured possession that would remain with him for the rest of his days.

The omens, on his return to England, were troubling. The first London case of 'Cholera Asiatica', a disease that could kill in a few hours, had been diagnosed not many days before his ship landed. The Central Board of Health had known it was coming, having tracked its lethal progression across Europe since June 1831.

John moved his family out of London to Totteridge, where they joined the six hundred residents who looked across the valley to fog-enshrouded London and breathed deeply of their own healthy air. The change didn't save his youngest son, although cholera wasn't the culprit. William was only twenty-one when he died of consumption, the wasting disease that seemed to consume from within; it would later be named tuberculosis for the knobbly growths that spread throughout the lungs, making it nearly impossible to catch any air. William wasn't alone in his suffering. Mary had the disease as well – as did their newly married eldest son.

John knew that New South Wales had a healthier climate, and that the long sea journey might prove beneficial. He had also heard that the economy was improving, and that the new governor, Richard Bourke, was more supportive of emancipists than his predecessor, Ralph Darling, a military autocrat whose harsh policies had alienated the emancipists and liberal gentry. In point of fact, so angered were the bitter conservatives by Bourke's liberal philosophies and religious tolerance that they had labelled him the 'convict's friend'. Climate, business opportunities, associates who appreciated him: it was right to return – permanently.

Far from casting him into oblivion when they dispatched him to the Antipodes, the Quakers had unwittingly nudged open a door of opportunity. It was a door that he would willingly walk through again when he could make such a choice for himself.

CHAPTER 13

If once upon a time in Potsdam an individual passed whole days in conjugating the verb ennuyer *[to be bored]:* je m'ennui – tu t'ennuis – il s'ennuis *&c., it is no less true that here the greater part of the population manifest a most devoted attachment to the verb 'to drink'.*

Australian Quarterly Journal of
Theology, Literature and Science (July 1828)

JAMES BACKHOUSE and his fellow missionary George Washington Walker were sitting glumly on board the *Henry Freeling* on 22 December 1834 when a voice hailed them. Evangelical Quakers, they had sailed into Sydney Harbour two days previously, still brimming with missionary zeal despite three tough years establishing a Quaker community in Hobart Town on the island of Tasmania. It was time to turn to their attention to the larger colony of New South Wales, to assess the merits of convict transportation and the conditions in the secondary penal settlements, and to support any Quaker coterie. When they had walked through Sydney's streets, however, they found a land of strangers: no familiar faces, no greetings from those who recognised their garb. They received warm handshakes when they visited the Wesleyan superintending the Missionary Society, yet queries about Friends worshipping in Sydney sparked nothing more than a regretful headshake. Their downcast group had gathered on deck for First Day worship, pleading for God's energy to help them begin all over again, when God answered their prayers.

'My name is John Tawell,' said the man who had called out to them. He immediately offered his services in any way that might help them, and invited them to his home in Macquarie Street to take tea with his wife.

As they enjoyed the Tawells' hospitality, one of the missionaries noticed a woman walking past dressed in Quaker attire, and pointed her out to his companions. Surprised, John remarked that he knew of no others who dressed in such a way, and hurried after her. She explained that her family had attended Quaker meetings in England and would be delighted to 'profess with Friends' in Sydney. Within a day of their prayers, the Quaker missionaries had assembled a congregation of five.

On Christmas Day, the Tawells worshipped with the missionaries on board the *Henry Freeling*, then they all retired to Macquarie Street for Christmas dinner. John was proving a godsend. Nearly every night, as the missionaries penned their diary entries, they mentioned having spent time with our 'kind friends' or 'dear friends' the Tawells. They dined frequently at Macquarie Street. They accompanied the Tawells on walks along the shores of Port Jackson and to meetings of the Temperance Society and Australian School Society.

The first shore-based meeting for Quaker worship in New South Wales was held at the Tawells' residence on Sunday, 4 January 1835, with twenty-two people attending. Together John and his new friends planned a public rally to be held in the old courthouse, and organised placards and handbills to be printed and circulated. Together they prepared the room, nailing planks to uprights to provide seating for up to three hundred attendees. 'John Tawell has been extremely attentive and useful in rendering us every aid in his power ever since our arrival,' Walker reported gratefully after the successful meeting. The missionaries' testimonies had been heart-stirring, and the room packed, with many turned away.

When the missionaries sailed again on 13 February for Norfolk Island, seven weeks after their discouraging arrival, they knew they were leaving their little group in capable hands. John would continue to hold meetings at his home, and build up a library of Friends' books for circulation among the convinced and the curious. Clearly, the roots of New South Wales Quakerism had been firmly tamped into Sydney's soil and would thrive under his benevolent care.

~~~

At last the Quakers needed him. John was delighted. But what could he do to show them how much Quakerism meant to him, and how much he had to offer? He thought deeply about the issue and in time had his answer. Among the many properties he had recently purchased was a £400-block in Macquarie Street situated opposite the Legislative Council chambers. There he would build a meeting house for the fledgling Quaker community.

The first Quaker meeting house in New South Wales was officially opened on 1 November 1835, with Backhouse and Walker in attendance. As they gathered outside, they saw a neat little building hinting at a classical influence, with two arched windows and a central doorway. A plaque announcing its year of erection sat above the entrance. A square stone inserted into the front wall proclaimed 'John Tawell to the Society of Friends', his munificence broadcast not only to the Quakers but to the wider community of Sydney. 'The building is all that a

Friends' Meeting House need be,' Walker exclaimed, 'simple, commodious and convenient.'

John lapped up the praise and appreciation, self-effacingly, of course. Then he told the missionaries that he and his wife had a grander vision. Since the building would be empty on weekdays, they were going to establish a girls' school. A non-denominational boys' school had opened its doors to 150 pupils earlier in the year but the needs of Sydney's girls had largely been ignored by the Australian School Society. The Quakers could fill the breach.

John had several goals in founding the school. Evangelicals believed in education for the masses for a simple reason: if children were not educated, they wouldn't be able to read the Bible – and thus would be unable to experience a direct connection with the word of God. Moreover, they needed direction in spiritual matters, as their parents couldn't be relied upon to provide such instruction. What better way to ensure religious indoctrination than school? Still better, education would provide a new set of opportunities and life expectations for these children. As the Quakers had long realised, education was a lifeline to hoist the poor out of the quagmire of poverty and misery. Others in Sydney – particularly those who exploited the masses' labour – feared that an educated poor might get ideas above their station, while some traditionalists fretted that educated women were a danger above all others. John, however, was committed to helping girls as well as boys receive an education.

The school opened in January 1836 under the management of a Ladies' Committee. Mary Tawell was one of its members. Her gentle kindness and charitableness had long impressed the visiting Quaker missionaries. Backhouse wrote home to his sister that 'Mary is the greatest comfort, a really valuable woman', and Walker felt a deep spiritual kinship with her. In fact, after the missionaries had returned to Tasmania late in 1835, Walker found her increasingly in his thoughts. Before long, he believed he had discovered why: Mary was gravely ill. 'My mind has felt much unity with her,' the distressed Quaker wrote in his diary, 'and her removal would occasion a great chasm. May the Lord be her help and stay in the time of trouble.' Five days later, another letter from John reported that the worst was over and Mary was much better. The Lord had answered their prayers.

~~~~~

Building a Quaker meeting house and establishing a girls' school wasn't enough, John decided. His encounters with Backhouse and Walker had inspired him to do more. How else could he show his devotion to Quaker beliefs and ideals?

The evils of drink were being denounced from pulpits across Britain, America and Australia, and Backhouse and Walker were passionate temperance advocates. To liquor they ascribed the social ills of the day, particularly the crimes that had exiled so many of their countrymen to Australia. As the missionaries journeyed around the country they initially preached temperance – until they saw the continuing havoc wrought by the 'evil nectar'. They began pleading not just for temperance but for abstinence. John was listening.

Three days after the Quaker missionaries returned to Sydney in February 1836, John wrote to Governor Bourke. He reported that his British agent had sent him five puncheons of Demerara Rum, four hogsheads of brandy and two hogsheads each of Jamaica Rum and Geneva Gin, as requested, and that these were currently stashed in the bonded stores awaiting John's payment of the exorbitant duties the government charged. He had a problem, though. 'I have of late taken a different view of the use of ardent spirits,' he explained, 'with regard to their lamentably demoralizing and physically bad effect.' He said that he couldn't in all conscience offer them for sale, so he made a suggestion. He would destroy the Demerara Rum and Geneva Gin. He would also convert the higher strength Jamaica Rum into the medically useful spirits of wine, and restrict the brandy to pharmaceutical purposes. He was willing to suffer the financial loss resulting from destroying the Demerara Rum and Geneva Gin if the government would release the liquor without requiring him to pay the usual duties. If they agreed, how should he destroy them?

'See no objection,' a government officer scrawled on the bottom of John's letter a few days later. 'The better way will be to take them out in a boat and stack them into the sea.'

At midday on 5 March 1836, the operation began. John, the two Quaker missionaries, and John Saunders, a Baptist minister and 'Apostle' of the New South Wales Temperance Movement, climbed into a government lighter already laden with seven barrels. Under the directions of a customs officer, crewmen rowed them into the deeper waters of Sydney Cove. Hands pushed the barrels to the side of the boat and tilted them. Six hundred and eight gallons of liquor gurgled from the barrels, glistening in the sunlight before vanishing into the blue.

Some of the onlookers nodded approvingly. Others gulped in horror. 'That's real murder,' cried a man sitting in a nearby vessel. Suddenly, one of the partly emptied puncheons tipped too far and plunged into the water, then surfaced and drifted near his boat. He paddled closer and dipped his horn into its opening, scooping out some of the liquor and lifting it to his lips – then spat out the salty rum and pushed away the puncheon in disgust.

'Even his vitiated palate rejected it,' wrote an amused Backhouse when he completed his diary entry, glorying in the day's achievement and naively expressing his satisfaction at witnessing triumph of principle over self-interest. 'A true patriot,' gushed the *Sydney Gazette*, declaring that Tawell had disposed of so many gallons of incipient misery, poverty and crime; the man deserved the thanks of present and succeeding generations for his noble vision. Sydney's citizens also used the opportunity to air their views. The religious used the 'rum tale' as a platform to preach God's word against drunkenness. The pragmatic complained about the loss of duties to the government coffers. The benevolent suggested that the rum should have been sold and the proceeds given to charity, while the shrewd recognised that rum consumption could only be reduced by degrees and that such an extravagant gesture would have no more effect than Molly McAlpine's attempt to sweep out an inundation of the ocean with her single broom. One literate drunk picked up his pen and, with shaking hands, pleaded with the highest in the land to work towards discouraging the vice by good example. 'I am not sober enough to write more,' he added regretfully, 'but I have a family, and I pray to God to protect them from the course of my misdoings.'

John's act had become a talking point for all of Sydney, providing publicity for the Quakers' temperance endeavours in a way that none in their small congregation had ever imagined.

Despite John's sustained support for the missionaries and his role as the linchpin of the town's Quaker community, he made no attempt to apply to the Friends for reinstatement. Devonshire House – the meeting that had expelled him, and thus the only meeting that could reinstate him to the Society – refused to readmit disowned members living in Australia, arguing that there was no recognised disciplinary body to oversee them there. Walker thought the argument absurd. Other Quaker meetings agreed with his assessment, readmitting those who proved their convincement to the missionaries' satisfaction. Nonetheless, if John wanted to be reinstated, he would have to return to England. Backhouse and Walker's witness was not enough.

Originally, the Tawells had no intention of returning to England. Their son John Downing Tawell and his wife Bethia had joined them in Sydney, having undertaken the sea journey to Australia in the hope of easing the symptoms of John Junior's consumption. Alas, Walker reported after meeting the young surgeon, 'he does not appear to have derived material benefit from the experiment, being still in a very weakly state.'

John Jnr practised medicine for a while, not appreciating the contagiousness of his deadly condition. With his father's financial support, he purchased a £5500 chemist business – then found that he couldn't manage all of his commitments, particularly as his wife was also experiencing bouts of ill health. His father offered to take charge of the chemist business and stock in trade. John Jnr drove a surprisingly hard bargain, a £300 annuity for life, arguing that the business was thriving and the stock in trade extensive and valuable. John was forced to sell the business, later complaining that he had made no profit from the sale having merely intended to help out his son. Their relationship deteriorated, and the surgeon and his wife left the colony a year later to return home.

Soon afterwards, with his son gone and Mary continuing to suffer medically, John decided that they should return to England as well. There, if he chose to do so, he would also have the opportunity to apply for readmission to the Devonshire House Quakers. This time he would be returning not only with God's blessings lining his pockets, but with the Quaker missionaries' gratitude embellishing their many letters home. This time he could walk into any Friends' meeting house with pride.

Over the following six months, John sold all but a handful of his properties, most for a profit. The sales created a new set of problems: what to do with the money. Most of the notes were promissory notes – a promise to pay – rather than government-issued banknotes. Only notes from a reputable business would be accepted by a British discounting house, an enterprise that would take a percentage of the note's cover value in return for providing cash.

John approached broker William Barton, who would later become famous as the father of Australia's first prime minister, and asked him to have £7000 worth of bills exchanged for notes he could take to England. John offered him the usual one percent commission. Barton approached several bill-brokers but the best they would offer was £5000.

'Friend,' John said disappointedly when Barton reported back, 'the offer is not enough. I was prepared to lose twenty or twenty-five percent on the bills to get away quickly, but that is too much to spare.'

Barton was surprised to find John on his doorstep a few days later. 'Friend,' said John again, 'I have been thinking that thou didst thy best in that affair; that it was not thy fault but my convenience that I did not elect to take the highest offer thou didst elicit, so here is thy commission on the best tender.' Then he laid a cheque for £50 on the broker's desk and walked out.

Barton marvelled at such a gesture – the sum was larger than the annual income of most colonists. He would repeat the story of John's generosity on numerous occasions in later years, long after the Tawells sailed for England in February 1838, never to return.

CHAPTER 14

Let he that is without sin among you cast the first stone.

John 8:7

❦

IN THE same month that John and Mary farewelled Sydney, Backhouse and Walker bade their own goodbyes to Australia and sailed for South Africa to continue their mission. Through letters and conversations over the following few years, they would learn of the difficulties faced by their 'dear friends' the Tawells in the aftermath of their arrival in England.

John and Mary chose Nash's visionary garden city, Regent's Park, for their new London home, leasing Cornwall Lodge (later the home of actress Lily Langtry), a minute's walk from Madame Tussauds. While the nearby park allowed John to indulge his passion for nature, Mary had little time to enjoy its pleasures. The brisk sea air hadn't cleansed her lungs as they had hoped. Consumption continued to eat the life from her.

John sought the best medical attention his riches could buy, approaching, among others, Dr John Elliotson, London's pre-eminent physician. Elliotson was the first British physician to use the stethoscope and was also a recent convert to the use of Dr Franz Mesmer's new hypnotism in his medical practice. Yet even such innovations failed to help Mary.

John asked a friend, Sarah Bacon, for the name of a reliable nurse to care for his ailing wife. He didn't want the usual types found in London's hospital wards or trailing Britain's

armies – dirty, foul-mouthed, ignorant sots. He wanted a superior sort of nurse, one who could minister to members of the
gentry. Mrs Bacon knew just the right person: a thirty-three-
year-old woman named Sarah Hadler. She was both respectable
and caring, and came with high recommendations.

Nurse Hadler took over sick-room duties, tending to Mary
as her wracking coughs and blood-stained handkerchiefs testified to her body's increasing debilitation. Mary lost the battle
on 12 December 1838. An obituary in the Quakers' *Annual
Monitor* reported that she 'filled her station by an exemplary
deportment, life and conversation, while her unassuming and
affectionate demeanour endeared her to those friends who were
best acquainted with her.' Thirty years previously, John had been
disowned by the Quakers for marrying this non-Quaker woman.
Now the Quakers mourned her as a very worthy woman indeed.

Within the following few months, John moved across
the Thames to Southwark, settling at 24 Bridge Street (now
Southwark Bridge Road), an area he knew well from his days
as a commercial traveller. He continued to attend Quaker meetings and joined the Peace Society. He renewed his philanthropic
pursuits, helping to found and fund a charity school in nearby
Chapel Place. His benevolence wasn't restricted to charitable
institutions, though. When the importunate son of a Quaker
friend hinted that he needed assistance in finding work, John
recommended him to one of his tradesmen, who immediately
offered the lad employment, declaring that John's word was
enough of a recommendation. When John then advanced the
lad money and helped him purchase the necessary gear (later
refusing to be reimbursed), they discussed Quakerism, with
John earnestly praising the rules and ordinances of the sect.
'The garb alone,' he added, 'will preserve you from many
temptations.'

'It is a hedge,' many Quakers claimed as a justification for continuing to wear their peculiar apparel, 'a hedge separating us from the people of the world, preserving us from the snares and temptations to which they are exposed, and keeping us in safety so long as we remain within its enclosure.' Not much of a hedge, a percipient Quaker memoirist would later admit, adding that if it had been high enough, as high as heaven itself, it might have kept out 'the enemy'. But, earthbound as it was, it offered no obstruction to the enemy's advances. Ultimately, the enemy was within.

~

John was still desperate to be readmitted to the Quakers, obsessed with the need to be accepted and respected by them. He planned his strategy carefully. On 4 December 1839, thirty years after being disowned, he wrote to the Quakers Meeting for Sufferings. 'For several months past, since my return from Sydney, I have had in contemplation to offer the Meeting House erected there by me in 1835.' He had mentioned the idea to Backhouse and Walker back in Sydney, proposing that they become trustees. They had agreed, helping him to prepare a list of four others who might join them in managing the trust.

'I do not possess the privilege of church fellowship with Friends,' John continued, 'but it is with love to the Society – and I would also trust with regard for its principles – by which I have been induced to make this offer as a free gift. My circumstances enable me to do this from a successful persevering industry in a respectable profession and business – a licenced apothecary and a chemist and druggist. There was no other party in Sydney who met as Friends that could have well afforded contributing to any hire of a room.'

On 3 April 1840, the Meeting for Sufferings officially accepted John's 'kind and liberal offer' and asked him to provide the necessary directions to enable the meeting house's transfer into the hands of the trustees. Three days later, John applied to Devonshire House to be readmitted to the Quaker fold.

Blatant vote buying? Crude opportunism? It seems astonishing from a man who was such a careful strategist. Yet in accepting his offer of the Sydney meeting house, the Friends were breaching their own rules, which stated that non-members were forbidden from contributing to Quaker funds. What was the offer of a property worth at least £800 but a proposed injection of funds, indeed an extraordinarily generous and beneficial one? Their decision must have seemed like an invitation to reapply for membership.

John had a pressing reason for wanting to rejoin the Quakers at this time. He had met Sarah Cutforth. Unless he was readmitted, they wouldn't be able to marry.

'We have received a letter from John Tawell applying to be reinstated in membership,' announced the clerk at the Devonshire House Monthly Meeting two months later. The usual head-nodding followed, along with remarks about his earlier perfidy, his penitence, his evident piety and philanthropy. A committee of three men was appointed to visit and confer with him.

Again and again John greeted his Quaker visitors and answered their probing questions, an intimidating process with much resting upon it. At the monthly meeting on 4 August the committee announced their verdict. 'We have several times visited John Tawell and after seriously considering the subject, do not think the time is yet come to accede to his request.'

Surprise greeted their declaration. 'Why?' everyone demanded. 'He has scrupulously paid all the debts he incurred before transportation, with interest, and has done his utmost to repair the known consequences of his former offence. He is a regular attender of our meetings for worship and has all the appearance of a consistent Friend. He is a rich and liberal man. Why so rigidly remember former offences? Why lose sight of that spirit of meekness which will restore the penitent offender?'

The grounds for such a judgement were not noted in the minutes, only the final decision – almost a foregone conclusion from the cautious sect. 'The meeting coincides with the committee's judgement,' declared the clerk, 'and requests them to inform him of their decision.'

The pain from the Quakers' face-slapping of thirty years previously began to throb again, made worse by his profound sense of injustice. More bad news followed. Sarah broke off their match. In the wake of this further disappointment, John relinquished his Southwark house and moved ten miles south of London to 1 Park Cottages in Croydon. The leafy suburb had become fashionable after the London–Croydon railway opened the previous year. But it wasn't popularity that drew him towards Croydon, rather proximity to his old mentor, Peter Bedford. Whatever the grounds for the Quakers' rejection, John saw it as another sign of God's wrath. By walking in the shadow of his venerable mentor, he yearned to rediscover his own pathway to righteousness, that is, to Quaker acceptance. And perhaps back into Sarah Cutforth's good graces, as well.

Despite her rejection, he hadn't given up hope. He rented an apartment at the King's Arms in Berkhampstead and regularly travelled there from Croydon, worshipping in the Quaker's High Street meeting house and attending meetings of the Tring and Berkhampstead Bible Society when he was in town. All the while, he continued to woo her.

⤳

Sarah faced a quandary. John wasn't officially a Quaker. If she married him, she risked being expelled from the security of her religion, from the comfort of her community. Yet marrying him couldn't really be considered 'marrying out' – not spiritually, anyway. He was committed to the faith, a man who 'professed with Friends', who espoused their beliefs and lived by their philosophies, a member in all but name. He had even built a Quaker meeting house and given it to the Friends – and they had accepted it, despite their own decrees. Surely they couldn't consider that marriage to him would be yoking herself to an unbeliever? The mental tug-of-war continued until, at last, Sarah reached her decision.

'Sarah Cutforth has given her company with an intention to marry a person not a member of our Society,' the clerk of the Women's Meeting announced in December 1840. Two months later, those appointed to visit Sarah reported that she had received them kindly but was still planning to marry. 'I hope that Friends will not be too hasty in putting the rules of discipline into practice,' she had entreated them, 'as I anticipate there is a probability that my friend will be reinstated into membership.' The women's committee continued visiting Sarah, while her friends admonished her in private – until it was too late. On 25 February 1841, John and Sarah wed in a civil ceremony at Berkhampstead's Registry Office.

At least they had married without the services of a 'hireling priest'. However Sarah had defied the Quakers' wishes in per-sisting with her plans to marry. With obdurate righteousness, they enforced their rigid rules. Sarah joined John in Quaker purgatory.

John moved into the Red House with his bride and

stepdaughter, having taken over its £60 annual lease a few months beforehand. Backed by John's wealth, Sarah no longer needed the income from her boarding school. She settled down to domestic married life, although this time she made certain of her financial security. She had John sign a marriage settlement, agreeing that her own assets would be held in trust for her and her children, and that John would assign her £6000 in Bank of New South Wales stock or sufficient stock in another company to provide her with an annual income of £600. Also, if she should predecease him, he was to pay her daughter a lifetime annuity of £200.

Strangely, John didn't fulfil the requirements of the marriage settlement. Perhaps he was keeping his options open until the New South Wales economy improved. The news from the colony wasn't good. Drought had struck again, starting in 1837 and worsening each year, a remorseless aridity that killed the grass, baked the earth, starved sheep and cattle and destroyed livelihoods. The British prices for Australian wool had remained strong until 1840, keeping the economy afloat, but when they slumped, and then the local wheat prices slumped and the rains still didn't come, the weakening economy collapsed. Land and stock became almost worthless, land proprietors and investors sank into bankruptcy, banks teetered, newspapers folded, and few had the money to buy the goods sent from England on speculation. Like the once-proud rivers of his second home, John's income stream was drying up.

Friends and acquaintances had long wondered about the extent of his wealth, with estimates ranging between £20,000 and £120,000. John himself boasted that he was worth £40,000 when he first returned to England and that he had doubled his fortune during his return trips. Later financial accounts would suggest that he was worth between £20,000 and £40,000 when he married Sarah, before the worst of the depression hit New South Wales.

Unfortunately, his wealth was still largely tied up in activities associated with the colonies: bank shares, property holdings, mortgages and shipping trade. They were difficult enough to manage from London, let alone from his home in Berkhampstead, so he regularly travelled into the city to conduct business. He was 'well known in the city' in the business euphemism of the time, a subscriber to London's Hall of Commerce and also a long-term member of the Jerusalem Coffee House. He visited the coffee house at least once a week to collect his mail and to read newspapers and transact business. He usually sat in one of the corner boxes on the left-hand side of the bar, where he enjoyed a coffee and toast. He rarely had company – not socially, anyway. These, of all people, knew his history. The word that he was a returned convict transportee had spread even before the ink on his membership papers had dried. His tainted background combined with his reserved disposition and peculiar attire made even the ebullient ships' captains steer shy of him. It was only back home in Berkhampstead, in the Red House, that he was lord of his fiefdom, loved and revered.

Despite the colony's slump, John filled his Berkhampstead home with servants, and lavished money and attention on his beloved wife and stepdaughter. Eliza was sent to a girls' school in London, while Sarah turned her energies towards the house, furnishing it with elegant simplicity. John concentrated on the extensive back garden, pulling out the beds of cabbages and greens Sarah had grown to feed her students, and donating them to the poor of the town. He tastefully redesigned the garden, erecting ornamental summer houses, a large conservatory filled with rare and choice exotic plants, and an aviary containing a variety of English and foreign species. Inside the house, he set up a natural history collection, which he proudly showed to visitors: case after case containing botanical specimens, shells, precious stones, birds and insects, eggs from Australian marsupials, a stuffed emu and penguin, a glass globe holding a preserved snake and a scorpion-filled bottle. His passion for natural history had already spurred him to join the Zoological Society of London, and there he rubbed shoulders with notables in the field. His knowledge and description of first-hand encounters with creatures that many would never see showered him with respect from his peers.

Meanwhile, John and Sarah, although barred from membership, continued to attend the Berkhampstead Quaker meetings for worship. John made sure that he didn't miss any of the meetings, sometimes travelling great distances to be present. Despite his devout exterior, he was however quietly rebelling. He felt the need to retaliate in some way against the Quakers for this latest snub. He didn't hand over the deeds for the Sydney meeting house – a touchy subject, no doubt, on both sides. A Tasmanian Quaker also complained that John was offering financial baits to birthright and disowned Friends to migrate to New South Wales.

John continued his benevolent pursuits in Berkhampstead and developed his reputation for philanthropy. He purchased medicines for the poor, and played an active role in local education and also in social and parish business. Yet some noticed an air of bustle and self-importance about him, as if he wished to make himself conspicuous, as if he hoped that his generous deeds would secure him an unwarranted status in the local community. One in particular watched and listened, a man who loathed the Quakers and everything about them, a twisted soul who would soon lash out at John with a vicious and unrelenting force.

Chapter 15

*See, see! There goes the fellow who has been so long
humbugging us with his sham honesty.*

Peter Cunningham,
Two Years in New South Wales (1827)

JOHN COMMENCED the year 1844 with a spirit of renewed
confidence. His son Henry Augustus Tawell had been born
healthy on 17 August 1843 – a relief to them all considering
the possible impact of a terrifying incident a few months
previously. John had climbed down from his phaeton and
handed the ponies' reins to an ostler, who then loosened the
bridle before stepping away for a moment. Something startled
the ponies – a hornet sting, perhaps, or a gadfly – and they
bolted with pregnant Sarah and her friend still on board.
Spotting a soft patch on the roadside, the quick-thinking
women had jumped from the carriage and tumbled away
from its wheels. Relief at Sarah's safety had naturally been
marred by concerns for the baby's well-being. The babe's
birth was a good omen.

John decided to apply again to Devonshire House for readmission. Among those appointed to visit and confer with him
was William Manley, who had served on the interviewing
committee four years earlier. At the February meeting, Manley
reported that they had talked with John but would like further
time to investigate. When the three men reappeared at John's

door not long after the meeting, he must have known that it didn't bode well.

'We were able to enter feelingly and with sympathy into his case,' the men at last reported, adding that John manifested an attachment to the Society's principles and that his conduct since their last investigation had been consistent with that attachment. 'However,' they added damningly, 'we have not been able to discover in him that abiding tenderness and self-abasedness of mind which true repentance for past outgoings leads into.'

Astonishment once again met the Quakers' report. Then came the questions and objections, the expressions of concern. 'Having had the full and deliberate consideration of this meeting,' the minutes of the wary sect finally reported, 'and though much interest and sympathy has been expressed towards him, yet this meeting does not see its way clear to accede to the application at the present time.'

Later rumours suggested that John's application had been demanding and that he had expressed no contrition for former offences. There comes a point, though, when one can apologise no more, when enough is enough. He had repented; he had shown his redemption through word and deed; he had repaid his debts; he had attended all their meetings for worship – indeed, he was the most habitual of habitual attenders – and he had supported the Quakers in every way possible. What more could they want?

Which was exactly what they saw: the simmering anger and frustration; the deep resentment that, no matter how hard he tried, they wouldn't grant him the respect and acceptance he craved. Because they knew that Quaker acceptance wasn't intended to meet his emotional needs, but to reflect his convincement of their spiritual beliefs and his acceptance of their moral codes.

The judgement was devastating. In dismissing his application for readmission for a second time, Devonshire House had ended his dreams of Quaker membership. This wasn't simply rejection; it was utter humiliation. The year hadn't begun well at all.

Despite the repeated rejections, John persisted in trying to ingratiate himself with the Quakers, somehow convinced that through his actions he could demolish concerns about his attitudes. In April 1844, he was one of two men appointed as surveyors of the highways of Berkhampstead parish, leading the editor of the *Bucks Gazette* to quip that under their 'able and judicious management there can be no doubt of having our *ways mended*'. It was a sly jab, but an unmistakeable one.

John's first action was to have a covering constructed over an offensive drain lying in front of the Quaker meeting house in High Street. The drain covering didn't last long. A heavy storm that June not only destroyed the covering, it washed the materials into the drain and blocked it, redirecting the waste waters across the turnpike road and beginning to cause damage. The turnpike trustees ordered him to remove the covering and clear the drain at once.

Egos clashed. The editor of the *Bucks Gazette* gleefully used the opportunity to have another dig at John and his fellow Quakers. 'But, alas!' he wrote, 'that all the patriotic exertions of this good man should be set at nought, reviled, abused and – can it be believed! – actually destroyed, annihilated – not one brick left upon another to point out to future ages the whereabouts of this masterly production of Quaker ingenuity and skill.'

John reluctantly obeyed the order, although declaring that the trustees were 'a parcel of damned fools and really did not know what was to their advantage'.

'It is quite evident that the trustees know nothing about roadmaking,' the *Bucks Gazette* responded. 'It strikes us that

the destruction of this magnificent work of art has its origin in
envy – they (the trustees) are jealous that the talents acquired
by this great and good man in foreign climes, a man who has
sacrificed so much for his country's good, and who was giving
the benefit of his hardly acquired experiences to the inhabitants of Berkhampstead, earning for himself at the same time
an honourable record in the archives of his country, a niche in
the temple of fame, and a blessing from every living creature
upon the face of the earth. These were too much for the trustees to stand by and see quietly and honourably acquired by
the surveyor of the highways and byways of Berkhampstead.'

The editor's mockery and references to John's felonious past
sharpened the nib of Miles's Boy's malicious quill. Protected by
his pseudonym, he sent letter after letter to the *Bucks Gazette*,
verbally lacerating John and deriding him for his ill-designed
drain, even suggesting he was misusing parish funds.

'A Little Boy' – no doubt local Quaker Richard Littleboy Jnr –
attempted to defend John against the ridicule of this 'mean,
malicious, pettifogging personage', claiming that Miles's Boy's
intention was merely to cast an opprobrious name upon a
worthy and unassuming man, and challenging him to take on
the onerous surveying duties himself if he considered his talents
superior. 'Dick' waded into the battle, claiming that Miles's Boy's
taunts and insults were the last resource of mental poverty and
literary meanness. Miles's Boy spat back and, for a moment, his
initial quarry was forgotten.

But not for long. Soon Miles's Boy suggested that the town's
'surveyor of the highways' liked the title as a reminder of certain
bygone days in New South Wales, when 'select parties firmly
united in their good work are agreeably engaged in mending the
highways and byways of their fellow countrymen' – a blatant
allusion to the chained road gangs of the penal settlements.

John stormed into the *Bucks Gazette* office in Aylesbury, demanding the identity of the malevolent Miles's Boy. The editor refused his request, explaining that those who wrote under a pseudonym did so to protect their identity, and that it was his duty to fulfil their wishes and to communicate their concerns. Naturally, the editor had no desire to shut down such a lucrative stream of vitriol. John threatened to take legal action and stalked out.

Behind the stoic face was a deeply troubled mind, a spirit sinking into a depression. John wrote to his missionary friend, James Backhouse, and twice visited his Quaker mentor, Peter Bedford. Neither realised that John was seeking a lifeline and failed to offer the spiritual guidance he so desperately longed for.

His financial burden was also becoming heavier. He admitted to the rector of Berkhampstead's St Peter's, a friend in philanthropy, that serious trade losses and the failure of an Australian bank had left him stretched. He intended to cut down his domestic expenditure and, in the next few months, he would be relinquishing his carriage and horses and discharging two of his servants.

All he had ever craved was wealth, respect and communion with the Quakers, yet as he caught the train to London on New Year's Day 1845, he knew that he could no longer claim to have achieved any of his heartfelt desires.

⌒

Although Berkhampstead was less than twenty miles from Slough, it was a circuitous route by rail. Sarah alighted at London's Euston Station then took an omnibus to Paddington Station. From there she caught the 4 p.m. train to Slough, the same train John had caught on New Year's Day.

Not that she knew when he had travelled there – or even

why. She wouldn't know the truth about anything until she had spoken to him. Yet that knowledge didn't stop the unanswerable questions from causing a brainstorm. Nor did it stop her from reaching one simple conclusion: that the shadows of his past had probably caught up with him.

It was 5 p.m. by the time she reached Superintendent Perkin's residence at Eton. When she entered the house and saw John, the hours of anguish and confusion overwhelmed her. After a while, when she had calmed enough to speak, she asked in a low tone, 'Oh my dear, what have you been doing?'

'Nothing,' said John earnestly, 'but I hope you will forgive me.'

They talked for some time, then Sarah showed him the newspaper report of the hearing. He read it with interest. Some hours later, as she prepared to depart, he asked her to leave some cash. She had only a sovereign, she told him miserably, and needed it for her journey home. After a harrowing farewell, she was taken to the railway station to begin the interminable trek back to Berkhampstead.

It was too dark to see the countryside passing by – not that she would have noticed it anyway. At least now she had some answers. He had said he was innocent. He had looked into her eyes and sworn that he was innocent, that the woman had poisoned herself. Fearing implication, he had fled from the house, needing no reminder that the burden of suspicion rested more easily on the shoulders of an ex-felon. Once the word 'convict' was mentioned, who would believe him when he declared his innocence?

She knew he was telling the truth. The shadows of his past had enveloped him again for sure. This was just one more ordeal he had to endure – that they all had to endure. When would it ever end?

Part 3

SUSPICION

This extraordinary affair, which is wrapt in the greatest mystery, has excited the most intense interest throughout this extensive neighbourhood.

The Times
(4 January 1845)

CHAPTER 16

Science has been accused of fostering crime by the facilities afforded for its perpetration; in her defence we can plead that science has deprived the criminal of all reasonable chance of escaping with impunity.

Journal of the Belfast Clinical and Pathological Society (1856-57)

AT SALT Hill, word spread that the doctors suspected poison, although the police hadn't found a suitable container that might have held a toxin. Concerned locals who resided along the Quaker's route between Bath Place and Slough Station searched their yards. In the garden behind the Windmill's front fence, someone found a little ounce phial, unlabelled, containing a tiny portion of light-coloured liquid. Had the Quaker tossed it over the fence when passing, the police wondered? They handed it over to Dr Champnes who was about to leave for London accompanied by Edward Weston Nordblad. Once there, they would rendezvous with William Bolton Pickering before paying a visit to the analytical chemist, John Thomas Cooper. Champnes opened his carpet bag and added the phial to its gruesome contents.

Cooper was in his laboratory at 82 Blackfriars Road, Southwark, on the Friday morning when the three surgeons arrived. For decades he had lectured in chemistry and medical jurisprudence, but had recently hung up his robes so as to work principally as a consultant chemist. A founding member of the four-year-old Chemical Society, he was also interested in the infant discipline of forensic toxicology – the study of deaths by poisoning.

Poison: it was a 'modern' weapon, in the popular Victorian imagination, a reflection of these sophisticated, enlightened times. Bludgeons and knives were considered the instruments of a more brutal age, crude expressions of violence that left visible traces on the victim's body. Poison, however, was subtle and devious, reflecting coolness and deliberation in its murderous design. Its traces were invisible to all but the experts, the surgeons whose eyes and olfactory senses were trained to notice the abnormal during a post-mortem examination, and the toxicologists, the archetype of the modern scientist – even the word 'scientist' had been coined only a decade previously – who used the tools of science to uncover poison's secrets.

They hadn't always been able to do so. Until recent times, poison was virtually undetectable, the weapon of choice for the assassin and for brutalised wives and hen-pecked husbands who craved an affordable 'divorce'. Indeed, for centuries, deterrence had been the only option available to the authorities in their attempts to combat the crime. Accordingly, the mandated punishment for such 'treason' under the Poisoning Act of 1530 was that the perpetrator should be boiled to death. A mere seventeen years later, the Poisoning Act was repealed, along with other treason acts, and a new punishment legislated. Queen Elizabeth's physician was castrated, disembowelled and quartered when suspected of attempting to poison her. He was later proven to have been innocent. Such brutality was no longer practised, because more humanitarian attitudes had seeped into British society, as well as into the legal system. Still, it was only with the advent of toxicology that the poisoner's terrain was no longer safe.

Toxicology was an offshoot of chemistry, which had been extracted from the clutches of alchemy and accepted as a science. As an increasing number of doctors began to study the medical properties and effects of chemicals for healing purposes, their trials and errors also ascertained what killed rather than cured. Those with mal-intent took heed, well knowing that it was easier to produce toxic effects than test for them. Then in 1813 a brilliant young Spaniard named Mathieu Orfila published his *Treatise on Poisons* and the science of toxicology was born. At long last, the law could turn its eyeglass towards the poisoner.

This advance proved timely. By the 1840s, 'poison panic' gripped the nation. Poisoning murders seemed to be epidemic. While poisoning still represented only a tiny fraction of homicides, the statistics were rising – although not because poisoning itself was being attempted more frequently; rather because specific poisons could at last be detected, and the poisoners prosecuted. In 1836, chemist James Marsh had told the world how to test for the best known and most accessible of the deadly poisons: arsenic – long nicknamed the 'inheritance maker'.

Poison's use within the home made it loom especially large in the public's fears. It was perceived as an unmanly crime – a cowardly, backstabbing woman's crime, evoking the phantasmagoria of Eve offering the tainted fruit to Adam, or of the evil stepmothers in the Brothers Grimm's bloodthirsty fairy tales who delighted in plying their wares to innocents.

Forensic toxicologists – the poison detectives – were the nation's saviours, engaging the enemy on the laboratory battlefield, exposing the weapon, unmasking the witches and sorcerers by shining the light of science upon them.

Surgeons Champnes, Nordblad and Pickering had all spent time in chemistry laboratories during their training and saw familiar sights as they walked into Cooper's lair: a huge skylight above bluestone work benches, a furnace and bellows, a coloured display of liquids on shelves lining the walls, along with racks of oddly shaped crucibles and test-tubes, retorts and other apparatus.

Champnes opened his carpet bag and carefully lifted out its contents. He placed on a bench the broad-mouthed pickle bottle containing liquid from Mrs Hart's stomach, the items from her table, her trussed stomach and part of her intestines, and the phial containing a few drops of a nearly colourless fluid. He then unsealed the pickle bottle. The noisome odour of partly digested food assailed them all.

As the items requiring testing were laid out one by one, Nordblad mentioned his suspicion that the woman had ingested oxalic acid, an industrial chemical used for dyeing, bleaching, ink manufacture and metal polishes. As a poison, it was quick acting and deadly.

Cooper was intrigued. He had never previously examined the stomach of a suspected murder victim. He picked up a piece of blue litmus paper and dipped it into the pickle bottle. On contact with the liquid inside, the litmus paper turned red – a sign of acidity. 'I think you are right in your conjecture that it contains oxalic acid,' he told the surgeons.

He collected a porcelain evaporating basin and asked Champnes to pour in some of the woman's stomach contents, then he poked through the viscous mass. He could see bits of meat and portions of apple without any obvious pips, but the remainder was unidentifiable pulp. The woman's digestive juices had dissolved most of her last meal.

He poured distilled water into the basin, swirling it through the pulp with a glass rod, then placed the basin on a heated sand bath, which cradled the bowl and allowed its contents to be heated slowly. Gently he stirred until the mixture bubbled, and continued stirring for a few more minutes. Every so often he sniffed the vapour wafting from the bowl – merely a stronger version of the previous foul odour. Eventually, he tipped the basin's contents into a paper filter placed inside a glass funnel and the liquid began to drip through to the glass container underneath.

As the filtering process would take time, he turned his attention to the beer bottle and glass tumbler taken from Mrs Hart's table. He dipped litmus paper into the two containers. Both pieces turned red. He then tested them for the presence of oxalic acid.

Chemists and toxicologists typically used reagents when testing for something unknown, substances that would react in a striking or characteristic manner, producing cloudiness or bubbles or a colour change or some other distinctive response that reflected the presence of a known substance. But when Cooper conducted the oxalic acid test, there was no reaction. It seemed that neither the beer bottle nor the tumbler contained traces of this toxic poison.

In the meantime, a small quantity of filtered liquid from the woman's stomach contents had collected in the glass receiver, so he returned to this liquid. Again he tested for the presence of oxalic acid, and again the results were negative. 'I feel quite certain that oxalic acid was not the cause of death,' he told the watchful surgeons.

As the liquid continued to filter, he settled on the dead woman's remains as his next subject. After Champnes untied the stomach, Cooper carefully examined the lining. He could see no evidence of corrosion. He decided to test for sulphuric acid anyway. Nothing.

Forget the acids, he decided. Extracting further small samples, he began testing for well-known poisons: baryta (barium hydroxide), which was used in homeopathic remedies; opium, a popular remedy for pain and sleeplessness; arsenic – odourless, tasteless and easily obtained, making it the weapon of choice for most poisoners; the salts of mercury, antimony, lead, copper and other metallic poisons. Still nothing. 'Well, if this woman has taken poison,' he announced to the three surgeons, 'it can be no other than prussic acid!'

Although Cooper had never examined the contents of a human stomach containing prussic acid and his knowledge of its effects on human tissue was only theoretical, he knew how to test for it. In fact, he had devised his own test. The only reason he hadn't already tested the woman's stomach contents for prussic acid was because he hadn't suffered his usual reaction when in its presence. Prussic acid had a peculiar odour like that of bitter almonds, an odour that produced a physical reaction in some people. For him, it caused an unpleasant and distinctive spasm at the back of his throat.

He tipped another sample of the stomach contents into the base of a retort – a piece of glassware shaped like an upside-down pipe with a sealed bowl. After adding a small quantity of dilute sulphuric acid, he sat the bowl on the sand bath and began heating the contents. The evaporated vapours condensed on the neck of the retort and flowed down into a glass bowl sitting underneath.

When a quarter of an ounce of clear liquid had distilled over, he poured the liquid into a test glass and added a grain of copperas, or green sulphate of iron. It was important that he stirred the contents long enough for the copperas to dissolve. He tipped in a small quantity of solution of potash – potassium carbonate – and continued to stir for a short while longer then left it to sit for a moment. Next, he added some muriatic acid (hydrochloric acid). Immediately, an intense shade of blue suffused the liquid – the colour known as 'Prussian blue'. The blue flush was as significant to a toxicologist as a garrotte to a police officer. Sarah Hart had died from the effects of prussic acid – or, to use its scientific name, 'hydrogen cyanide'.

Cyanide was an accidental discovery, as so many scientific discoveries are. In 1704, a colour maker from Prussia's capital of Berlin had tried to create his usual red pigment using potash and copperas, but it so happened that his latest batch of potash had been contaminated with blood-derived animal oil. Instead of red, he produced the first synthetic blue dye – his 'Prussian blue'. Later that century, a German-Swedish chemist produced an acidic solution from the dye which he called 'Scheele's prussic acid', an innocuous name that little reflected its deadly nature. When its chemical composition was later determined and a chemical family name required, the term 'hydrogen cyanide' was coined – *kyanos* being the Greek word for blue.

The French physiologist, Francois Magendie, found very weak doses of cyanide useful in treating coughs and nervous-system disorders such as epilepsy. Other doctors followed his lead, although there were many accidental overdoses. In a Paris hospital, fourteen epileptics who were dutifully lining up to receive their medicine were given half an ounce of French Pharmacopoeia, which was one part prussic acid to nine parts syrup, instead of Magendie's own formula of one part acid to 128 parts syrup. By the time the eighth patient was opening his mouth to suck from the spoon, the first was dead. There was no antidote.

Medically, cyanide works rather like a garrotte, as it prevents the absorption of oxygen at a cellular level. The poison attacks every vital organ at the same time, the only uncertainty being which organ will succumb to it first. Yet many doctors continued to prescribe it, and newspapers provided graphic accounts of tragic overdoses. Those with a criminal intent took note.

Cooper knew that the prussic acid produced for commercial purposes came from the blood and horns of decomposing animals, and that all animal substances contained prussic acid's essential ingredients of hydrogen, carbon and nitrogen. So he needed to make sure that the experimentation process itself hadn't produced the prussic acid from these raw ingredients.

Rather than using a sand bath to heat the liquid, he added salt to a water bath to increase the boiling temperature from the usual 212 degrees Fahrenheit to 226 or 227 degrees. An adaptor kept the glass receiver as far as possible from the furnace, while folds of wet blotting paper kept the receiver itself cool. When an ounce of clear liquid had distilled over, the chemist and the surgeons sniffed the liquid but they still couldn't detect the odour of prussic acid. Yet when Cooper applied the prussic acid test, the distinctive colour again suffused the liquid, enough to tint it a much deeper, stronger shade of blue. So why couldn't they smell the prussic acid? The men speculated that the odour of beer and digesting food might be too powerful, or that the prussic acid was administered in one of its relatively odourless forms – perhaps the salts of prussic acid, which hadn't the pungent odour of its water-based sibling.

Leaving the test results in the receiver, Cooper picked up the tiny phial found in the Windmill's garden. A sniff detected the odours of camphor and acetate of ammonia. The blue litmus paper dipped into the remaining drops produced no reaction. The prussic acid test – nothing. Clearly, the phial had not held the prussic acid that had killed the woman. He washed out the phial and poured in the blue sample from his second experiment, corking it up for preservation. He had already discarded the results of his first hasty trial.

By this stage, he was hurrying. The coroner had requested the results as soon as possible, but testing for unknown chemicals was time-consuming, and they had already been at the work benches for five or six hours. The weak winter sunlight was fading; there was little more they could do now. The bottle, tumbler and bun would have to wait until another day. Before finishing though, as a control experiment, he poured some distilled water into two phials, adding a few drops of prussic acid to one and testing both for prussic acid. The two phials, one containing a light blue liquid and the other colourless water, were packed away in Champnes carpet bag, along with the proceeds of the second experiment and all the other goodies the surgeon had brought with him.

After the surgeons departed, Cooper continued distilling the stomach contents. With an out-of-town commitment the following day, he decided to add nitrate of silver to some of the distilled liquid to ensure that the highly volatile prussic acid did not escape. Nitrate of silver separated the cyanogen from the precipitated substance, forming an insoluble white substance called cyanide of silver. This would prevent decomposition during his absence, enabling him to experiment further at his leisure.

This wasn't simply a fascinating case. Britain's justice system required him to be thorough and conclusive. The fate of the suspect might hinge upon the results of his experiments. He had a sacred duty to the suspect in addition to the dead woman.

CHAPTER 17

*The dead woman has spoken and science has presented
itself as interpreter.*

Examiner
(19 January 1856)

❧

SHORTLY BEFORE 10 a.m. on Saturday, 4 January, a small
covered carriage drew up outside the Three Tuns tavern. The
crowds lining the roads turned to ogle the occupants. Was
it him?

Police Superintendent Samuel Perkins stepped down from
the fly followed by a man dressed as a Quaker. The crowd went
quiet as all eyes focused on the suspect, the tension in the air
palpable. The two men stepped warily towards the crowd, which
separated as if by silent command. The men hurried into the
public house, aware of the vulnerability of their exposed backs
as the crowd closed tight behind them.

The inquest room had filled long before the commencement
hour. Perkins could see Reverend Champnes and a number of
magistrates and other county worthies among the chattering
throng. As John surveyed the room, he spotted his London
solicitor, William Bevan, and newly appointed counsellor, J.J.
Williams, sitting at a table.

The previous day John had sent two letters by special messenger. One was to his wife. The second letter authorised Bevan
to employ a defence counsellor. Mr J.J. Williams, a barrister

and special pleader who worked the Oxford Circuit, accepted the appointment. That same day, around midday, he arrived at Superintendent Perkins's house to discuss John's case with him. He reassured John that he would be well represented when the inquest resumed.

As John continued looking around the room he saw that the jury had not yet assembled, nor was the coroner present. He pulled out a handkerchief and wiped his face. Glancing at a clock, he said coolly, 'I find we are too early for them.'

The keen eyes of nine reporters scrutinised him. Some were well-known members of the local press, others from the prestigious London newspapers. One scribbled: 'There is a sinister squint in one of his eyes which added to a very jaundiced complexion gives his countenance an air of quiet villainy.' Others were kinder and made allowances for nature's unfortunate lottery.

Perkins steered John out of the inquest room and into the back parlour, ordering a constable to stand guard outside the door – not to prevent John from escaping but to protect him from the mob. Yet even the constable's steely-eyed determination and his hand hovering near a truncheon failed to deter those desperate to see the suspected murderer close-up. It would be a long and trying day for them all.

Finally, shortly after 10 a.m., Coroner Charsley arrived and announced that the hearing would resume. The clerk called out the jurors' names then advised that Mr Montague Chambers and Mr J.J. Williams were representing the prisoner. Except that Chambers was nowhere to be seen. He had failed to arrive as planned on the nine o'clock train from London.

'Might the proceedings be delayed for half an hour,' Williams pleaded, 'as it is probable that Mr Chambers will arrive by the next train from town?'

The coroner ignored objections from a couple of jurymen and adjourned the inquest for another hour. When Chambers still hadn't appeared by 11 a.m., the coroner called the first witness, Surgeon Champnes.

The pressmen clenched their pens in irritation. 'As Surgeon Champnes's evidence is most important,' one reporter grumbled, 'it is necessary to mention that from the low tone of voice in which he spoke and from the very clumsy way in which he gave his testimony generally, it was with difficulty we could catch his observations. The coroner and the counsel for the prisoner frequently remonstrated with him but to little purpose.'

The bashful young doctor was not enjoying the experience of testifying: the questioning was merciless. The news of the experiments at Cooper's laboratory hadn't leaked to anyone, so the jury and spectators were feasting on his words, however low in tone they might be. 'We first tested for oxalic acid but found none,' he recounted. 'We then tried the test of sulphuric acid but found none; we then tried the test for arsenic but found none; we then tried the tests of lead and copper but still there was no exhibition of poison resulting from these tests. We then tested for prussic acid and the result proved that poison to be present.'

To this, the courtroom erupted, the excited chattering intermingled with frustrated whispers: 'What did he say? What did he say?'

'It might not, however, have been prussic acid by itself,' Champnes admitted after the room settled, 'but that poison in conjunction with some salt nearly allied to it.'

'Was the poison of the nature to cause death?' the coroner asked.

'I cannot say,' Champnes said with some hesitancy, 'but I have every reason to believe so.'

'That is evidence,' Coroner Charsley said to the jury. 'The witness says, in his opinion, that the poison present was sufficient to cause death.'

A voice from the defence table interrupted him. 'Mr Champnes did not go so far as to say that that was his opinion,' Counsellor Williams rebuked the coroner, 'only that he had every reason to believe so.'

Coroner Charsley turned back to the surgeon. 'Are you now of opinion that the poison exhibited was sufficient to cause death?'

'I am of that opinion,' Champnes confirmed.

'Can you say what quantity of poison was taken by the deceased?'

'I cannot.'

The coroner continued to question Champnes, asking if he had smelt prussic acid on Sarah Hart's breath at the time of death or from her body during the post-mortem examination. Champnes said that he hadn't. Charsley asked if he could determine how much poison was in her stomach or how it had been administered. Champnes explained that it had probably been administered as a liquid, and that prussic acid acted very quickly, although of course the speed depended upon its strength. The quantity found in Mrs Hart's stomach would likely have caused a rapid death, he said.

'Did you analyse the contents of the bottle found in the deceased's room?' the coroner asked.

'No, I did not. There was not time to do so.'

'Can you, in conjunction with Mr Nordblad, do so now?'

Surgeon Nordblad interjected, 'The analysis will take a considerable portion of time.'

Williams took the opportunity to pipe up, 'Is it likely that the inquest will be adjourned as, from the importance of the enquiry, I am anxious for the presence of my leader, Mr Chambers?'

The coroner refused to adjourn the inquest. He had already made enough allowances for the importunate defence. Instead, he invited Counsellor Williams to cross-examine the witness.

John's barrister asked Surgeon Champnes if Mrs Hart's lung adhesion might have caused her natural death when she became overly excited, but the surgeon refused to accept this suggestion. Williams then turned his attention to the prussic acid experiments, asking if he was correct in thinking that the poison, if responsible for the woman's death, should have caused congestion or some other effect on the brain.

'It would have an effect upon the brain, certainly,' Champnes agreed, 'but that effect would not be visible at the post-mortem examination. It would not be a congestion of the brain, but a paralysis of it.'

'He has already said that in his direct examination,' the annoyed coroner interrupted. 'He said that the brain was not affected.'

'That is exactly the reason why I put this question,' Williams retorted. 'Now I beg to ask the witness, if there would not be a difference in the state of the brain, however slight, where poison had been taken?'

'I think there would be a difference,' replied Champnes hesitantly. He was soon forced to admit that he had little knowledge of acid poisons.

The following witness, Surgeon Nordblad, had a better understanding of chemistry in general and of prussic acid in particular, and wasn't as intimidated by the courtroom environment. Firmly, he told Coroner Charsley and the jury: 'From the entire absence of disease, from the manner of the deceased's death and from the presence of this poison, I can come to no other conclusion than that Sarah Hart died from the effects of prussic acid, or an allied salt such as cyanuret of potassium. These salts have not the odour of prussic acid but both would destroy life in one or two seconds or from that to a quarter of an hour, according to its strength.'

'Can you say what quantity of prussic acid was taken?' the coroner asked.

'No, I cannot.'

'But you do say that enough had been taken to produce death?'

'Certainly,' Nordblad declared, although no such evaluation had been made during the testing.

The coroner then asked if he could quickly analyse the liquor in the bottle. Nordblad explained that this was impossible, that it had taken five hours to test the stomach contents.

'It is important to have the liquor analysed,' the coroner advised the jury. He then announced to the entire room that he would adjourn the inquest until they could obtain the results of such an analysis.

Juryman Captain Wood cried out, 'Certainly it is most important that this should be, for the prisoner appears to be a knowing hand ...'

Cries of 'Oh! Oh!' overrode him.

'It is an impropriety to make such an observation,' Charsley roared, adding that the comment was uncalled for and might prejudice the rest of the jury.

When the courtroom quietened, Counsellor Williams asked, 'Will you allow the prisoner to see his solicitor?'

'I have no objection,' said the coroner, 'but it must be in the presence of Superintendent Perkins, the officer who has him in charge.'

'I trust that the coroner will be satisfied if the officer stood outside the door so the prisoner should not be able to make his escape,' Williams ventured.

'Oh no, that will not do,' the coroner chided him. 'The prisoner must not be out of sight of the officer.'

'I am sure,' hinted Williams, 'that the officer is far too respectable a man to wish to hear anything that passes between the prisoner and his legal adviser in the interview.'

The coroner agreed, and turned to Perkins. 'All you have to do, and all I wish you to do, is to take care that the prisoner is never out of your sight.'

At this late stage of the proceedings, Mr Montague Chambers burst into the room and took up the cudgels. Could John's property be restored to him as it had no connection with the proceedings? The coroner agreed that John would require some money to support himself while his case came to trial, and offered to release the twenty-two shillings in silver and copper coins found in his pockets – but no more. Chambers then asked if the prisoner could be provided with a copy of the depositions.

'Everything which has transpired has already been so admirably reported in the public papers,' Coroner Charsley responded dryly, 'as to render copies of the depositions almost unnecessary.' He refused Counsellor Chambers' request and told the jury that the hearing would recommence at 10 a.m. the following Wednesday.

⁓

John had remained in the back parlour throughout the day's proceedings, avoiding the gaze of his companions. He maintained the implacable reserve bred into him through years of silent Quaker 'professing', although some occasional restlessness reflected his natural tension. At long last Superintendent Perkins received word that the inquest had again been adjourned, and that he was to take the prisoner back home with him.

With policemen flanking him, John walked out of the inn towards the fly. The crowds parted, hushed again but now menacing, the smouldering tension of a mob not quite certain of its target, not yet baying but quietly growling.

Chapter 18

*There is a curiosity implanted in our nature which
receives much gratification from prying into the actions,
feelings and sentiments of our fellow creatures.*

Sir Walter Scott,
Quarterly Review (1826)

VICTORIAN BRITAIN loved a good murder. Sarah Hart's death
uncapped the pens of pressmen across the country. The first
reports of the 'Salt Hill Murder' landed on the nation's breakfast
tables only thirty-six hours after Sarah's death. Updates followed
almost daily for weeks. Suspect John Tawell soon became a
household name, a morsel to be chewed over as dinner-table
detectives analysed and theorised, eager to decide the merits
of the case for themselves.

Why such fervent interest in murder and murderers? cried
men of letters, including the likes of Charles Dickens and
William Makepeace Thackeray. Of course, in centuries past,
when murder was punished by revenge or recompense, it was
just another premature death reckoned from a violent and unfit
world. In later years, when the law came to impose its supreme
will, murder was merely one of many crimes punishable by
death. With the recent relaxation of the Bloody Code, murder
had become – in practical terms at least – the only act that sent a
criminal to the gallows. Now it seemed as if everyone was trans-
fixed by news of the crime and, in particular, its perpetrators.

The image of a criminal swinging from the gallows underpinned some of the curiosity. Unleashed passions added to
the allure. 'There is a latent devil in the heart of the best of
men,' wrote a mid-century psychiatric manual, 'and when the
restraints of religious feeling, of prudence and self-esteem are
weakened, the fiend breaks loose.'

Evangelicals, alienists (psychiatrists), judges, and others
concerned with the greatest good had long preached that way-
ward behaviour, criminal or otherwise, expressed a willingness
to give in to imperious impulses, and that such passions must
be controlled. 'If they fail to do so,' a jurist thundered, 'they
will be punished for it.' By Queen Victoria's reign, Britain had
grown quite proud of its calm, rational, disciplined, some would
say 'civilised', state.

But the latent devil was curious too. For just a moment he or
she lived vicariously through the unleashed passions of others.
That's why, of all the murderers whose crimes were described
in the country's newspapers, the nation's breakfast tables were
most intrigued by the seducer-murderer.

The pressmen hadn't taken long to decide upon the likely
relationship between the Quaker suspect and the dead woman.
'It has been stated that the eldest child of the unfortunate Sarah
Hart, a boy about five years of age, bears a close resemblance
to the prisoner,' *The Times* observed, adding coyly, 'The public
will be able to form their own opinions as to the nature of the
connexion which existed between the unfortunate woman and
her "friend", the party in custody.' Few minds were left struggling over the implications of a friendship between a transported
felon and a virtuous maidservant.

Virtue was the foundation stone of Victorian morality.
Victoria's mother, the Duchess of Kent, had sheltered her
daughter from any association with her uncle William's bastard

children, and had been insistent on Victoria's utter sexual propriety. In the community, the respectable woman had come to be revered, the fallen woman despised, considered responsible for her own ruin for allowing herself to be 'plucked' too soon – unless, of course, she had been plucked by a philanderer.

The legacy of the Prince Regent and the other naughty libertines had been cast into the social hellfires. A 'gentleman' was now law-abiding and self-disciplined, a husband who respected women and the institution of marriage, a pillar of society, a mirror of his country's civilised state. Still, the seducer was the villain of popular melodrama, and Britain loved to loathe him.

The populace also loved a good poisoning case as much as they feared poisoning. 'It keeps brains puzzling and hearts throbbing and betting books going until the verdict is given,' reported one contemporary. The thought that the man who heartily shook your hand at church, or the woman who kissed your child's cheek, might have a demon lurking inside – that was the very definition of passions unleashed. It chilled, it captivated, it titillated.

With its ingredients of suspected murder, seduction and poisoning, the Salt Hill Murder inevitably whetted Britain's appetite. The suspect's peculiar circumstances – wealth, respectability, Quaker affiliations and return from transportation – combined with his extraordinary apprehension by means of the electric telegraph, made for a piquant concoction, too much of a temptation not to gorge upon. And the newspapers kept feeding their readers new and even more tantalising morsels.

In truth, the newspapers themselves were partly responsible for the public's insatiable hunger. The ability to supply deliciously gruesome details had spawned a continuing desire for gruesome details, and for more scandals and drama to alleviate the mind-numbing dullness of everyday life. The fascination with murder also coincided with an era of cheaper printing and transportation costs as well as broader literacy. The newspapers soon encroached on the market once fed by the broadsides, recognising that crime and sensation drew readers and paid bills.

Some felt the need to justify their reportage. 'In giving the fullest narration of the mysterious circumstances which have created so intense an excitement in the public mind, it is far from our intention to pander to the vitiated taste, already too prevalent, for horrors,' wrote the pompous editor of the *Railway Bell*. His reason for laying before his subscribers at great cost the very best information he could procure about the Salt Hill Murder, the very best pictures he could pay an artist to draw, was the journalist's usual catchcry: 'We are only doing our duty, and are returning in some degree the generous patronage awarded us by a discriminating public.'

Some papers flagellated themselves. 'Nostra culpa. Nostra maxima culpa,' groaned the Roman Catholic *Standard* after months of detailed reportage. Most were unapologetic, aware of their customers' appetites and the financial rewards for sating them. Day after day, week after week, the press continued to provide reports about John's case until they could wring nothing further from the story.

The press was particularly interested in John's reaction to his situation and, anonymously, Superintendent Perkins was happy to oblige them. 'Tawell maintains an almost total silence,' wrote *The Times*, 'and appears at all times to be fidgety and ill at ease. He is extremely restless at night, obtaining but little sleep till towards the morning.'

John was handcuffed and chained to the bedpost. Most likely, his night-time restlessness was caused by physical discomfort as well as trepidation, and his eventual sleep that of exhaustion.

'He appears considerably more depressed in spirits than previously,' the reports continued as the days passed. 'His sighs and moans, his quivering lip and restless eye clearly indicate that he is suffering the most intense mental anguish, although there is a manifest effort on his part to appear to treat the matter with stoical indifference.'

John knew that his case wasn't looking good. One paper reported: 'From the inquiries Tawell has made as to his mode of conveyance from Slough to Aylesbury, he appears to anticipate the result of the coronial inquiry.'

Aylesbury was the seat of the county assizes. This was the court responsible for trying the more serious crimes, the felonies – among them rape and murder.

⁓

Back in London, chemist John Thomas Cooper had returned to his laboratory to continue with his experiments. He tipped the cyanide of silver that he had produced the previous day into the base of a small retort and poured in a dash of very dilute muriatic acid, then held the retort over a heating lamp. He carefully distilled the contents into a receiver before testing them again for the presence of prussic acid. This time he knew that the liquid would be suffused with the distinguishing shade of blue, as both he and his assistants had smelt the pungent odour of prussic acid wafting up during the distillation process. A second, quite different, experiment had also revealed the presence of prussic acid, with two markers this time: odour as well as colour.

Similarly to ensuring the accuracy of a mathematical calculation, the well-trained chemist then reversed the experiment, precipitating the acid with nitrate of silver, which again formed what appeared to be cyanide of silver. He didn't stop there. He attempted to dissolve the cyanide of silver in cold nitric acid, without success – a good sign for his hypothesis. He succeeded in dissolving it when he used boiling nitric acid, then he burned the resulting gas, watching it produce the rose-coloured flame that was characteristic of cyanide of silver.

He had confirmed and double-confirmed the results of his initial experiments. Without a doubt, Sarah Hart had the deadly poison prussic acid in her stomach at the time of her death. As to how it got there – well, that wasn't his question to answer.

Cooper was able to tell the two Slough surgeons the results of his experiments when they returned to his laboratory the following day. Again Champnes opened his carpet bag and lifted out the items still needing to be tested. Cooper picked up a new addition, a piece of burnt paper that had been discovered in Mrs Hart's fireplace. He moved it under a light and inspected it carefully, noticing a faint circular mark. He rubbed it between his fingers. 'It looks like leather or paper,' he told the surgeons, 'but it is hard to tell as it burnt quite black. It is so discoloured from the effects of the smoke that it is even impossible to tell the original colour.' He handed it back to the surgeon, who stowed it in his bag.

By this time, Champnes had laid out the porter bottle, glass tumbler and remains of the plum bun. Using the salt-water bath, Cooper carefully distilled the contents of each, watching the resulting liquids trickle into the receiver. Although he had three times as many substances to distil, the testing process was faster as he knew what he was looking for. He added a pinch of copperas, a sprinkling of potash, a dash of muriatic acid. Tensely, they all watched the first test glass. Nothing. The second – nothing. The third – nothing. The blue flush refused to brighten any of the liquids distilled from the items found on the dead woman's table.

To be thorough, Cooper tested the porter and bun for oxalic acid and a couple of other popular poisons. He did the same for the other phials found in the woman's house, again without success. Clearly, she hadn't ingested the poison through any of these sources.

Having finished his experiments, Cooper tightly corked the bottles and sealed them with a piece of bladder tied over with string. As he handed Champnes the pickle bottle containing the remainder of Mrs Hart's stomach contents, he advised, 'Keep it in a cool dark place for further investigation should it be deemed requisite.'

All the while, the three-pronged police investigation had been continuing. The piece of burnt paper or leather found in Sarah Hart's fireplace was among the recent breakthroughs. Another was a list of Bible verses, which included Genesis 4:7, Psalms 4:2–5 and Isaiah 1:16–19. These were written in John's neat handwriting, with the remark at the bottom:

> *The word* men *is generally used, but the sense is meant for both men and women, because it could not be properly put, and we must, in reading the Scriptures not expect to be satisfied with so doing, unless we seek to endeavour to seek in our own minds for that spirit in which they were written for our instruction. J.T.*

The police opened a Bible and flipped through the pages until they found each of the verses listed. One was an injunction from Ephesians against fornication or adultery, Chapter 5, Verse 5: 'For this ye know, that no whoremonger, nor unclean person, nor covetous man who is an idolater, hath any inheritance in the kingdom of Christ and of God.' Another, also from Ephesians, advised husbands to love their wives as they loved themselves, as Christ loved and gave himself for the church. Otherwise, they contained the usual Biblical injunctions against sin, as well as the advice to trust in and seek mercy from the Lord.

A seducer to his seduced? If so, perhaps these verses indicated that he had recognised the error of his philandering ways and was endeavouring to convince himself and his ex-mistress that it was God's wish that he should devote himself to his wife. Or were these the words of a man oblivious to his own hypocrisy?

From the statements of witnesses, the police had also managed to trace John's movements on the day of Sarah Hart's death.

That New Year's Day, his Berkhampstead train arrived at Euston Station shortly before midday. Soon afterwards, he was seen hurrying past the recently built Victoria Hotel, his cheeks and eyes downcast. From Euston, he caught an omnibus into the financial heart of London where he alighted at the junction bordered by the elegant, fortress-like Bank of England, the re-erected Royal Exchange building and the lord mayor's Mansion House – the same spot he would alight that night with Sergeant Williams on his tail. On his midday visit, he then hastened along Cornhill to the Jerusalem Coffee House, where he sat at his usual table and ordered his usual coffee and toast. As he waited, he inquired about ships from the colonies. He learnt that his ship of interest had arrived but without his desperately wanted £700 remittance.

Shortly after 2 p.m., he walked the short distance to 62 Lombard Street, the banking house of Messrs Barnett, Hoare and Co. As a long-term customer, he was well known among the clerks and directors of this Quaker-owned establishment. He approached clerk Henry Swaythe and asked to draw a cheque for £14. Swaythe found the ledger with John's account details and checked the balance – it was overdrawn. He looked up at the Quaker standing before him and explained the problem.

'I have permission from Mr Gurney Hoare to overdraw the account,' John told him.

Swaythe knew there had been no objection when the account was first overdrawn so he took the gentleman at his word. He handed over the money – in gold – and jotted the details in the ledger.

John returned to the Jerusalem Coffee House around 3 p.m., the busiest time of day. Some 150 to 200 men congregated there, mainly merchants who had left their counting houses to hear the news, or to talk with ships' captains and shipping agents before heading to the Exchange or home for the day. Wending his way through the crowds, John approached waiter John Kendall. 'What hour does thee close the door at night?'

'Eight o'clock,' Kendall replied.

'I am going to dine at the west end of town and cannot be back until half past nine o'clock,' John said. 'I have a greatcoat and a parcel which I wish to leave.'

Kendall agreed to take charge of the items, although it was an odd request. London was suffering an extremely cold winter, with daily temperatures rarely rising above freezing, and those who could afford a greatcoat were glad to be enveloped by its warmth. Still, he had no concerns about complying with Mr Tawell's request as he resided above the coffee house. He explained that the door would be closed but that he would listen out for his knock.

From the coffee house, John walked back to the Bank and

caught an omnibus to the temporary terminus of Paddington Station, situated on the western side of Bishop's Bridge Road. There, he approached railway clerk Henry Gratton, who was officiating at the first-class counter that afternoon, and asked for a ticket on the 4 p.m. train to Slough. Warned that the train was about to leave, he hurried to the departure platform and climbed into one of the first-class compartments.

From Slough Station, he had a twenty-minute walk to Bath Place, past the Windsor Road junction on the left leading to Herschel House, past Mr Botham's Windmill Inn on the right and, a bit further along, the often rowdy Three Tuns tavern. Around 5 p.m., he reached Sarah Hart's cottage and entered, closing the door quietly behind him.

―◠―

Catherine White was standing behind the Windmill's bar an hour or so later, decanting wine and other beverages to the guests enjoying the inn's hospitality. 'Botham's', as it was affectionately known, was still a favourite resting place for those who disdained the speed and cinders of rail travel in favour of a more ponderous journey by horse-drawn carriage – and for those who simply enjoyed the district's soothing environs.

Every so often, the door would burst open and someone shuffle through, a weary workman or a traveller seeking accommodation for the night. Catherine glanced up when another guest came through the door and over to the counter – Sarah Hart from Bath Place.

Sarah preferred the Guinness porter available from the Windmill rather than the beverages from the nearer Three Tuns, and was willing to walk the seven hundred yards to the Windmill to purchase it. The two women were around the same age and they chatted for a few minutes as Catherine tipped the porter into a bottle and corked it. Sarah didn't say why she was purchasing the porter, although she did request the loan of a corkscrew. Handing her a rather bent one, Catherine said, 'Would you return the corkscrew and bottle as soon as you have done with them?'

'You may depend upon my bringing them back in the morning,' Sarah assured her as she headed out into the darkness again.

Salt Hill gardener William Marlow was trudging towards the Windmill when Sarah trotted past a short time later. 'Ah, Marlow, is that you?' she sang out.

'Why, Mrs Hart,' he replied, 'what are you running so fast for?'

'I have got a friend come in and I have been for a little porter for him,' she replied gaily, waving aloft her bottle as she dashed by, her pattering feet and flapping skirts soon swallowed within the evening's gloom.

When next seen by a local, only a short time later, she was sprawled on the floor drawing her last breaths. As to what happened in the intervening period, it was still a mystery.

Chapter 19

Look to yourself and heed this warning that I give you!
Your day is past, and night is coming on.

Charles Dickens,
Nicholas Nickleby (1839)

***

'CAN I have a plate of bread and cheese and a glass of brandy and water?' asked the rabid teetotaller after being installed in the Three Tuns's back parlour on the morning of Wednesday, 8 January. John and his police escort had just run the menacing gauntlet after the now-familiar fly clip-clopped back to Salt Hill for the resumption of the inquest. The crowds lining the streets and converging on the tavern were even larger on this third day of the inquest. The pundits expected a verdict by the day's end, and the Salt Hill community wanted to be there for the announcement.

The pressmen managed a quick word with the suspect's police escort. 'John Tawell appears to be in a state of considerable nervous excitement,' *The Times* reporter wrote, 'and to keenly feel (although he makes every attempt to suppress the emotions under which he labours) the hazardous situation in which he has placed himself.'

The press had already reached their verdict. Had the jury as well?

'It will be the recollection of the jury,' Coroner Charsley declared at 10 a.m., 'that the proceedings were adjourned until today in order that the contents of the bottle and tumbler found on Sarah Hart's table might be analysed by the professional gentlemen in whose custody they had been placed.' He then called Surgeon Nordblad, who pushed through the crowds to reach the witness stand.

'Since the last examination,' Nordblad told the coroner and jury, 'I have, in conjunction with Mr Champnes, analysed the contents of the bottle found on the table in the room of the deceased, and the contents of the tumbler and the bun.'

The room was so silent that the reporters could almost hear the frisson of tension as the surgeon paused to take a breath. 'They contain no poison of any description,' he said.

A wave of disappointed mutters enveloped the room.

John's defence counsel wasn't disappointed, however. Far from it. He had been reading up on prussic acid. He asked the following witness, the less knowledgeable Surgeon Champnes, if he was aware that prussic acid could sometimes be found in human urine.

'I was not aware of that,' the young doctor admitted. 'It may, I believe, be evolved from the human body during the process of decomposition without having been taken into the stomach.'

Meanwhile the sounds of banging doors and muttering voices were creating a disturbance at the back of the room. The voice of a court officer rose above the din. 'An inspector of the London police has arrived and has something of importance to communicate to you,' he announced to the coroner.

'Whatever the inspector has to say to me it must not be said in public,' the coroner ordered. 'I will see him out of the room privately at a subsequent stage of the proceedings.'

The officer was already threading his way through the

room. When he reached the coroner, he whispered something in his ear. Despite craned heads and pricked ears, nobody could hear what the officer said – the information that he considered important enough to interrupt the inquest against Coroner Charsley's wishes.

A short time later, the coroner concluded the Crown's case without alluding to the police officer's appearance. He then asked if the defendant's counsellors wished to produce any witnesses.

Montague Chambers attempted to earn his hefty retainer. 'You were kind enough, sir, as I understand, to state to my friend Mr Williams on the last occasion that at the close of the case you would permit me to say a few words.'

'I cannot permit you to make a speech for the defence,' cautioned the coroner. He explained, patiently, that defence counsels were allowed to cross-examine witnesses and produce evidence but not to make a speech that might influence the jury. 'Have you any witnesses to call for the defendant?' he asked again.

'I beg to observe,' the wily barrister countered, 'that there is no person present who could be correctly described as a defendant. This is a court to inquire into the cause of death of one of the queen's subjects, not the guilt or innocence of any party. On the evidence as it now stands, there is so much doubt with regard to any individual, that ...'

'I must interrupt you,' said the annoyed coroner. 'You are now doing the very thing which I said you must not do.'

'I am very sorry if I am going beyond the line,' Chambers wheedled, 'but I understood that, on the last occasion, you told my friend Mr Williams that we should have an opportunity of addressing the jury.'

'I never intended to have said so,' the bewildered Charsley replied, 'and I have no recollection of having done so.'

'You never did say so,' came the surprising rejoinder from Chambers's off-sider, Mr Williams. 'My learned friend Mr Chambers must have been misled by an erroneous report.'

The coroner's head swivelled abruptly towards Williams. Instead of thanking him for correcting his colleague's misapprehension, he berated him. 'You addressed the jury on Saturday during my absence which was excessively irregular. If I had known you were going to do so, I would have excluded you from the room!'

Williams spluttered with indignation, vehemently denying having done so. He explained that he had merely made some observations to his neighbours after the court's adjournment and if some jurors were among them … well, he couldn't help it if they had heard him too.

Chambers slipped in an apology, adding – at excessive length – that if the coroner did not wish him to address the jury he would bow to the decision. He still felt that the case involved great mystery and doubt, however.

'Are there any witnesses for the defendant?' the coroner barked once more.

'Not any, sir,' Chambers admitted at last, then again reminded the jury that there was no one in the room who could strictly be called a defendant.

Waving off the lawyers and their ploys, the coroner turned to the jury and began to sum up the case. He stated that the evidence proved that Sarah Hart had swallowed a poison deadly enough to destroy life in a few minutes, and that the evidence also suggested that she hadn't wilfully destroyed her own life. While the court had been offered no proof regarding the identity of the poisoner, he believed that sufficient evidence existed for them to make their own inferences.

He then described the case against John Tawell, referring in particular to his agitation upon leaving Mrs Hart's place. Why would anyone leave another person in the agonies of death without giving any alarm? The evidence was circumstantial, of course, and should be treated with caution; however, he had learnt that cases based upon strong circumstantial evidence were often more reliable than those founded upon the testimony of a single witness who might be motivated by ill-intent. He reminded the jury that coronial courts were convened to determine only whether or not the suspect had a case to answer. 'The secrecy with which such crimes are committed should not ensure impunity to the offender,' he concluded. 'Ponder well the evidence and return a verdict which will satisfy public justice and your own conscience.'

~

'How long do you think they will be now?' John fretted to his counsellors, who had retired to the back parlour with him while the jury deliberated. When told it could be half an hour or even longer, his agitation increased.

The noise from outside was impossible to ignore. Coroner Charsley had ordered everyone to leave the room so the jury could discuss the case in private. The crowds swarmed around the entrance to the tavern, desperate to be close to the door when it reopened. Those who had spent time in the inquest room knew that it could accommodate only a fraction of the people striving to get in.

'How long now?' John asked again, an unanswerable question offering nothing more than a moment's break from the unbearable strain. Eventually, fifty minutes after the room had been cleared, a court officer announced that the jury had reached its verdict. John and his legal representatives were invited to enter first, then the tavern doors would be opened to readmit the public.

The reporters squeezed among the crowds outside were the most determined to get back inside the makeshift courtroom. They were desperate to hear the verdict first-hand and capture their impressions of the suspect's reaction. Their readers demanded so; their jobs as well. A judicious shove here, an elbow there, was most definitely called for. They pushed their way into the inquest room, and pushed some more until they had won a vantage which offered a clear line of sight to the suspect's face.

As the coroner asked the jury for its decision, the pressmen kept their eyes fixed firmly on the suspect. A pause followed as the foreman took a deep breath, then he announced: 'Wilful murder against John Tawell for poisoning Sarah Hart with prussic acid.'

There, before them, they witnessed no emotional reaction at all. Tawell presented a mask of fortitude. The ordinary spectators in the room were humming in agreement with the jurymen, although a few voices cried, 'Poor fellow! Poor fellow!' Still Tawell showed no reaction. His self-control was extraordinary. One reporter wrote: 'A person unacquainted with the circumstances would have taken him for a casual spectator.'

Even John's lawyers were astounded, having heard his constant fretting during the jury's deliberations. They realised that John was wearing a mask, a public persona that slipped as soon as he returned to the back parlour. A glass of brandy and water revived him from his collapse. For the next hour, while Coroner Charsley completed the necessary paperwork, John and his counsel had their heads together, making plans for his future trial.

The throng refused to leave the vicinity. It made no difference whether they had observed with their own eyes the suspect's uncaring countenance when the verdict had been announced, or if instead they'd paced outside after the inn's doors had been slammed in their faces. Now others joined them, drawn like wolves towards the scent of prey. For ninety minutes they hung around the Three Tuns. Sombre conversations about the inquest soon gave way to glad bantering, a seemingly light-hearted melody of post-thespian pleasure. Occasionally, there was a jarring note, a discordant interruption as they remembered why they were there and who they were waiting for.

Eyeing the crowd were nine or ten policemen, the local police force's numbers having been bolstered by Inspector Wiggins and some other members of the London Metropolitan Police. The shrewd coroner had suspected they would need the Londoners' assistance. The bobbies tuned into the noise, recognising its tone. They thumped their top hats into place and patted their trusty truncheons, then planted themselves outside the tavern doors.

Around 3.30 p.m., the doors slowly opened. 'There he is! There he is!' voices screamed. A horde of angry faces loomed in front of John, their mouths spitting abuse.

The policemen immediately surrounded the frightened prisoner, trying to protect him from clawing hands and kicking boots. The enraged crowd threatened to overwhelm the small band representing law and order, whose usual duty was to catch suspected villains, not protect them. A few bystanders leapt to their assistance, fighting off the besieging throng. The constables managed to forge a pathway. Behind their protective buffer, John stumbled towards the waiting carriage and scrambled inside.

The mob surrounded the carriage, continuing to screech at him. The women's strident tones were the ugliest and their language the most profane. The driver cracked his whip, urging his horses into a gallop, but even that didn't stop the crowds. For a quarter mile, they chased after the carriage, yelling and hooting, flinging stones and handfuls of dirt. After a while, as the carriage picked up its pace, they panted to a halt and the shrill voices died away.

Darkness fell as the carriage rattled along the narrow country roads, through villages of thatched cottages clustered around a 'steeple house', startling the ducks kipping near their frozen ponds. They travelled for fourteen miles, slowing as they drove into Amersham, about halfway between Salt Hill and Aylesbury, where they pulled up outside the three-storey Griffin Inn. The horses needed watering and so did the passengers. John ordered tea and a mutton chop which he ate with relish. He had remained silent through much of the journey and kept his own counsel while he ate. After finishing, however, he turned to Superintendent Perkins and said with some bemusement, 'I can't think what the people made such an uproar about at Salt Hill as we were coming away. Oh dear!'

From Amersham they picked up the old Roman road to Aylesbury. It was nearing 8 p.m. when their horses' hooves clattered across the ancient town's cobblestones. Aylesbury was a lively market town during the daytime; however, at this hour on a cold winter's evening, it was almost eerie. The shops were shuttered and the stalls packed away, the streets hushed. Only the skinny cats remained, letting out the occasional plaintive mew as they slunk into the darkness.

As the carriage pulled into Market Square, John saw his new home. Built the previous century, the red-brick, two-storey county hall served also as a courthouse and a prison. The prison itself was situated behind and partly underneath the hall, and had recently been condemned as inconvenient, insufficient and inadequate. A new building was in the planning stages, not that John would see it – whatever the outcome.

The police superintendent refrained from mentioning that the balcony in front of the second storey's large middle window was known as 'the drop' – the place where the condemned fell to their death. Instead, he bade John farewell and handed him into the custody of the appropriately-named Mr Sherriff, the governor of Aylesbury Gaol.

⌒

'Will thee accommodate me with a comfortable bed and a room to myself?' John asked the gaoler as they walked through the prison.

'No relaxation in the discipline of the prison can be allowed in your case,' Sherriff informed him. 'You must submit to the same rules which are adopted towards the other prisoners.'

Heaving a great sigh, John followed the gaoler to his assigned quarters. Sherriff ordered one of the turnkeys to search him – another regulation – and then locked him in the cell for the night. John discovered that one of his requests had been met, albeit unintentionally: he had the room to himself. He took off his greatcoat and slept in his clothes as he had nothing else to sleep in. By morning he looked haggard and careworn.

Over the next few days, his composure returned. Perhaps he had noticed a couplet on one of the prison's walls, inscribed a couple of decades earlier after a prisoner was judged not guilty of murder through insanity. It proclaimed:

If you have done murder and wish to get clear,
Take care and be tried in Buckinghamshire.

CHAPTER 20

This is one of the most curious cases of circumstantial evidence which late years have produced.

Pictorial Times
(11 January 1845)

⁂

THE WORDS whispered in the coroner's ear on the final day of the inquest were most important to be sure. The police had made a momentous discovery in relation to the poison.

Superintendent Perkins and his fellow police officers knew that the courts faced colossal difficulties in convicting suspected poisoners, particularly when the toxicologists couldn't identify the lethal substance used. The discovery that prussic acid had killed Sarah Hart was a critical lead that might help them forge a solid link in their chain of circumstantial evidence. They needed more to ensure justice, though.

After the inquest had adjourned on the previous Saturday, Perkins wrote to London's Commissioners of Police, asking them to order their beat constables to visit all the druggist shops throughout the metropolitan district, particularly in the Cornhill and Paddington neighbourhoods. They were to enquire if a Quaker gentleman – aged about sixty, whiskerless, light haired, light complexioned and about five feet six inches tall – had recently purchased prussic acid or any other poison. Boldly inscribing the letter 'In haste', he requested that they report back to him as soon as possible.

This type of needle-in-the-haystack approach was one of the few strategies the police could use in these infant days of crime detection. Fortunately, they had graduated from the deductive strategy of an earlier era – torturing a confession from the suspect – although that technique had proved quite successful, statistically speaking, that is. Either the suspect confessed and was then executed, or died during the interrogation. Case closed.

Superintendent Perkins was one of the new breed of policemen who applied intelligence to their attempts to discover clues. He recognised that the prussic acid was probably purchased from an apothecary, and that the suspect was so attached to his Quaker identity that he wore his distinctive garb everywhere. Wisdom suggested questioning all the London apothecaries though, naturally, there were problems with this approach. They might be searching in the wrong place.

Perkins's letter reached Colonel Charles Rowan, Joint Commissioner of the Metropolitan Police, on Sunday, 5 January. Rowan advised that he would conduct such an investigation and that the results would be forwarded to Eton before the inquest resumed on the following Wednesday morning.

Commissioner Rowan had leaflets printed. He ordered the beat constables to leave them at the apothecary shops they visited in case another assistant, not then in attendance, had served a suitably peculiar gentleman. By this time the police had learnt that John resided in Croydon some years earlier, and had recently visited friends in Northampton, so the order was broadened to cover those districts as well. Reports began filtering back that the constables were having little success. Apothecaries in Croydon, the city proper and Westminster were all shaking their heads when asked if they had received a request for prussic acid from a Quaker.

One Croydon apothecary, a Quaker named Drummond, admitted knowing John Tawell. In fact, he had seen him only six or seven weeks before. Drummond told the constable that he thought little of their chances for success. 'It is useless for you to make these inquiries as John Tawell could mix the article up himself, he having been in the profession.' His disheartening comment was being repeated by apothecaries across the city.

Drummond did offer one suggestion, though: that the constable should call upon Peter Bedford, John's old friend and mentor, who still lived in the district.

Bedford was home. He told the constable that John had visited him the same day he called at Drummond's. His stated reason was that he wanted to hand over a small sum of money, a very small sum in fact – a mere twelve shillings and sixpence – reportedly collected at Berkhampstead for an institution abroad. John had stayed for an hour, talking about his family. What was curious, the old psychic murmured, was that this was John's second visit in a matter of weeks, the other visit also to pay a tiny sum towards the same overseas institution. Yet his return journeys probably would have cost more than the donations. What was also odd was that these visits came after two years with no contact.

One policeman had more success. A Mr Robinson at 71 Paradise Row, Chelsea, reported that an elderly man answering the suspect's description had twice visited his shop within the previous three weeks to purchase prussic acid, although the man had not been dressed as a Quaker. Robinson told the constable that he had refused the man's request and would recognise him if he should ever see him again.

The troupe of constables continued to tramp the streets. Based merely on the number of apothecary shops in the metropolis, Londoners were most definitely attached to their 'physic'.

It was no wonder that some were lamenting the lack of stricter regulations regarding access to deadly poisons.

Then Police Constable Edmund White called at an apothecary situated at 89 Bishopsgate Street, just a few minutes' walk from Cornhill.

Manager Henry Thomas had been working at the counter of Surgeon Hughes's apothecary on the previous Wednesday when a man dressed in Quaker garb and a greatcoat walked in. Thomas recognised him. He was a regular customer. Some months earlier, the man had mentioned that he was once a chemist and druggist abroad, although Thomas had already known of the man's connection with the industry, having been told so by another staff member. They felt an affinity with their own and asked few questions when receiving requests for medical preparations.

'Can I have two drachms of Scheele's prussic acid?' the Quaker asked, pulling from his pocket a small half-ounce phial. He handed it over and said that it could be used to fill the order.

Thomas looked at the little phial and saw that it carried a 'Scheele's Prussic Acid' label with details of strength and dosage. He held the phial in one hand and grasped its tiny glass stopper with two fingers of the other and pulled. The stopper wouldn't come out. He tugged and tugged but it was stuck fast. 'I'll get you one of our own,' he said to the customer, who appeared to be in a hurry.

Locating a similar-sized phial, he filled it with Scheele's prussic acid as requested, rather than the weaker London Pharmacopoeia brand. He picked up a printed label marked 'Hydrocyanic acid (Scheele's Strength)' and was about to fill in the details when he was interrupted.

'You need not put a label on the bottle,' said the Quaker, adding that he required the acid as an external application for varicose veins. He rubbed his leg as he mentioned his affliction.

Thomas knew that prussic acid was sometimes prescribed for such a condition and that the Quaker had in the past mentioned his condition when purchasing medicines. Nevertheless, he ignored the remark and completed the label, explaining, 'We never send medicines out without it.' Any apothecary worth his scales knew the dangers of unlabelled medicines, particularly a bottle containing a poison as deadly as prussic acid. He placed a small piece of white leather over the top and attached it securely, then wrapped the phial in white paper and handed it over.

The Quaker fished out the required four pence and laid it on the counter. As he left the premises, Thomas jotted down 'hydrocyanic acid' and '4d.' in his poisons book, as he was legally obliged to do.

But there was more, he told the jubilant peeler. That wasn't the last time he saw the customer. The Quaker returned the following morning, Thursday, 2 January.

'Can I have two drachms more of prussic acid,' the Quaker had asked as he reached the counter. 'I had the misfortune to break the other bottle.'

Since the Quaker's visit the previous day, Thomas had managed to extract the glass stopper, so he retrieved the labelled phial and filled it with prussic acid. Again he covered it with a piece of white leather and wrapped it with white paper, although this time he charged the customer eight pence, four for the prussic acid and four for the previous day's phial. Again he jotted the details in his poisons book.

He had thought nothing further of the purchases until Constable White pushed the printed leaflet into his hand. After recounting his story to the policeman, he pulled out the shop's

The Quaker John Tawell, with his usual mask of sphinx-like inscrutability, in a portrait published in the *Go-a-head* journal.

Tawell wore the traditional Quaker 'costume' – a plain dress reflecting a belief in a simple life. Published in Rudolf Ackermann's *The Microcosm of London* (1808–1811). Courtesy of the Kean Collection / Getty Images.

Left: Prisoners like Tawell on their way to a hulk moored off Woolwich dock, where they would remain until transferred to a convict ship bound for Australia. Engraving from *The Malefactor's Register*. © The British Library Board.

Right (top): The first Friends Meeting House in New South Wales was Tawell's 'gift' to his beloved Quaker brethren. Published in James Maclehose's *The Picture of Sydney and Stranger's Guide in New South Wales for 1838*.

Right (bottom): 'I desired liberty; for liberty I gasped; for liberty I uttered a prayer': Tawell's 'humble' appeal for a ticket of leave from his sentence. Courtesy of State Records of New South Wales.

Paddington Station, the London terminus of the Great Western Railway, as it looked on New Year's Day 1845. © Science & Society Picture Library via Getty Images.

Left: The dawn of the information age: a Great Western Railway advertisement for the electric telegraph's services between Paddington and Slough. © Science & Society Picture Library via Getty Images.
Right: The two-needle telegraph that Thomas Home operated at Paddington on that fateful New Year's Day – so simple, yet so powerful. © Science & Society Picture Library via Getty Images.

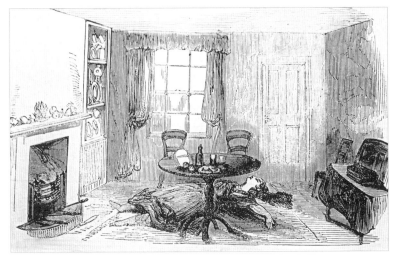

The scene in Sarah Hart's parlour when she was found, as depicted by the newspaper *Railway Bell*. A Guinness bottle, plum cake and other refreshments are shown on the table, which indicates that the drawing was based on secondary reports.

Sarah Hart's cottage (second from the right) in Bath Place in the hamlet of Salt Hill, near Slough. Published in *Railway Bell*.

A crowd begins to gather outside the Three Tuns inn, the site of the inquest into Sarah Hart's death. Published in *Railway Bell*.

Baron James Parke presiding over Tawell's trial in the court house in Aylesbury, Buckinghamshire. The renowned barrister Fitzroy Kelly would earn the nickname 'Apple Pips' for his bravado performance in defence. Published in *The Pictorial Times*.

FATAL FACILITY; OR, POISONS FOR THE ASKING.

A 'poison panic' gripped England in the 1840s – and the court heard the alarm bells. Here, *Punch* magazine satirises the availability of opium and arsenic. A child asks, 'Please, mister, will you be so good as to fill this bottle again with lodnum, and let Mother have another pound and a half of arsenic for the rats (!)', to which the 'Duly Qualified Chemist' replies, 'Certainly, Ma'am.' © Punch Limited.

Aylesbury market square with the court house in the centre. The great balcony, from which condemned prisoners fell to their doom, can be seen above the ground-floor arches. Published in *The Pictorial Times*.

EXECUTION
OF JOHN TAWELL,
AND FULL CONFESSION, TO HIS WIFE, IN A LETTER
Of the Murder of Sarah Hart.

Aylesbury.
This morning, 8 o'clock.

At an early hour this morning, the sheriffs, with their usual attendants, arrived at the prison, and after partaking of some refreshment, proceeded to the condemned cell, where they found the reverend ordinary engaged in prayer with the wretched culprit.

After the usual formalities had been observed of demanding the delivery of the body of the prisoners into their custody, Tawell was conducted to the press-room, where his irons were struck off. The executioner, with his assistants, then commenced pinioning his arms, which operation they skilfully and quickly despatched. During these awful preparations he sighed deeply, but uttered not a word. At a quarter before 8, all the arrangements having been completed, the bell of the prison commenced tolling, and the melancholy procession was formed; —

actions. After living 15 years in Sydney, he returned home, where he has been endeavouring to gain admittance as a member of the Society of Friends, to which body he belonged before his transportation, but they would not admit him. During his first wife's illness, the deceased nursed her, whence arose their illicit correspondence.

COPY OF VERSES.

GOOD people all of each degree
Attend to what I shall unfold,
It is a dreadful tragedy
Will make your very blood run cold.
Your heart aches with grief will bleed,
When you this cruel tale shall hear,
There's not been done so vile a deed
Since the days of Courvoisier.

John Tawell is my name 'tis true,
In wealth and splendour once I've dwelt,

... sort of scream, and saw the prisoner chemist, and was formerly lecturer ill and vomitted about a hand coming out of Mrs. Hart's house. on chemical justi I said, I am afraid my neighbour is Champneys and t ill; but the prisoner, who appeared men called on in

COPY of VERSES.

Pre-printed souvenir execution reports were standard fare for the 'gutter' press, to be pulped in the event that the condemned was reprieved. If the prisoner refused to ease concerns about whether justice had prevailed, the press never let the truth get in their way – Tawell's confession to his wife was never drafted. Courtesy of Buckinghamshire County Council.

Inset: The grim reaper visits Tawell as he pens verses to his wife – another fantasy of the press.

"PARTIES" FOR THE GALLOWS.

HORRID MURDER

FULL PARTICULARS DREADFUL MURDER PORTRAIT OF MURDERER

With the community so desperate for information about Tawell and his case, *Punch* launched some of its typical darts. The boy demands, 'I vonts a nillustrated newspaper with a norrid murder and a likeness in it.' © Punch Limited.

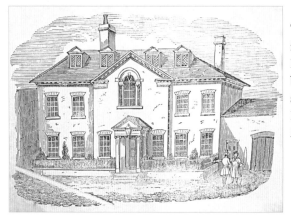

The Red House
in High Street,
Berkhampstead:
beloved home or
serpent's lair?
Published in
Railway Bell.

Sarah Tawell in old
age. Ever a devout
and charity-minded
Quaker, she chose to
support Sarah Hart's
young children in
the years after their
mother's death.
Courtesy of William
Rowntree.

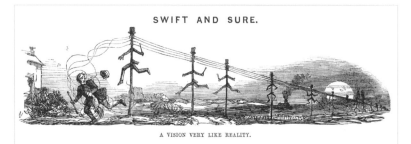

SWIFT AND SURE.

A VISION VERY LIKE REALITY.

The electric constable uses 'God's lightning' to avenge the deaths of the
innocent: *Punch* opined, 'No wonder the murderer is nervous, when he
is, literally, very often "hung upon wires."' © Punch Limited.

poisons book and pointed to the two purchases. The delighted copper left soon afterwards to report his discovery, returning the following day to obtain Henry Thomas's statement in writing. The apothecary manager again described the consecutive purchases but this time he referred to his customer as 'a medical gentleman, for many years an apothecary'.

Thomas's statement found its way to Inspector Wiggins who read it with astonishment and frustration. If the customer was truly John Tawell, he must have been apprehended not long after purchasing the second phial of prussic acid. In fact, he must have had the phial in his pocket when they questioned him at the Jerusalem Coffee House. Regrettably, they hadn't searched him until much later, after they had travelled across London to Paddington railway station and all the way back to Slough.

Wiggins's superintendent had one concern about the apothecary's statement. He scrawled on the bottom: 'Get further enquiry to be made to ascertain if he is indeed a medical gentleman and, if so, whether he is or is not the party in custody.'

Meanwhile, on Wednesday morning, the final day of the inquest, a police inspector caught a train to Slough. He was under orders to inform Coroner Charsley that a man answering John Tawell's description had purchased prussic acid on the day of the murder.

Inspector Wiggins was ordered to investigate both possible sightings, although a couple of days passed before he found time to do so. He visited Mr Robinson of Chelsea and questioned him closely about the elderly man who attempted to purchase prussic acid. Later, he wrote in his daily report: 'He does not answer the description of the prisoner John Tawell.'

He had more success when he visited Henry Thomas at 89 Bishopsgate Street. He later reported: 'I am of opinion that John Tawell is the person who purchased on two occasions prussic acid from him.' He also suggested to his superiors that Mr Thomas should be sent to Aylesbury Gaol to see if he could personally identify Tawell as the person who purchased the poison.

⌒

In the aftermath of John's indictment and the discovery of his presumed purchases at the apothecary's shop, Superintendent Larkin of the Stoke and Burnham Division decided to search John's house at Berkhampstead to see if he possessed any bottles of prussic acid. It was a belated decision, but these were the early days of crime detection – so early, in fact, that detectives were only a recent addition to the London Metropolitan Police force, and none had been assigned to Sarah Hart's case.

A charming mistress greeted Larkin when he arrived at the Red House on the morning of Friday, 10 January. Mrs Tawell invited him inside and offered him every courtesy, including her daughter's assistance. As Larkin explored the house, he discovered a medicine chest full of bottles, phials, powders and potions – at least one hundred different medical preparations. Some were from the Bishopsgate apothecary, the remainder from other London and country druggists. Presumably Tawell did indeed supply Berkhampstead's poor with medical preparations, as reports claimed. Or perhaps he was a hoarder, or a hypochondriac.

Tawell's stepdaughter helped Larkin pack the drugs into a hamper, and he carted them back to Slough for examination. Surgeons Nordblad and Champnes immediately tested them but could discover nothing poisonous in any of the confiscated preparations.

⌒

Nearly a week passed before Henry Thomas was asked to identify the suspect. On Sunday, 12 January, Superintendent Perkins travelled to London to interview the apothecary manager and, on the following afternoon, escorted him to Aylesbury. By the time they arrived, the prisoners had been locked in their cells for the night, so they were refused permission to enter the gaol.

When they returned early the following morning, Mr Sherriff walked with them from one cell to another. Henry Thomas eyed inmate after inmate but couldn't identify any of them as the prussic acid purchaser. Eventually, in a cell containing a number of prisoners, Thomas's eyes lit on one particular man. 'That's the man who bought the poison,' he said quietly, pointing to John Tawell.

His words, though, were caught betwixt those of the prisoner himself. With a look of confusion, John said to the man pointing at him, 'I think I have seen thee before.' He tried to talk further with the visitor but the officials told him to be quiet. A moment later Perkins and Thomas retreated from the cell.

'I have so clear a recollection of the features of the prisoner,' Thomas told the police superintendent afterwards, 'that I can swear most positively to his being the person.'

Of course, John's Quaker attire would have helped.

~

When the news broke that Henry Thomas had identified John Tawell as the Quaker who purchased prussic acid on the day of Sarah Hart's death, the apothecary manager stared down claims of irresponsibility in selling such a deadly poison. The *Morning Advertiser* published his letter to the editor justifying the circumstances of the sale:

> *Fearing from the statements in your paper of yester-*
> *day that the public may be inclined to take a wrong*
> *view of the matters relative to the murder at Salt Hill,*
> *I should feel particularly obliged by your stating that*
> *Mr Tawell was well known as a medical practitioner;*
> *also that he did not call at 89 Bishopsgate Street for*
> *fourpennyworth of prussic acid, but that he brought*
> *a phial with a regular label (Scheele's prussic acid,*
> *stating full dose and particulars on it) such as is usu-*
> *ally kept by medical gentlemen, and wished to have*
> *two drams of the acid in it. I served him with two*
> *drams, knowing his profession, and charged him 4d.,*
> *the usual price for such an article to practitioners.*

Other London papers expressed concerns over the official handling of the case. 'The most remarkable feature in this extraordinary and serious matter is the want of vigilance on the part of certain authorities,' blasted the *Weekly Chronicle* on 25 January. 'So far back as Monday last the prisoner was identi-fied by Mr Henry Thomas as the purchaser of the prussic acid, yet no attempts have been made to secure his evidence. Many people expected that the magistrates of Slough would have instituted a more complete and rigid investigation into the circumstances of the case.'

The *Weekly Chronicle*'s complaint was unjust. The authori-ties had already secured Thomas's evidence. In point of fact, the investigation was progressing very well indeed. They had discovered the so-called weapon. They had connected the weapon with the suspect. They had even identified a motive.

Wiggins had numerous avenues to follow in this compli-cated investigation and determining motive had been one of them. While it wasn't necessary for the prosecution to explain a suspect's motivation, the authorities had learnt from bitter experience that juries found it easier to convict if they could understand what might have driven a suspect to commit a crime. The failure to satisfactorily convince a jury that the suspect had a reasonable motive was too often responsible for generating a reasonable doubt.

On the day after John's committal, Inspector Wiggins called at the banking house, Messrs Barnett, Hoare and Co. in Lombard Street, to inquire after his financial situation. 'John Tawell has previously had cash to a large amount in our hands,' they told him, 'but at present he has overdrawn his account.'

Money. As a motive it was so simple, so primal, so easy to explain to a jury. In his report dated 15 January, Wiggins wrote complacently: 'I believe this makes the case complete against the prisoner John Tawell.'

Naturally, it would be advantageous if they could uncover the victim's relationship with the deceased, although that wouldn't prevent their case from proceeding to trial. In the courtroom, a murder case was not really about the victim, only the killer.

Chapter 21

Men's vows are women's traitors!

William Shakespeare,
Cymbeline

AS THE undertaker slid the lid over Sarah Hart's cheap coffin and tightened the screws, she disappeared from view. No daguerreotype of a grave matron adorned her mantelpiece. No miniature captured her bright smile. Perhaps a lock of hair had been cut away, or a whiff of fragrance lingered on a handkerchief or frock. Otherwise, her children had nothing to remind them of the mother who had lovingly tucked them into bed one night, then vanished from their lives. All that remained were the children themselves, their faces bearing hints of her pretty looks, their manners a testimony to her mothering skills. What was to become of them?

Orphaned children were typically the responsibility of their own birth parish, however the Salt Hill community didn't want Alfred and Sarah to be separated and sent to the respective orphanages or workhouses. Charity had a stiff price, as the caring and suffering well knew – from reading *A Memoir of Robert Blincoe* and *Oliver Twist*, if not from their own bitter personal experience.

The community rallied to save Sarah's children from that fate. The Farnham Royal authorities decided that the bairns would remain in Mrs Ashlee's temporary care while they established a subscription fund in their names, hoping that the charitably minded would dig deeply into their pockets. Mr Botham of the Windmill offered to act as fund keeper. One of his long-term guests, a lady named Wombwell, assumed responsibility for fund-raising. The children's guardian angel was well known in the fashionable world for her beauty and amiable disposition. Deeply moved by the children's plight, she vowed to befriend them until they were claimed by relatives or friends, or could be placed in an educational asylum.

The tally increased daily. 'Liberal contributions' from the wealthy; pennies and ha'pennies from the less well-to-do. Still no one claimed the children.

The newspapers half-heartedly attempted to uncover the mystery of Sarah Hart's origins and to capture her essence. They forgot to gather the obvious details of physical appearance – height, hair and eye colouring, complexion, physique – although they did refer to her prettiness. Their readers might also have discerned from the post-mortem testimonies that she was pleasantly plump. As for character, they merely said she was well liked and a good mother. Again, any perceptive reader might have realised, from the remarks about her chattiness as she purchased her final bottle of porter, or her neighbourly greeting as she ran through the darkness towards the safety of her own hearth, that she had a bubbly gaiety, an infectious friendliness.

Sarah Hart the corpse was of much more interest to the pressmen.

⌒

After the midday meal on Thursday, 9 January, Salt Hill's citizens tugged on their black coats and armbands and buttoned up their well-worn mourning frocks. In ones and twos they left their homes and converged on the notorious cottage in Bath Place, where the undertakers and pallbearers were hefting Sarah's coffin onto a cart. Mrs Ashlee stood nearby, gripping the hand of Sarah's bewildered little daughter. Young Alfred, the chief mourner, was holding onto another woman, recognised by those who had attended the inquest as Sarah's friend from London, Mrs Mary Ann Moss.

The cart carrying Sarah's coffin lumbered off around 2.15 p.m., followed by other carts and carriages and a long straggling line of mourners. The children had been hoisted into one of the carts, their little legs unable to endure the two-mile walk from Bath Place to Farnham Royal's parish church of St Mary's. As the mourners neared the plain Gothic structure, they could see Reverend Antrobus in his funereal robes waiting at the church's entrance to console them.

'I am the resurrection and the life,' Reverend Antrobus intoned as he walked into the church, followed by the pallbearers carrying Sarah's coffin. The two black-garbed women with their young charges joined them, as well as those from the funeral procession who could squeeze into the modest church. 'The Lord giveth and the Lord taketh away; blessed be the name of the Lord,' he told the dazed faces of the little boy and girl as he stood in the pulpit reciting the service for the burial of the dead. 'In the midst of life we are in death,' he later chanted as the pallbearers prepared to lower Sarah's coffin into the grave hacked out of the almost frozen earth. 'We commit her body to the ground, earth to earth, ashes to ashes, dust to dust.' The two children were gently urged to throw sods onto the unlabelled wooden box lying below them in the hard, unforgiving ground.

The coffin bore no name or description, not even a date of death. No one knew who she really was. They were certain of one thing, though – that her name was not really 'Sarah Hart'.

⸺

As Salt Hill mourned, the mail box at the Police Commissioners in London filled with letters. They included suggestions and tips as well as the usual diatribes against police authority. It had taken a long time to establish a metropolitan police force because Britain feared such state-controlled power. Additionally, memories still lingered of a certain shiny blade that had thumped all too frequently across the Channel half a century earlier.

Two anonymous letters, dated 9 January, were among the pile delivered to the Police Commissioners that day or the next. Both referred to the mystery surrounding Mrs Hart's identity. One letter coyly suggested that the bobbies contact a Mrs Bacon of Wilmington Square, Clerkenwell, and also a Mr Robinson, now of Stoke Newington but late of Wilderness Row. The pair might be able to provide some helpful information.

The letters were forwarded to Inspector Wiggins for investigation. He first travelled to Clerkenwell, where he found Mrs Sarah Bacon at home at 6 William Street, just off Wilmington Square.

Was the sight of a police officer on her front step one that Mrs Bacon had been dreading? Had she tried to convince herself that 'Sarah Hart' was not the servant Sarah Hadler she had introduced into John Tawell's household six years previously as a nurse for his dying wife?

⸺

Mrs Bacon had discovered the truth about their relationship in 1840, when she took tea with John at his Southwark home. She couldn't help but notice the roundness under Sarah's apron as she served them. After the housekeeper cleared the table and returned to the parlour to sit beside them, Mrs Bacon aired her thoughts. 'I know what you are going to speak about, Sarah. You had better begin.'

Distressed, Sarah jumped up and fluttered about the room, saying that it wasn't the case, trying to vindicate her master.

The shrewd matron wasn't fooled. 'If I say any more than what is right,' she responded pointedly, 'the law is open and Mr Tawell might punish me.'

John laughed. 'I am about to be admitted a Friend and to marry Mrs Cutforth,' he explained, 'and if these things are rumoured about, it will make a very great difference. I should not like such things to be talked about.' Turning to Sarah, he admonished her: 'Do not excite yourself so much.'

They discussed the available options. John agreed to support Sarah and her child. The earnest young mother-to-be, concerned more for her master's well-being than her own, then said, 'I will be dead to the world from this time. No one shall know what has become of me, not even my own mother.'

The boy, Alfred, was born in May 1840, a month after John sent off his application for readmission to the Devonshire Meeting. A few weeks later, shortly after the Meeting ordered its members to interview him about his beliefs and penitence for past wrongs, Sarah fell pregnant again.

<hr/>

What on earth possessed him? A desperate need to fill the void left by his wife's death with the quintessentially life-affirming act – or was it simply lust?

And her? Kindness, perhaps. Empathy for a distressed soul. Maybe even an awareness that in meeting the needs of this pious Quaker she might acquire a husband, bear children, find her own place in the world, rather than remaining in service, pandering to the whims of others.

Whatever led their eyes to meet, their gazes to linger, their bodies to move towards each other, it wasn't a momentary lapse, instantly regretted, hushed over, paid off, forgotten. Rather, Sarah had continued to work for John – and warm his bed – for nearly two years after his wife's death, even after he had begun courting his future wife.

~

Ticking that interview off his list, Inspector Wiggins headed north to Stoke Newington to visit the second person mentioned in the anonymous letter. 'I have been informed by Mr Robinson,' he would later write in his report, 'that he has known the prisoner John Tawell for more than twenty years, he being his agent in England the whole of the time that John Tawell was abroad. Tawell had two sons both now dead and the widow of the eldest son now resides at Islington. Mr Robinson saw the deceased Sarah Hart some years ago, but has not seen either for the last two years.'

John's eldest son had continued to suffer dreadfully from consumption in the aftermath of his return to England, and his relationship with his father had deteriorated further. Reports from Berkhampstead said that John Jnr had once been found lying in a state of exhaustion on the roadside nearly opposite the Red House. He purportedly told the nightwatchman that he had called at the Red House but that his father refused to see him. He died on 28 April 1843.

Wiggins was satisfied with the results of his investigation. The shadows hanging over Sarah's past had at last lifted. Clearly she was not the wife of one of John Tawell's sons, nor were her children his grandchildren, as she had told Mrs Moss. Clearly, the pressmen's suspicions regarding their relationship had been correct. Now all he required was a response from Superintendent

North of the Gravesend Police confirming the claims made in the second anonymous letter.

That letter had been helpfully blunt: Sarah's real name was Sarah Hadler, the correspondent claimed, and her mother, Mrs Hadler, lived at 7 Bath Street, Gravesend. 'It is well known,' the letter continued pointedly – and ungrammatically, 'that Sarah Hadler been kept secreted from her friends these last five years by John Tawell.'

⁓

London's outermost shipping port was a bustling riverside town of fifteen thousand, packed to the gunwales with cosy inns and brisk supply shops. Shipping ports attracted unsavoury types and Gravesend was too busy for the police to know those who kept out of mischief. When Superintendent North received Inspector Wiggins's letter, he despatched a constable to the coincidentally named Bath Street, to call at number seven. The Hadlers didn't live there, the residents told the constable. They lived at number eight.

Thomas Hadler was one of the town's three blacksmiths and ran his own small smithy. The couple could afford a few luxuries, such as a London daily newspaper. On Friday, 10 January, Thomas's wife Grace had read the final report of the coronial inquiry into Sarah Hart's death, and had learnt of John Tawell's committal. The suspect's name was unusual and familiar, a name from her missing daughter's past. Of course, 'Sarah' was a common name and her daughter had no children. Surely, the dead woman could not be her daughter.

Then there was a knock on her door.

⁓

Sarah was her illegitimate daughter, the distraught mother revealed. She was born in 1805 at Chatham, eight miles east of Gravesend, and had carried Grace's maiden surname, Lawrence, during her childhood years. Beyond this, Mrs Hadler did not refer to Sarah's father. He was probably one of the many sailors or soldiers – the 'vanguard of liberty' – who had passed through the strategically positioned Royal Navy dockyard town when Napoleon's menace loomed large and England geared itself for war.

Around Sarah's ninth birthday, Grace had married Thomas Hadler and moved with him to the little village of Chalk near Gravesend. There, Sarah's stepfather found work as a blacksmith, probably at the High Street forge that inspired Charles Dickens when he wrote *Great Expectations*. Sarah's mother provided her with three half-siblings during the family's years at Chalk; another four came after they moved to Gravesend. Sarah also received a good education and a respectable grounding in the evangelical Wesleyan Methodist faith.

At some stage during these years, or more likely after going into service in London, Sarah first encountered Sarah Bacon, the woman who would later introduce her to John Tawell. Curiously, most of Sarah's employers during her years in service were Quakers: John Walker and his family at 9 Wilderness Row, Clerkenwell, then down the road at number thirty-three, Joseph Robinson. Later she worked for the Scotts in Charterhouse Square, leaving there in 1838 to enter John Tawell's service. The community of London Quakers was small, and auctioneer Joseph Robinson was at that time acting as John Tawell's agent while he was abroad. In the past, Robinson had been one of William Cutforth's creditors and had signed his widow Sarah's removal order when she left London for Hemel Hempstead, a dozen years before her marriage to John Tawell. As for Mrs

Scott of Charterhouse Square, she was Sarah Cutforth's sister. Had John's future wife and future mistress ever met during the years Sarah Hadler had served these Quaker families?

Mrs Hadler told the police officer that she had last seen her daughter a year or two after she entered Tawell's service, when Sarah travelled to Gravesend for a few days before returning to his home in Bridge Street, Southwark. Soon afterwards, her daughter's letters had ceased. She had always wondered if her daughter had gone abroad with a family, and feared that she would never hear from her again or even learn what had happened to her.

~

On Tuesday morning, 14 January, Grace and Thomas Hadler began the long journey to farewell their daughter, firstly by boat to the London docks, then by omnibus to Paddington where the old couple walked into the police station and asked for Inspector Wiggins. From there, they took the Great Western Railway train to Slough – perhaps their first train journey as the railways hadn't yet reached Gravesend – then by fly to the Christopher Inn at Eton. There the county magistrate, the Reverend Mr Carter, was presiding over a magistrates' meeting regarding Sarah Hart's death, while Mr Long, the solicitor recently appointed to manage the case, was meeting with the witnesses.

Carter paused the proceedings. He immediately despatched a letter to Reverend Antrobus of Farnham Royal. Sarah Hart's body was to be exhumed, the magistrate ordered, so her mother could identify her.

As Reverend Antrobus directed the gravediggers to heft their spades and dig up the coffin they had buried only five days before, other local residents were receiving orders to attend the exhumation. Surgeon Nordblad, Surgeon Champnes, a Windsor doctor, the jury foreman and the parish churchwarden all converged on the Farnham Royal graveyard. The thump of spades hitting the hard earth drew them towards Mrs Hart's grave. They hurried along the churchyard's narrow paths, past humble headstones trimmed with wilting posies and granite monuments inscribed with the names of local notables. They couldn't help but notice the clusters of villagers who had already arrived, keen to participate in the next act of this tragic drama.

A fly pulled up to the churchyard and the black-garbed couple descended. Reverend Antrobus ushered them into his vestry room, stoking a fire to provide warmth and remaining with them to offer some spiritual comfort.

Outside, a loud thwack signalled that a spade had struck its target. Dusk had long set in by the time the gravediggers lifted Sarah's coffin to the surface and laid it next to her grave. Assisted by some spectators, they carried it to the church porch and placed it on trestles near the vestry-room door. While breaths vaporised and cold hands fumbled at the screws securing the lid, someone knocked on the door and asked the Hadlers to come to the porch.

The surgeons and officials stepped back to give the Hadlers room. The gravediggers pulled the lid away. Grace braced herself and tentatively looked into the coffin. Tears began to trickle down her lined cheeks as she lifted her hand and reached into the coffin, gently caressing the porcelain cheek, little changed because of the winter's cold. 'Oh my poor dear dear child!' she wept. 'My poor daughter!'

All around her, men surreptitiously wiped their eyes and stared fixedly at the ground.

Once Grace had looked upon her daughter's calm features for a few minutes, comforting arms led her away. The lid was screwed back down and the coffin carried back to the gravesite. Sarah Hadler was returned to her final resting place in the bleak little graveyard at Farnham Royal.

From the graveyard, the fly carried the Hadlers to Bath Place where they were introduced to Sarah's friend and neighbour, Mrs Ashlee. It was nearing bedtime when the two motherless tots first gawped up at the faces of their grandparents.

What was to be done with them? In her initial grief, Grace said that she couldn't afford to support them. However, over the following days, as their bewildered faces tugged at her heartstrings, she decided to take them back to Gravesend. She would care for them – in the short term at least – while Sarah's financial affairs were settled and other arrangements could be made. A few days later, with bags in tow, the ageing grandparents and trusting little boy and girl left Slough for ever.

⤙◠

While John had financed six servants and a carriage and horses, Sarah's stash of pawn tickets had grown larger. Her pile of unpaid bills was larger still, but there was no money in the house to pay them.

During her days in Salt Hill, Grace and her daughter's friends had approached a local broker and asked him to value her possessions. He offered £9 for them all, a sum that would cover only a fraction of her debts. Not good enough, they told him. Instead, they decided to auction them.

'Sale of the furniture and other property of the late ill-fated victim, Sarah Hart', announced the catalogue, advising that the auction would take place at Sarah's Bath Place premises on Friday, 24 January. It was a clever plan. Victorian Britain loved visiting a 'murder site', more so than most other grand exhibitions of the day. Crowds thronged to Bath Place on the day of the auction, feasting their eyes on her clothes and her toiletries, her furniture and her kitchenware, reaching out to touch each article, no matter how ordinary or dull.

The canny auctioneer had divided Sarah's possessions into sixty-five lots, recognising that many locals would willingly purchase these goods with little inherent value simply because of the awful circumstances. Sarah's friends were relieved by the result – nearly £23.

Sarah's prize possession, her watch, was not among the items auctioned. Despite her straightened circumstances, she had valued it too much to pawn. Superintendent Larkin had found it among her things when he searched her house. Upon reporting his discovery, he was ordered to retain it and produce it if necessary at Tawell's trial. The watch was a special numbered piece, silver, with the initials 'S.H.' engraved on the back, made by London's eccentric watchmaker, Sir John Bennett. Larkin and the other inspectors suspected that it had been a gift from John Tawell during happier times.

Without the sale of Sarah's watch, the bounty of the auction was not enough to cover all her debts. After deducting the rent, the remainder would pay only fifteen shillings in the pound to her various small creditors, mainly the neighbourhood tradesmen. Nothing would be left over for the care of Alfred and young Sarah.

Part 4

FASCINATION

As for the crime of murder, it is extraordinary how a very little time lessens its horror. At first, society is in a convulsion of terror at the act. A few days pass; paragraphs appear declaratory of the respectability of the accused. Every hour he becomes an object of increasing interest and every hour the mark of blood seems fading upon him.

Punch (1845)

CHAPTER 22

The language of experiment is more authoritative than any reasoning.

Alessandro Volta, as quoted in Marcello Pera,
The Ambiguous Frog (1991)

THE LUXURY of John's first night in Aylesbury Gaol – alone in a cell – didn't last. The gaoler moved him into a cell housing two or three other prisoners, a more typical arrangement. John pleaded for special treatment and offered the appropriate temptations. He had long ago discovered that money greased the wheels of bureaucracy, particularly in the privately run prison systems – except this gaoler refused to oblige him.

One prison regulation was pleasing. It allowed him to pay the neighbouring White Hart Inn to provide meals. The inn was not only one of the most convivial drinking houses in town, it had an excellent cook too. However, the regulations restricted the amount of wine and beer he could purchase: no drowning of sorrows, no sleeping the sleep of the innocent, for the accused. Instead, his nights were long, interminably long – the prisoners were locked up from 6 p.m. until 8 a.m. – and his sleep was restless and broken.

Over the following weeks, a sense of camaraderie developed between John and another inmate, a butler named William Wilder, who was confined in the same cell. Wilder was charged with breaking into and burgling the house of his master, an assistant schoolmaster at Eton College, who had known the butler for twenty years, employed him for six and trusted him completely. One of Wilder's confederates turned Queen's evidence, revealing that it was a 'put up' burglary, and that they had committed numerous crimes during their mutual employment there.

John and his new-found friend discussed their prospects, each agreeing, indeed certain, that they would both be acquitted. John decided to help his cell-mate. 'I will engage thee as my servant to live with me at Berkhampstead,' he told the delighted butler. He made arrangements for them to travel together to his residence at the conclusion of the assizes. It was never too early to plan for the future.

Many in the town believed that John's cheerful air – admittedly dashed for a short time after Henry Thomas identified him – and his certainty that he would secure an acquittal were proof of his innocence. Others simply hoped that justice would be satisfied without the people of Aylesbury having to face the horrors of a public execution.

⁓

John's family and Quaker friends didn't forsake him during his weeks in Aylesbury Gaol, although some newspapers reported otherwise. His wife and stepdaughter visited the day after his incarceration and regularly journeyed there afterwards. Sarah always spoke cheerfully and confidently of his acquittal, both to John himself and to others of her acquaintance.

Many of her friends, having weighed the evidence, cautioned her to consider the worst, to prepare herself in case he was convicted. She immediately escorted them to the door. 'How could you suppose my husband to be so great a sinner?' she demanded, before closing it behind them.

'Of course, latterly,' observed the *Weekly Dispatch*, 'she has had few friendly visits of this nature.'

Quaker friends from Berkhampstead also visited John, and Mr Sherriff allowed them to meet with him privately. 'Their communication greatly tendered him – poor Man!' wrote another friend. 'Whether he is cleared by law or otherwise, his situation is deplorable.'

Some Quakers distanced themselves, of course, declaring righteously, indignantly, that John wasn't in fact a Quaker, that while he might wear the garb of a Friend he had been expelled long ago and repeatedly spurned when he applied for re-admission. Once, twice, thrice they denied him.

Britain crowed with disdain. The Quakers and their 'expulsions'! The man professed the Quaker faith, wore the Quaker garb, spouted the Quaker speech, worshipped at Quaker services, registered his children births in Quaker registers and buried his family in Quaker burial grounds. He had built a Quaker meeting house, was welcomed at Quaker dining tables, slept in Quaker lodging houses and provided free hospitality to those attending Quaker monthly and quarterly meetings. Not a Quaker?

'Thus it always is,' rebuked one newspaper reader. 'No sooner is a Quaker charged with any offence than out comes a notice that he is "no longer a member of the Society". But what sort of Christianity is this? One of the first duties of religion is the reformation of the wicked. Yet here is a body, calling themselves Christians, making a merit of casting forth the sinner to perish without help to repentance and salvation!'

Ten days after John's committal, 18 January, was the day of the Aylesbury County Meeting. Carriages and horses brought smartly dressed members of the gentry and magistracy into town. While the women gossiped and shopped, the men discussed the county's affairs. Afterwards, some of these worthies ambled down to the town's gaol.

'We are here as visiting magistrates,' they announced self-importantly, 'and have come to inspect the gaol.' The guards dutifully unlocked the doors and the men marched inside. They glanced into a couple of cells, then asked to be led to Tawell's. 'Step outside for our inspection,' they ordered him. As the bemused inmate left his cell and stood waiting for their next command, the magistrates picked up their spy glasses and inspected him as if he were a prime piece of horseflesh up for purchase – or, more likely, an old hack they were considering putting down. Then they turned their backs on the inmate and joked among themselves as they walked out of the building.

'Such vulgar curiosity and impertinence!' John bitterly complained to the gaol's governor.

'It cannot be remedied,' Mr Sherriff told him. 'These visiting justices have a command and superintendence in the county gaol superior to my own, even though I am the governor and county gaoler.'

Ironically, such power had been granted to the magistrates in response to the Quakers' own efforts in the years since John's earlier incarceration in Newgate. Aghast at the state of the gaols and the treatment of prisoners, several prominent Friends, most especially Mrs Elizabeth Fry after her visit to Newgate in 1814, had pushed for prison reform. They had been moved by 'the filth, the closeness of the rooms, the furious manner and expressions' of the prisoners – conditions that were 'indescribable'. The resulting legislation, championed by none other than Robert Peel in his 1823 Gaols Act, allowed regular visits from chaplains and required justices to visit prisons and forward quarterly reports to the Home Secretary; this helped to improve prison conditions considerably. Certainly, though, the justices' freedom, indeed their *obligation*, to inspect local prisons was never intended as a source of entertainment.

When the news reached the desk of *Punch*'s editor, he queried bitingly: 'We ask the curious magistrates and gentry whether, having spied their fill at an accused murderer, they did not quit the gaol much more satisfied, more amused, than if they had paid their shilling at Madame Tussauds?'

⁓

By late January, the date of the Buckinghamshire Spring Assizes had been set: the week commencing 10 March 1845. Two notables had also been appointed as prosecutors: Mr Sergeant John Barnard Byles, the leader of the Norfolk Circuit, and Mr Michael Prendergast, a special pleader for the same circuit. With the nation's attention focused on the prosecution, these men knew that they couldn't afford any mistakes. Realising that they required more information about the prussic acid that had killed Sarah Hart, the prosecutors' assistants approached chemist John Thomas Cooper and asked if he could determine exactly how much prussic acid had been in her stomach contents.

'I have not the means in my possession of doing so,' Cooper told them. 'Mr Nordblad and Mr Champnes possess almost everything relating to the matter.' He reflected on the situation for a moment, then added, 'I think it possible, if I had the remainder of the stomach contents and if they were contained in the same bottle in which they were originally brought, I might be able to do so. I have a distinct recollection of about the height at which the matter stood in the neck of the bottle.'

Forensic toxicology was only in its infancy of course. Precision, thoroughness: these were yet to intrude into the lay consciousness, or even to dictate the scientific rigour necessary when a life was at stake.

On Saturday, 8 February, Surgeon Champnes delivered the tightly sealed pickle bottle to Cooper's laboratory. He didn't remain to watch the experiment itself. Before opening the bottle, Cooper filed a notch on the side to mark the height of its contents. He then used a salt-water bath to distil the remaining contents of the deceased woman's stomach, having previously poured a solution of silver nitrate into a receiving bowl to fix the prussic acid right at the moment it touched the surface. After discounting for a slight contamination with silver chloride, he estimated that he had produced 1.43 grains of cyanide of silver.

Afterwards, he poured water into the pickle bottle until it reached the notch, enabling him to measure how much fluid the bottle had held prior to the current experiment, and then to estimate how much fluid the bottle had initially contained. Making a few calculations, he decided that the woman's stomach contents had originally contained 1.002 grains of real hydrocyanic acid, the equivalent of twenty grains of Scheele's.

'Some may have been lost by absorption or exhalation, or by the transfer of the contents of the stomach to the bottle,' he wrote in his report, explaining that prussic acid was highly volatile and always diminishing. 'It is more than probable that the quantity was more than I estimate. But from my experiments I am satisfied that there must have been at least a grain of real prussic acid in the stomach.'

⟶

Mr Cooper was not alone in undertaking additional investigations. Of the three doctors who had assisted with the initial examinations, Edward Nordblad was the most knowledgeable and the most curious. On 18 February, he set up his own investigation. During his training, he had observed the effects of prussic acid on dogs, cats and goats; this time he decided that two dogs would suit his purpose. He fed them normally at 2 p.m. and five hours later began his experiment. He poured beer into two containers, then added a measured dose of Scheele's acid: into one, twelve grains of pure acid; into the other, three grains of pure acid – that is, twelve times and three times the amount Cooper estimated was in Mrs Hart's stomach. He smelt both containers but couldn't detect the distinctive, bitter almond smell of prussic acid.

At exactly 7 p.m., the same time that Sarah Hart had died, he put both containers on the floor. The dogs lapped up the beverage. A minute later, both collapsed. He knelt down and smelt their breaths, yet again unable to detect any odour of prussic acid. Four minutes later the dog with the stronger dose died; another five minutes passed before the second dog was dead too. He put their bodies in an outhouse to sit overnight.

The following day at 1 p.m., the same time that Mrs Hart's dissection had begun, he smelt the dogs' breaths. He prided himself on his acute sense of smell, yet still he couldn't detect the distinctive odour. He opened up their stomachs and smelt the usual sour odour of partly digested food, but no prussic acid.

The medical texts were wrong – according to his own olfactory senses, anyway. He would be able to testify to that effect at Tawell's trial.

~~~

John's solicitor was busy preparing the defence's case. Expecting astronomical expenses, Bevan arranged to release more of John's overseas funds and to assign all his property to trustees for his wife's benefit – although, as he explained to his client, if convicted, his whole estate would be forfeit to the Crown.

John signed the paperwork on 31 January agreeing, among other assignments, to pay an annuity of £13 each to his two illegitimate children. Many newspapers claimed that the settlement provided nothing for the children, refusing to credit John – or his solicitor – with any humanity. It was still a paltry sum, though, particularly when he had agreed under his marriage contract to pay his stepdaughter £200 annually in the event that her mother predeceased her.

Solicitor Bevan had already banked the remittance that arrived from Sydney not long after John's committal. This was the money John had been hoping to receive when he travelled to London on the day of Sarah Hart's death, and it totalled £700. Fourteen years' worth of payments to Mrs Hart and her children. The money had arrived within two weeks of the day he was supposed to have murdered her ... to save himself, according to the police, a paltry £13.

Swiftly, 'reasonable doubt' was once again established – in the minds of some, at least. True, the man had broken the legal code by soliciting forged banknotes, but that was thirty years ago and, in the aftermath, he had paid society's price and redeemed himself. True, he had also breached the moral code by sleeping with an unmarried woman – but, if that was a crime, half the men in England would find themselves in gaol! Moreover, he hadn't committed adultery and had supported the woman and her offspring thereafter, which most fornicators failed to do. Forgery, fornication: it was a giant leap from there to murder, all the more so for a pious and evidently Quaker man with £700 at his disposal.

Bevan retained two additional, learned solicitors, one for his chemical expertise and the other for his knowledge of the locality. He also retained barristers Montague Chambers and J.J. Williams to continue John's defence. A new appointee, Fitzroy Kelly would lead the team, however.

Kelly was the Edmund Kean of Britain's courtroom theatre, the most highly paid and successful barrister of the Victorian age. Strikingly handsome, exceptionally intelligent, earnest yet lively, energetic and hardworking, he was a wordsmith who could reduce technicalities and complexities to easily understood terms, a skilled amateur actor, a courtroom performer who compelled and persuaded – who won. His fees reflected his exalted status: a retainer of 300 guineas.

In the following weeks, though, each of John's barristers backed out in turn. Chambers and Williams claimed engagements elsewhere on their respective circuits, while Kelly reported receiving a heavy brief in a Maidstone case to be tried the same week as the Aylesbury assizes. 'The spirits of the prisoner, which had been pretty good, appeared considerably to fail him as soon as he learnt that Mr Fitzroy Kelly would be unable to undertake his defence,' reported the press. Bevan appointed two other barristers and convinced Fitzroy Kelly to stay on, with special arrangements made to allow Kelly to attend both the Aylesbury and Maidstone trials.

The defence's responsibilities included subpoenaing witnesses and retaining experts. The medical practitioners and chemists brought onto the defence's team included some of the most eminent in the capital. With the support of such powerful – and expensive – men, John was said to again be looking forward with confidence to the result of his trial.

Sarah was as well. She knew that her husband was innocent. She also had the utmost confidence in his legal team. As she ate her Sunday dinner at the White Hart on the weekend before his trial, she remarked to the staff, who were sending John's dinner to the gaol, that this would be the last Sunday dinner he would eat in that place.

Although she had applied to the High Sheriff for five seats in the courtroom, her family and friends had dissuaded her from attending, convincing her that it would only increase her suffering. She continued to assure them of her certainty in his innocence, to talk about having him home again – very soon. As she planned the revitalising holiday they would take after his return, she tried to believe that her world could and would return to normal.

Because, in the moment she had read of her husband's apprehension for murder, the walls of her privacy had collapsed. Passers-by slowed as they neared the Red House, some gathering in clumps on the footpath, gawking as if its well-known facade had been transformed into some sort of malevolent host, as if they could see evil seeping from the cracks around its doors and windows. When she left her home, their eyes followed her, some questioning, others condemning, casting judgement on this willing dweller in the serpent's lair.

Could it get worse? A few days prior to the trial, her misery turned to mortification. While travelling by carriage to Berkhampstead Station, her two ponies abruptly stopped in the middle of the road. Usually docile and compliant, they refused to budge. The secretly watchful began to stare openly as she tried to whip the ponies into action, then to cajole them, but they remained mutinously still. In the end, she climbed down from her carriage and walked towards the station, trailed by the murmurs of the superstitious: 'It is a foreshadowing of evil!'

⌒

Meanwhile, Buckinghamshire's sheriff faced an organisational nightmare. The assizes had experienced nothing like the excitement and anticipation surrounding Tawell's trial for as long as anyone could remember – if at all. Moreover, this case was proving particularly difficult in terms of preparation. The trial date would not be confirmed until the Assize Commission opened the week beforehand, although Wednesday, 12 March, was the date they were expecting. The trial would last at least a day or two, a particularly extended period for a criminal case, which would create further complications as the witnesses had to travel to Aylesbury, mostly from a distance of thirty to forty miles. The witnesses would require seats in or near the court-room, and accommodation for a night or two, perhaps longer. To make matters worse, so many people had applied to attend the trial that even if the courtroom were five times its size, he wouldn't be able to fit them all in.

The sheriff printed notices of the stringent regulations to be observed in the court during the trial and made arrangements to increase the available space, but he knew that many would be turned away. They would not be happy.

John was busy making his own preparations for the trial and its conclusion. He had already ordered a new suit of clothes and arranged for it to be delivered to the White Hart on the Thursday morning. A carriage would also await him outside the inn. He would depart Aylesbury triumphantly, returning immediately to Berkhampstead, where he planned to give a celebratory dinner.

During his preparations, the White Hart's proprietor popped in to see him. John shook his hand and expressed his appreciation for the meals and kindness, adding, 'I shall soon shake hands with thee, old boy, on the other side of these walls.'

CHAPTER 23

*May not the assassin be considered as a sort of public
player, an heroic victim self-doomed for the agreeable
excitement of a most civilised nation?*

Punch (1845)

IN THE stately homes of the gentry, and in the humbler abodes
of merchants and labourers, in the streets and shops, the market
square and courthouse, nothing else was talked about. It was a
constant buzz, 'Tawell … Tawell … Tawell'. The mere mention
of John's name electrified the town of Aylesbury.

Yet 'John Tawell' was not the only name printed on the calendar of the Buckinghamshire Spring Assizes. Eighty Aylesbury
Gaol inmates were to face the judge. Most had been charged
with burglary or housebreaking, or with stealing food or other
cheap articles – 'in which cases,' wrote the concerned editor of
the *Aylesbury News*, 'there is reason to fear the unfortunate fel-
lows were starved to the commission of crime or were perhaps
driven to the county gaol by the harsher discipline and more
stinted diet of the union workhouses'. Three cases involved
physical assault, and another three murder or attempted murder.
But none of these had captured the nation's attention like John
Tawell's.

The 'jolly' assizes began on Monday, 10 March, with all
the pomp and ceremony of a public extravaganza. One after
another, groups of Aylesbury prisoners were taken up to the

dock, John's cellmate, William Wilder, among them. Sometime
later, the news filtered down that Wilder had been convicted.
John was astonished. 'Well, it's very extraordinary,' he said with
confusion. 'I hardly know what to think of a Buckinghamshire
jury after this.'

He soon regained his spirits and confidence in his own
acquittal, however. When Wilder returned to the cell moaning
about the fate awaiting him, John said complacently: 'Well, be
of good heart. You will find Sydney a very pleasant place and
I have no doubt, after a little time, you will manage very well,
as I did.'

By Tuesday afternoon, crowds were converging on Aylesbury
from adjacent towns and villages, even as far away as London,
determined to grab the best seats in the house. Courtroom hear-
ings were reality theatre, with tales of tragedy and sometimes
comedy, always conflict and uncertainty, writ on the lives of
fellow citizens. They were skirmishes between different ver-
sions of the 'truth', games played out by skilled adversaries.
Murder trials were the most exciting of them all, a gladiatorial
fight to the finish.

The astute proprietor of the White Hart Inn had enticed
locals to provide a hundred beds in nearby houses for those he
couldn't accommodate in his own roomy premises. Soon every
inn was full, every spare bed occupied, and still they came. No
one could remember a busier time.

In light of the onslaught, the local newspaper's editor tried
to prepare the inhabitants and potential jury members for the
big day. He warned of the dangers of being influenced by the
city pressmen and by the public opinion they whipped up, and
even remonstrated with the London reporters about the tone

of their coverage. Serving as a juror was an important duty, the *Aylesbury News* advised, particularly when the mandated sentence was death. It was easy for jurymen to fall into the trap of believing that the evidence must be strong against the defendant or he wouldn't have been indicted, to be convinced of his guilt simply because he stood in the dock. On the other hand, those horrified at the thought of consigning a fellow human to the gallows might unwittingly overlook vital evidence from the prosecution and give too much weight to anything offered by the defence. Implacable attitudes could send an innocent man to the gallows, or let a blackguard go free.

Instead, the jury was advised to dismiss from their minds everything they might have heard about the case and to attend only to the evidence presented in court. 'Strictly speaking,' admitted the editor, 'the amount of evidence that would convict a man of stealing a penny loaf ought to be sufficient to convict another of murder, because in neither case ought a verdict of "guilty" be returned without due evidence. But in common cases, the jury will be satisfied with a moderate amount of probability, while in cases of murder nothing short of the actual impossibility of the prisoner's innocence ought to induce a jury to consign him to the hangman.'

⁓

Wednesday, 12 March dawned, a bitterly cold morning with a severe frost and piercing wind. Any other day, Aylesbury's residents might snuggle into their blankets and snooze for a bit longer, but not this day. By sunrise, the town was a frenzy of activity and excitement. Pedestrians and equestrians continued to arrive in the market square, all intent upon reaching the county hall, to get as close as possible to the knave whose fate was about to be determined.

Handbills were circulated through the crowds stating that no one except the reporters would be allowed into the courtroom without a ticket. Naturally, the mob had little interest in such formalities.

The sheriff had arranged for the magistrates, lawyers, witnesses and reporters to be admitted through the Magistrates Chamber door, but he hadn't allowed for the size and tenacity of the crowd outside. No one could get through. His constables and javelin-men were stationed at the top of the stairs – the constables with their truncheons, the javelin-men with their menacing pikes – but they were too far away to help those fighting their way through the mob.

The sheriff ordered his men to create a pathway. One step at a time they descended. They prodded – and when that failed, whacked – the resistant throng, until they succeeded in clearing the stairs and forming a corridor of armed implacability. Those required or allowed into the courtroom were at last able to enter the courthouse.

The difficulties did not end there. In the hall leading to the staircase stood three or four officials, testy and officious, delighting in obstructing the passage of those permitted to enter. 'Ruffianism is not too strong an epithet to apply to the behaviour of these jacks in office,' wrote one angry reporter, 'for they were not content with annoying gentlemen, but actually assaulted them. It is to be hoped that they will be called to account by the justices who have control on these occasions.'

The press's accommodation? 'Nothing could be more unsatisfactory or unsuitable,' raged another reporter. 'After a struggle of more than half an hour's duration, destructive to clothes and almost fatal to life and limb, we fought our way to a miserable little corner of one of the galleries.' The front seat was too far from the rail to allow ease of writing, the back seat too high to serve as a chair, and far too many reporters were crammed into the small area. At least, though, they were away from the mob.

Outside the courthouse's public doors, the scene was like the crush at the hustings of a hotly contested election. Yelling, jesting, shouting, hooting. 'It beggars all description!' wrote one appalled reporter who had been caught up in the crowd. The officials refused to open the doors any earlier than 9 a.m., the session's commencement time. It was a foolish decision. When the doors at long last opened, the frenzied rush was like a jet of steam erupting from an over-boiled kettle, propelling the javelin-men from the bottom to the top of the stairs. Almost instantly, the standing area in the courtroom was filled. Still the mob kept pushing. Both the outer hall and inner hall were packed out, with bodies forcing open the folding doors that separated the two rooms.

And the noise! It would be impossible to conduct a murder trial with the racket created by such a huge unruly mob. The under-sheriff realised that the folding doors would need to be closed. To do so, however, they would need to eject many of the spectators who had fought so hard to get into the building. He made the necessary order and another battle began. 'Stand back! Stand back!' cried the javelin-men as they attempted to drive back the hordes, their words accompanied by loud knocks on nearby pates. Several staves were broken, and a few heads injured, but in the end the crowds retreated. The javelin-men closed the folding doors. The session could begin.

Magistrates thronged the bench. The defence and prosecution teams pushed papers around the lawyers' table, their large numbers preventing anyone else from sharing their prime space. The reporters stood upstairs in the Petit Jury gallery with some of the jury-in-waiting. Soon the clerk called the court to order and announced that Mr Baron James Parke was about to enter the courtroom.

A short elderly man in gown and powdered wig strode across to the bench. He swept the room with his piercing brown eyes, then sat facing the court. He was a celebrated figure in legal circles, a highly respected judge who would later be eulogised, in Britain and abroad, as one of the greatest judicial minds. His mental acuity in grasping difficult points and disentangling complicated facts, in clarifying every aspect of the law, was considered remarkable even among his peers. Grave without being pompous, courteous but not patronising, he was an able adjudicator in these courtroom battlefields. The barristers knew that he would attend closely to every stage of the proceedings, and that he would rule wisely. They also knew that they risked freezing to death while he did so.

Baron Parke had a well-known fetish – fresh air – which he insisted upon partly to alleviate the noisome odours of the unwashed masses who invaded his courtroom, and partly in the naive hope that their diseases might escape rather than infect him. His fetish often proved a hardship on a bleak winter's day, yet as the attendants flung open the windows on 12 March, the audience in the Aylesbury courtroom were grateful for the frigid but refreshing air washing over them.

Then a murmur ran through the court: 'He is coming.'

CHAPTER 24

Hypocrisy is the cloak which conceals modern acts
of turpitude, as dark nights were trusted to for the
concealment of the bloody deeds of old.

G.W.M. Reynolds,
The Mysteries of London (1845)

JOHN TAWELL appeared as if from Hades itself, a black-garbed figure rising up from the bowels of the building through the entrance in the centre of the dock. He looked around with a steady confidence, curious, seemingly unconcerned, then talked for a moment with the gaoler.

The spectators craned to get a glimpse of the notorious villain. As he took off his distinctive Quaker hat – newly purchased for the occasion – and placed it beside him on the dock rail, they could see what everyone else had seen: no horns or forked tongue, just a gentleman with long greyish hair pushed back from his forehead, a white face, a slight cast to his left eye, and the normal signs of age including wrinkled cheeks and busy lines around his mouth. 'It was the face of a man whose course of life has been uneasy and chequered,' one reporter decided, 'and whose brain has seldom been idle.'

The Clerk of the Arraigns read out the indictment, a simple document containing only one count. 'John Tawell, not having the fear of God before his eyes and being instigated by the devil, did wickedly and with malice aforethought, on the first of January at Salt Hill, make an assault upon one Sarah Hart and cause her to take two drachms weight of prussic acid, well knowing the same to be a deadly poison, and he did force the said Sarah Hart to take into her body the said poison, by the operation of which poison she fell mortally sick and did then and there die.'

Pausing for a moment to allow his words to sink in, the clerk then asked: 'How say you: are you guilty with respect to that murder or not guilty?'

The man dressed in the garb of the honest and trustworthy Quakers responded loudly and firmly: 'Not guilty.'

Baron Parke ordered that the jury be sworn. John listened attentively. 'You can object, if you please, to any of the jurors by challenging,' the judge advised. John took up the invitation. He and his counsellors challenged thirteen prospective jury members before the required twelve were selected. 'It was a jury of plain countrymen,' the *Aylesbury News* would write appreciatively, 'of twelve farmers possessing nothing but common sense.'

The jury selection hadn't been easy. The commotion outside had prevented the prospective jurymen from hearing their names called. The crowds on the wrong side of the folding doors had mutinied, scuffling with the court officials as they kept trying to push through the doors. 'Keep back! Keep back!' The under-sheriff's distinctive voice could be heard above the hubbub. 'I can't!' voices shouted in return, distracting the attention of everyone in the courtroom. Again came the distinctive thwacks, and the bellows of pain.

The commotion continued for much of the morning, only easing as the mob decreased in size. Snow had begun to fall, which helped to numb the enthusiasm of those who hadn't made it through the front doors. As they plodded home or to the nearest pub, and as those closest to the inner doors stepped back from the thrusts of the javelin-men, those at the rear found themselves propelled outside into the snow. Before long, they left as well. At last, the officials were able to slam the outer doors. The trial could proceed uninterrupted.

⟿

'The prisoner at the bar stands indicted for the most serious crime known to the law – the crime of wilful murder,' said the lead prosecutor, Sergeant Byles, as he stood and faced the jury. 'In cases of this kind you are not to expect direct and positive evidence, as no man who meditates the crime of assassination by poison fails to take precautions. No eye sees death poured into the cup, sees the passage of the deadly poison from the hand that administered it to the body of the murdered, save that which is All-seeing. All that a human tribunal can do is to gather together the circumstances of the case and form as just and con-scientious a judgement as is possible for fallible mortals to do.'

He recounted the story of Mrs Hart's death and her sus-pected murderer's capture by means of the electric telegraph. 'Quick as the train went,' he told the spellbound audience, 'the signal was there long before the train arrived at the London terminus!' It was a reminder of the pivotal role played by the electric telegraph – the 'electric constable' as it would soon be nicknamed – in delivering Tawell into the hands of justice. It was also a reminder that this strange machine had powers that seemed almost magical, as if they had all been transported into the mysterious world of a Brothers Grimm fairy tale. Trains; telegraphs. Truly, they were living in amazing times.

Byles then summarised the evidence he would present to the court, the evidence he claimed would prove that the gentleman standing in the dock was a murderer. His simple speech had no rhetorical displays or dramatic flourishes, and therein lay its brilliance. It was exactly the type of introduction that would appeal to the jury of plain countrymen who preferred working things out for themselves, who would not take kindly to being patronised by an arrogant Londoner. An indescribable hum of applause infused the courtroom, the type of orderly acknowledgement, wrote one reporter, that was heard in a Presbyterian or Unitarian chapel when a preacher was particularly eloquent. One spectator with legal knowledge was overheard muttering to a neighbour, 'It's a fearful array of facts.'

The lead prosecutor sat down leaving his off-sider, Mr Prendergast, to take over. Prendergast rose and called his first witness, Mrs Ashlee. As she walked to the witness box, John's barrister asked the judge if his client might be accommodated with a seat.

'Prisoner, do you wish to sit down?' Baron Parke asked.

'Yes,' said John gratefully. 'I should be much obliged as I have long had a varicose affliction in my legs.'

The legal practitioners in attendance dipped their metaphorical hats at Tawell's clever barrister. Kelly had scripted the dialogue, coaching John to testify at the start of the trial – without breaching the rules preventing him from testifying at all – regarding his medical problems and, by unspoken extension, his need for medical preparations that would relieve the associated discomfort. Having laid the groundwork in such a natural way, it would be easier later to convince the jurymen that Tawell possessed certain preparations for medical rather than malevolent reasons. His words also alluded to age and infirmity, conditions that might spark a feeling of sympathy in the jury, perhaps another slim doubt. Every doubt, tiny though it might be at first, was a nick in the chain of circumstantial evidence. And as England's pre-eminent defence counsellor well knew, a case based upon a chain of circumstantial evidence was never as strong as one buttressed by eye-witness testimony, so enough nicks in the chain could break it.

An usher ejected a nearby spectator from his comfortable repose and carried the chair to the dock, positioning it so John would still be facing the jury. John seated himself then leaned forward, resting an elbow on the bar and propping his chin in his hand. He slipped the other hand into his warm pocket. As he looked up again, Sarah Hart's neighbour, Mrs Mary Ann Ashlee, was stepping into the witness box.

Mrs Ashlee was dressed in deep mourning – a poignant reminder of the tragedy at the heart of the courtroom trial. 'Between four and five o'clock on the day of Sarah Hart's death, I saw the prisoner go into her house,' the gentle neighbour began. She proceeded to describe how the evening had begun like any other, and should have ended and been forgotten like any other, but for the twist of fate that had plucked her from obscurity and splashed her name across the nation's newspapers. That twist of fate had made her story of crucial relevance to the legal system as well as a subject of fascination among the public. She had been asked to repeat it, exhaustively, until the most minuscule details and suppositions were indelibly imprinted in her memory as fact.

Mrs Ashlee was one of many witnesses who testified that day, most having already appeared at the earlier inquest. Some testified to having seen Sarah Hart shortly before her death or while she was dying, others to John's movements in the afternoon or evening of her death. Some described their own involvement in sending the timely message along the telegraph lines to London, or in apprehending the prisoner and hearing him declare that he hadn't been at Slough that night, that he didn't know anyone there.

Then Police Superintendent Samuel Perkins, the man who had lodged John at his home for nearly a week until the inquest jury reached its verdict, took the witness stand. He began to describe an incident that had happened on Friday, 3 January, the day John received visits from both his lawyer and his wife, the day before the coronial jury sat for the second of three sessions to hear evidence regarding Sarah Hart's death.

—◠—

It had been a busy morning, that Friday morning, with letters being dispatched to Tawell's wife and solicitor, and a visit from one of the barristers who would represent John in court the following morning. After the barrister departed, Superintendent Perkins and his prisoner sat down to eat their midday meal. An idle conversation began, the usual innocuous nothings, until John tossed in, between bites: 'That wretched and unfortunate woman once lived in my service for two years and a half, or nearly so. I suppose thee did not know that, Perkins?'

The startled officer replied cautiously, 'I did not know it, but I had heard so.'

'She left my service about five years ago,' John continued, as Constable Hollman entered the room. The Farnham Royal constable was also a temporary resident at Perkins's house, and had left the room only a few minutes beforehand.

Perkins interrupted John, warning: 'Mind, we are both police officers and what you say I will have to report to the coroner tomorrow.'

'I have no objection,' said John, and blithely continued his tale. 'I have been in the habit of sending her money, but I have been pestered with letters from her when I was in London and I was determined to give her no more money. She was a very good servant when she was in my service but she was a bad principled woman, a very bad woman. She wrote to me to say that if I did not send her some money she would do something – she would make away with herself.'

'Have you got these letters?' Perkins asked.

'No, I don't think I have. I never keep such letters as those.'

John pushed on with his story, explaining that he had travelled to Salt Hill on New Year's Day to tell Mrs Hart that he would send her no more money. When she had asked for a drop of porter, he sent her out to purchase a bottle and they both enjoyed a glass. Then the trouble began.

'She had in her hand a very small phial, not bigger than a thimble, and she held it over the glass of porter, and said, "I will! I will!" She drank part of it and threw the remainder into the fire and began to throw herself about in such a manner ...' and John imitated her actions by moving his shoulders to and fro as if in convulsions. 'Then she lay down on the hearthrug and I walked out.'

The astonished policemen sat there dumbfounded. They hadn't expected such a revelation.

'I should not have gone out if I thought she had been in earnest,' John continued remorsefully. 'I certainly should not have left her.'

Was he telling the truth? Superintendent Perkins immediately ordered another search of Sarah Hart's fireplace. Constable Hill and Superintendent Larkin scooped the cinders into a box and took them outside into the garden where the dust and ash could do no damage. Carefully, they sifted through the box's contents. There. A little piece of burnt paper. Constable Hill picked it up and peered at it. Despite its blackened state, he could see a circular imprint like a bottle rim. Had the paper covered the top of a glass phial that had since melted in the fire? He sent it with Surgeon Champnes on his second visit to the chemist, but Cooper reported that the paper was too blackened to be useful.

———

John's defence team mentally winced at their client's ill-advised admission. It was all very well for John to try and defend himself, to provide his own account of the night in question; however, he had made the prosecution's job easier for them. No wonder J.J. Williams, the lawyer who had counselled John to make such a statement, had claimed commitments elsewhere and jumped ship.

John's new barrister, Fitzroy Kelly, wasn't going to let Perkins's startling revelation enter the court record unchallenged. He questioned whether Superintendent Perkins might have improperly drawn such an admission from John. He even questioned the honesty of his 'recollection'. 'Didn't you say in reply to a question on the second day of the inquest as to whether the prisoner had told you anything, "No, he was very close."'

'I did not say so to anyone,' Perkins replied indignantly. 'On the morning of the last day of the coroner's inquest, I told the coroner that I had information to give of the conversation I have detailed, and I understood him to say that he wouldn't take any more evidence. There were no witnesses under examination then or subsequently.'

Constable Hollman was the next witness to testify, and he largely confirmed his superior's statement. Hollman wasn't a party to Perkins's communication with the coroner, though, so the questions as to when exactly the coroner was informed, and why John's revelation wasn't raised at the inquest, were left unsubstantiated.

John had remained calm and composed as he listened to all the witnesses, and to the evidence stacking up against him. He had the best counsel money could buy, backed by the expert advice of eminent doctors and physicians, so he was still quietly confident that he would triumph in court. During the various testimonies, he whispered frequently to his solicitors and barristers and even to the gaoler. Sometimes he mentioned statements made by the witnesses. On two or three occasions he spun around and stared balefully at a witness, an abrupt movement that was particularly noticeable as his back was customarily to the witness box. It drew the court's attention towards him and sparked curiosity as to what might have interested or alarmed him. Occasionally he rubbed his face and seemed fidgety and restless, but by this time most of the jurors and spectators were feeling the same. They had been sitting – or, in most cases, standing – for many hours.

Around 3 p.m., after the policemen had testified, the judge allowed the jury to retire for refreshments. From their eyrie, the reporters looked with amusement at the goings-on in the various levels of the courtroom: the tiers of human heads rising one above another in the different galleries, the anxious spectators running to the privies yet also trying to ensure that no one stole their space. Several were unable to get back up to the galleries by the stairs, so those below hoisted them onto sturdy shoulders so they could climb over the gallery railing. They had no need to worry about the crowds outside. The snow flurries had driven away even the most resolute, and the area outside the county hall was blanketed by a silence almost as remarkable as the previous commotion.

During the break, John's composure transformed into a levity bordering on impudence. He was a man seemingly without a care in the world. Laughing, he stuck his hat back on his head, saying that he was doing so now that the judge was absent as he felt very cold from so many windows being kept open.

He chatted to his counsellors and to the man who brought his dinner from the White Hart. He even jovially invited the waiter to visit him at Berkhampstead after the trial. 'I am offering no idle employment,' John assured him. 'I fully anticipate the pleasure of entertaining all my friends and I will cordially welcome you among the number.' He also talked and laughed with spectators standing in the space between the dock and the counsel's table, some of whom would later take the stand as his character witnesses.

Up in the gallery, some of the reporters were questioning the value of John's legal team. What was he paying for, indeed paying a prodigious sum of money for? Fifteen witnesses had testified without any interesting or valuable cross-examination coming from his side. 'No attempt has been made to break it down on the part of prisoner's counsel,' wrote one reporter, 'which makes people wonder whether any defence is really to be attempted and what that defence could be.'

~

'I am a surgeon at Salt Hill,' Mr Henry Montague Champnes told the court a short time after the session recommenced, before recounting his own experiences on the night of Sarah Hart's death. When he described the following day's post-mortem examination, he made a surprising declaration: 'I smelt the odour of prussic acid the moment I opened the body. I made a remark to that effect. Neither Mr Pickering nor Mr Nordblad did, however. It was not a passing conjecture of mine. I was positive of it.' As the surgeon continued to testify, he was forced to admit that his knowledge about prussic acid was primarily theoretical and that, yes, the authoritative texts, such as Taylor's *Medical Jurisprudence*, all reported that the bodies of prussic acid victims exhaled strong odours of the acid which, if death was rapid, could even be smelt in their blood and mouth.

Most of the courtroom spectators were merely there for the entertainment, but a few brows furrowed at Champnes's declaration that he had smelt prussic acid's distinctive odour at the post-mortem examination. Those who had attended the January inquest or had carefully perused the inquest reports knew that Champnes and Nordblad had then testified that they hadn't smelt prussic acid at the post-mortem. The doctors had also testified that it took many hours of chemical testing before prussic acid was discovered because its distinctive odour had not been smelt by them or the chemist, so the prussic acid test had been left until last. Champnes's admission that the odour *should* have been smelt – according to the medical authorities – explained why he, and later William Pickering as well, were now testifying that they had indeed smelt the prussic acid while performing the autopsy. Of course, if they testified otherwise, the defence could use the same medical authorities to argue that the prussic acid found in Sarah Hart's stomach contents had probably been liberated during decomposition and testing, and that her cause of death was consequently unknown. That being the case, it raised a very large reasonable doubt as to whether she had actually been murdered – just the type of reasonable doubt that John's lawyers were hoping to cultivate in the jury.

Yet John's legendary barrister, Fitzroy Kelly, failed to home in on these 'discrepancies', to question the surgeons' veracity and thereby undermine the credibility of these critical witnesses. What indeed was Tawell paying for?

Surgeon Champnes stood in the witness box for an extended period that afternoon, questioned, among other things, about prussic acid deaths in general and the amount of the chemical necessary to kill an adult. Where along the medicine–poison continuum did this particular chemical turn from tonic to toxin?

One moment Champnes rambled on about grains of pure prussic acid, the next about grains of London Pharmacopoeia or Scheele's; one moment he referred to drachms or drachmas or drams, the next to minims or drops or ounces. He described one death from eighteen grains of Scheele's, another from three-and-a-half drachms, and the deaths of the seven French epileptics from seven-tenths of a grain of pure prussic acid. It was confusing to the judge and bewildering to the jury, and left most of the audience scratching their heads. How much prussic acid did it *really* take to kill a person? The substance of his answer was that less than one grain of pure prussic acid – that is, less than fifty grains of London Pharmocopaeia or twenty grains of Scheele's – would kill a human.* Or so he thought. 'The exact dose is not determined yet,' he admitted.

Fitzroy Kelly then cross-examined the young country surgeon. He led him to admit that prussic acid could be found in stone fruit and seeds, among other substances, and that commercial Prussian blue was made from the blood, bones and horns of animals. Kelly then picked up *Watson's Lectures on the Practice of Physic* and said, 'Do you agree with this? "A blow, a fall, an electric shock, a teaspoon of prussic acid may cause death, and leave no vestiges on the nervous system!"'

'Yes,' Surgeon Champnes agreed.

For the first time, the discerning could see where John's legal team was heading in tackling his defence.

The indefatigable Baron Parke preferred to extend the court day for as long as possible, so it was around 7 p.m., ten hours

---

* London Pharmacopoeia was 2 parts pure prussic acid to 98 parts water while Scheele's was 2½ times stronger at 5 parts prussic acid to 95 parts water.

after the session commenced, before he announced that the court would adjourn for the night.

The pressmen would later grumble that it was all very well for the judge and legal teams to continue after sunset, as they had been supplied with candles. Stuck up in the press's 'most admirably inconvenient gallery', as one reporter would later snipe, 'we were in perfect darkness during the last half hour'. The candles down below exacerbated their difficulties. The flickering patches of light dazzled those looking down upon them, intensifying the darkness of the upper gallery and creating even more difficulties for the note-takers.

With so many witnesses still to be examined, Baron Parke suggested resuming at an earlier hour the following morning. 'Eight o'clock?' he asked, looking around the courtroom. Naturally the barristers, jurymen and court officials agreed to his suggestion. He then told the jury that he was sequestering them. They would have to remain in the custody of a court bailiff as he couldn't permit them to be separated until the case was finished. Beds would be made available for them at an inn.

One juror called out in alarm, 'But shall we not be allowed any provisions?' The courtroom regulars laughed at his naive inquiry.

'Oh, certainly, gentlemen, you shall have everything you require,' Baron Parke assured them, then thumped his gavel and left the bench.

In the aftermath, John and his counsellors spent some time discussing the day's proceedings. As they prepared to leave the courtroom, John said to one of them, 'Where are you going when you leave here?'

'I am going to the White Hart where I am staying.'

'Do you think,' John asked, 'that there would be any objection to my accompanying you?'

Quickly controlling his amusement at the assumed ignorance of his client ('for it must be assumed', he would later declare), John's legal adviser gently dismissed the suggestion. Instead, the turnkey returned John to the bowels of the building, Charon guiding him back to Hades.

Chapter 25

That's carrying the joke rather too far.

Captain Frederick Marryat,
Snarleyyow, Or, the Dog Fiend (1844)

THE SECOND day of John's trial arrived, again bitterly cold and already snowing. The lessons of the previous day had been well learnt by everyone. Many locals chose to wait for the newspaper reports, knowing that the witnesses' testimonies would be transcribed word for word. The local editors, in particular, would respect their desire to hear for themselves the testimonies of the witnesses and the judge's ruling.

The under-sheriff decided to open the doors much earlier, preferring eager spectators walking calmly into the courtroom over a rampaging mob. The courtroom filled in an orderly fashion, a stark contrast to the day before. The reporters' complaints had also been heeded: the understrappers at the doors were less officious and their own facilities improved. Contented, the pressmen pulled out their notepads and glanced around, absorbing the atmosphere and trying to put names to faces. They could see several Quakers among the assembled audience, and numerous medical men, both with the law officers and in the crowds.

John had enjoyed a restful night's sleep. After dressing himself, he gathered his belongings and sent a messenger to confirm that his suit would arrive that day at the White Hart, and that a carriage would await him outside the inn. He had been informed that the court would sit until the verdict was handed down, and he was determined to leave Aylesbury as quickly as possible in the aftermath.

A turnkey escorted him into the dock and provided him with a chair. He sat in the corner nearest the witness box looking as composed as he had previously, although his hands betrayed a certain nervousness. Every so often, one would creep up to his mouth – a classic posture of alarm or consternation.

'I am a practical chemist,' John Thomas Cooper began, the first witness on this second day of the hearing, 'and was formerly a lecturer on chemistry and medical jurisprudence.'

Men like Cooper played a critical role in Britain's attempts to combat the poisoning epidemic that seemed to have taken hold of the nation's households. While the results of a beating, stabbing, shooting or garrotting were visible to most and easy to describe to a jury, the results of a poisoning were generally invisible to all but a handful of specialists. When these experts attempted to explain their transformation of the invisible into the visible, though, the words they used were often intangible, occasionally unintelligible, creating a legal quandary. How could a jury, drawn from those whose criteria for attendance was merely that they were voters and men of good standing in the community, understand such evidence – let alone send a man to the gallows – when it was the sole basis of proof? This impasse was a helpmate to the cunning poisoner. However, medical jurisprudence was teaching doctors and scientists the type of information required in a courtroom and the best strategies for turning the intangible into the tangible, something the jury could see for themselves.

'Messieurs Champnes, Pickering and Nordblad called on me and produced a bottle full, or nearly so, of the contents of a human stomach,' Cooper continued. He then described, in mind-numbing detail, the procedures used to test Mrs Hart's stomach contents and the other contents of Champnes's gruesome carpet bag. He sparked the court's interest again when he reached down to his side and picked up his bag. Opening it, he pulled out a piece of broken glass. 'The bottle which contained the Prussian blue I had produced from the sand bath has unfortunately been broken,' he told the court, remorsefully. 'My bag fell from the table yesterday and the bottle containing the first result from the sand bath was broken. But here are the remains.' He held up the piece of glass. The judge, jury, barristers, reporters and nearby spectators could all see traces of a blue stain.

Cooper placed the glass on the rail in front of him and reached again into his bag. 'Here is the produce of the water bath,' he said, holding up a small bottle. Everyone could see that it contained about an ounce of deep blue liquid, the colour generally known as 'Royal' or 'Prussian' blue. It was the toxicologist's equivalent of a blood-stained dagger. A satisfied 'aah' rumbled through the courtroom.

Then came a critical question. Could Cooper have produced the prussic acid in the testing process itself?

~

Some weeks beforehand, as Cooper had ruminated on the results of his experiments, he had an alarming thought. Apple pips! He had noticed partly digested apple in the dead woman's stomach contents although he hadn't noticed any pips. What if the pulpy mass had included chewed-up apple pips? And what if these had produced the prussic acid found after the distillation process? Bitter almonds were well known to produce traces of prussic acid but, as far as he knew, no one had tested apple pips. He decided to conduct his own experiment.

Cooper approached his cook and asked for the pips of fifteen apples. After bashing them slightly to bruise them, he tipped them into a retort with distilled water and applied the same degree of heat as in his previous experiments, although he used a lamp for heating purposes rather than a bath. Having distilled about an ounce of liquid, he applied the same tests to determine if the process of distilling apple pips alone could produce any traces of prussic acid.

It could.

After Cooper finished describing his experiment to the rapt courtroom, he reached into his bag again and pulled out another ounce bottle. He held it up for a moment so everyone could see it, then placed it next to the first bottle. The liquid in the second bottle was only a faint shade of blue, much lighter than the first. The crowd chorused another satisfied 'hmmm'.

'The quantity of prussic acid contained in it is unappreciable,' Cooper announced firmly. 'I do not think any chemist could estimate the quantity, it is so small.' He then reminded the court that he hadn't seen any apple pips in Sarah's stomach contents and that the essential ingredients found in prussic acid existed in all animal substances, though not as prussic acid itself. It required furnaces with searing temperatures of six hundred or seven hundred degrees to liberate the prussic acid from animals for commercial use.

Still, doubt was pushing its foot through the door he had just opened. Fitzroy Kelly asked if the results might be different if the apple pips had been macerated. Cooper couldn't say. 'Bitter almonds sometimes yield more prussic acid without maceration than with,' he added. 'It depends on the distillation process.'

'I ask one more question,' said Kelly. He picked up a tome from his table and flicked through the pages to find a marked spot. 'Do you agree with Taylor in his *Medical Jurisprudence* that "the odour of prussic acid, which is said to be peculiar, may be found when all other tests fail to prove the presence of that acid."'

'I do not believe it!' Cooper replied emphatically. 'As far as my experience goes, it would lead me to the contrary conclusion.'

'But, if I understand rightly,' Kelly pushed him, 'you don't smell prussic acid at all, but feel its effects in another way?'

'Sometimes it has produced a spasmodic contraction about my throat, without my smelling the odour. At other times I have distinctly perceived the odour of it. It depends, I think, very much upon the state of the nasal organ at the moment.'

The judge interjected, asking Cooper whether he had any doubts about the presence of prussic acid in Mrs Hart's stomach, and whether he had any doubts that prussic acid might exist without being smelt.

'None whatever,' Cooper replied.

'Was there enough prussic acid in the contents of Mrs Hart's stomach to have caused her death?'

'I am not aware of what quantity of prussic acid destroys life,' Cooper admitted, 'as I have no practical knowledge on the subject. The case I am most familiar with is that referred to yesterday as occurring in the French Hospital where the epileptic patients died from seven-tenths of a grain. From my experiments, I am satisfied that there must have been a full grain of pure prussic acid in her stomach.'

⁓

Taking a break from the lengthy scientific evidence, the prosecution called to the stand Charlotte Howard, the unwed mother who had left her baby in Sarah Hart's care. The spectators' interest quickened. Those who had monitored the story via the newspapers hadn't heard Charlotte's name before. Who was she and why was she testifying?

Charlotte briefly described her connection with Sarah Hart then continued: 'I remember Mr Tawell coming down to Bath Place on the 30th September last. Shortly before seven o'clock in the evening, Mrs Hart let him in. She did not expect him that evening. I did not see him but I heard Mrs Hart say, "Here's my master". I also knew it was he by his voice. He was there about ten minutes when Mrs Hart called me and told me to go and get a bottle of stout from the Windmill. I did so and brought it in. I was then told by Mrs Hart to go and get a sheet of paper from Mrs Ashlee. When I came back with the sheet of paper, Mrs Hart took it from me and returned into the front room where Mr Tawell was and remained about a quarter of an hour before he went away. Mrs Hart then came out of the front room and said to me, "Oh, I'm so very ill! I was obliged to tell my master to go, for I can scarce stand."

'She looked dreadfully ill,' Charlotte told the stunned court. 'She retched a good deal and complained of her head being very bad. She said: "I drank only a little glass of porter. I am sorry that I drank it all at once for immediately upon having it I felt my head giddy and was sick instantly." She went upstairs to bed directly after she told me she was ill. She was so bad that she would have fallen had I not held her up.'

Charlotte attended Sarah during the night while she vomited violently again and again, purging her stomach of all its contents. The following day Charlotte cared for the children while Sarah remained in bed, complaining of feeling giddy and ill.

'On coming downstairs,' Charlotte continued, 'I observed the table in the room where Mr Tawell had been. On it were thirteen sovereigns, the bottle of which half the porter was drunk, and two glasses.' She took charge of the money, taking it up to Sarah's room and stashing it in her drawer. She threw out the partly drunk porter but drank some of the remaining bottled porter and gave some to the children. 'It did not make me sick,' she added, 'and it did not sicken them either.'

For a moment, astonishment silenced the room. As the magnitude of Charlotte's revelation sank in, everyone seemed to gasp at the same time, an endless in-drawn breath. Then the whispers began: awe, horror, concern, delight. What excitement; what drama. It was the best entertainment they had enjoyed in a long time.

In such a status-conscious society, it was easy to discredit some witnesses. John's barrister asked Charlotte about her marital status.

'I am not married,' she replied defiantly, 'nor was I when I had the child.'

Kelly then asked what the doctor had said when Mrs Hart was taken ill at that time.

'She had no medical advice,' Charlotte admitted, her response suggesting that Sarah was not ill enough to call the doctor. Those who knew the state of Sarah's finances realised that she hadn't sought medical advice because she couldn't afford it.

Edward Nordblad was the next witness, a more experienced surgeon than Champnes. He had heard the testimonies of Sarah's neighbours regarding the events of 1 January, he told the court, and believed that their descriptions of her symptoms indicated sudden death. 'If they appeared after drinking I should think there was poison in the draught. I should have suspected either prussic or oxalic acid as I know of no other poison that would produce death so suddenly and rapidly.'

As for Charlotte Howard's revelations: 'The symptoms

described are precisely those of a dose of prussic acid, short of death. Sickness, vomiting and headache are symptoms attendant upon anything disagreeing with the stomach. I have seen dogs vomit after taking prussic acid and the analogy between them and human beings is perfect.'

'You speak rather *dog*matically,' Fitzroy Kelly quipped, as he stood up to commence his cross-examination. A splutter of laughter rolled through the courtroom. For a moment, as John turned to look at the witness, a smile teased his face, then he pinched his mouth and spun back to face the jury.

Kelly then jokingly chided, 'You say, sir, that the analogy between dogs and human beings is perfect. Is porter the proper drink of dogs?'

'No,' allowed Nordblad, then redirected the court's attention to the seriousness of the occasion. 'It was used as a medium for the poison.'

Nordblad described his experiments on the dogs and answered further questions about the effects of prussic acid. 'Less than one grain of pure prussic acid will destroy life,' he informed the court, 'but I am not chemist enough to say that more than one grain was found in Sarah Hart's stomach.'

To questions about the medicinal uses for prussic acid, Nordblad advised that it was mainly prescribed for diseases of the skin and cancerous eruptions, and that the average dose was five minims of Scheele's – that is, about one-twentieth of a grain of pure prussic acid. 'I have never heard of prussic acid being administered externally for varicose veins,' he added. 'I should think it useless.'

With a flourish, Fitzroy Kelly handed Nordblad a piece of paper.

'You have no right to hand him a paper, except to refresh his memory,' the judge admonished the barrister. Kelly explained that it was one Dr Addison's prescription for prussic acid which had been written out for the prisoner.

Nordblad glanced at the piece of paper. 'This is a proper prescription for varicose veins,' he admitted. 'I agree that prussic acid may be applied successfully to such afflictions, to alleviate pain.'

Kelly had one more question: 'Might not death have arisen from the effects of water being poured down the deceased's throat?'

'It might,' admitted the experienced medical practitioner.

⟶

When apothecary manager Henry Thomas took the stand to testify about John's prussic acid purchases, Kelly also handed him Dr Addison's prescription for his assessment. Thomas read the piece of paper and recognised Addison's handwriting, agreeing that prussic acid was a suitable application for varicose veins or for ulceration arising from some other cause.

Then Thomas, who had been called to support the prosecution's case, proceeded to disagree with the testimonies of the preceding medical and scientific witnesses. He said that he did not believe that Scheele's prussic acid could be mixed in a drink and consumed and not be smelt after death, and that porter was unlikely to disguise the smell. 'I killed a parrot for a lady a few days before Mr Tawell called on me,' he added, by way of an explanation. 'It was ill and the lady wished to have it killed. I put about thirty drops of Scheele's prussic acid into water which I put into a glass syringe, and I injected it down the bird's throat. There were three women present and they were compelled to leave the room, the scent was so strong and suffocating. The bird was afterwards stuffed.'

Just to be certain, he had conducted his own prussic acid experiment prior to the court case. He mixed thirty drops of acid with eleven ounces of porter and sniffed it. The odour of prussic acid was slightly perceptible, he told the members of the jury.

Confused countenances looked back. Despite the testimony of the 'experts', both medical and scientific, nobody could agree as to whether prussic acid would always or only sometimes be smelt. Nobody was certain about the amount of prussic acid required to kill a human. None of the witnesses had previously seen a human victim. All were at the mercy of the textbooks – of second-hand experience – and the textbooks themselves disagreed with each other. What information could they rely upon? Indeed what information *should* they rely upon in coming to a verdict?

Putting prussic acid into porter wasn't Henry Thomas's only experiment. Under the guidance of Mr Lievesley, a lecturer at the London Hospital, he had also tested the pips of fifteen apples, using a salt-water bath, diluted sulphuric acid and sulphate of iron. 'I obtained two grains and a quarter of cyanide of silver,' he told the court, 'or nearly half a grain of pure prussic acid.'

Unmeasurable according to an expert who used one testing process; possibly deadly according to another who used a different procedure. Of course, both experiments also presupposed that someone would gobble fifteen apples in a single sitting, pips included, or even more unlikely, only the pips of fifteen apples. Still, the ramifications of the testimony were grave. Indeed, according to some reports, for a short time afterwards the apple industry slumped … until common sense prevailed.

Then Henry Thomas was handed a gallipot holding the piece of burnt material from Mrs Hart's grate. He examined it closely. 'This is paper, not leather,' he said, looking back up at the jury. 'I always use leather to tie on the bottles. This would be too small entirely if it were leather to cover the bottle.'

Kelly said to the judge, 'My lord, Mr Cooper also thinks it is paper.'

The apothecary's response was disappointing for the prosecution as it broke the tenuous link connecting John's purchase of the prussic acid with the crime scene and, by extension, with the prussic acid found in Sarah's stomach. Yet the prosecution was not concerned. Their case was strong.

One by one the remaining prosecution witnesses took their turn in the witness box, some testifying at length, others for only a few minutes. Around 1.30 p.m., Sergeant Byles announced that the prosecution's case was closed. As it was a convenient time for refreshments, Baron Parke decided to adjourn the court for fifteen minutes.

John used the break to take a spectator to task for rudeness. Although the courthouse's great doors had been closed all morning to prevent congestion, those with passes to the courtroom had been permitted to enter. By late morning the court was so crowded that several gentlemen were granted permission to stand in the dock with John. One raised his eyeglass and stared at John as if he were an insect requiring dissection. When the court adjourned, John walked over to him and demanded, 'Why does thee stare at me so, sir? Am I not a human being like the rest of thee?'

Astonished, the gentleman could only stammer, 'I beg your pardon. I did not wish to stare offensively.'

John then turned and briskly descended from the dock to the prison. It was time for his dinner.

'Can I have a glass of brandy and water?' he asked the gaoler. Mr Sherriff refused permission but allowed him some wine with his sandwich. John had a few swigs but failed to finish it, so he carried it back to the dock with him and placed it on the floor nearby. Again, as he waited for the judge to return, he chatted to those around him. Recognising a face in the crowd, he beckoned the man over, saying as the man approached, 'How d'ya do? How is your dear wife?' Anyone unaware of his identity would have thought he was passing time with a close friend during the intermission between two acts of a delightful play.

His mood changed instantly when one of his fellow dock-dwellers stepped near his wine bottle. The temperance advocate remarked firmly, 'Take care! Mind my grog!'

CHAPTER 26

*'I may be a hypocrite,' said Mr. Pecksniff, cuttingly, 'but
I am not a brute.'*

Charles Dickens,
Martin Chuzzlewit (1844)

AROUND 2 p.m. Baron Parke returned to his seat and resumed the session. The courtroom thrummed. They were about to hear from the great Fitzroy Kelly, the man extolled as one of the best advocates in the land. What could he say to undermine the 'fearful array of evidence' the prosecutors had presented to the court?

Kelly paused for a moment, his head bowed, his eyes glittering with tears, then he looked up and spoke in a quiet, troubled voice: 'I address you under a pressure of responsibility which I am scarcely able to bear and I hope that you will pardon me if, from feeling so deeply, I betray a momentary weakness. I hope I will be able to impress upon you what I consciously believe to be true, that you are being called upon to send to his last account one who has just stood at the bar a living and breathing man, not upon sworn evidence, nor upon the truth of any facts whatever, but depending wholly upon theory and what is found loosely and inaccurately reported in books. I will show you that if you act upon such evidence, you will commit a most fatal mistake.'

It was a dramatic beginning, eloquent, moving, even rather alarming. Kelly had just forced the jury to confront the niggling concern they had tried to push behind them: the confusion about the medical and scientific evidence presented by the prosecution, a confusion made worse by the fact that the prosecution's own witnesses had disagreed with one another.

Kelly then pulled the two skeletons from John's closet, mentioning his recent illicit behaviour and his felonious past. He cautioned the solid countrymen sitting in the jury box not to equate behaviour, however blameable, with acts far exceeding them in villainy. He explained that while John had behaved immorally, he had atoned for his sins by paying Mrs Hart one pound sterling a week ever since. As for the prosecution's claim that financial difficulties drove him to kill her: although John's bank account had been overdrawn at the time of Mrs Hart's death, he had received seven hundred pounds a very short time later, enough to support her and her children for fourteen years. 'Considering his circumstances, would saving such a sum be a sufficient reason to commit murder?' Kelly asked the twelve puzzled faces in the jury box.

Regarding John's previous criminal offence, Kelly stated that it was not at all one of cruelty, and that John had atoned for his offence by a life of industry, kindness and bounty. Nevertheless, that period of John's life was the key to his subterfuges, as he would explain in more detail later.

First he would discuss the scientific evidence. 'Before the prosecution can call upon you to condemn the prisoner to death,' he advised the jury, 'it must be proved that the deceased died of poison, and that the poison was prussic acid taken into the stomach. But this evidence is not only defective, it is entirely divested of certainty.'

Kelly mentioned the discrepancies between the witnesses' evidence and the confusion in the literature regarding many critical factors in the case. Should the surgeons have smelt prussic acid, did they actually smell prussic acid, should they have observed prussic acid-induced changes in Sarah's organs, did prussic acid produce a succession of screams like Sarah's or only one 'death scream', as the literature suggested? How much prussic acid was required to kill a human, how much prussic acid was originally in Sarah's stomach contents, how did it get there? So many questions needed answers but the prosecution hadn't provided them.

He asked why the prosecution hadn't called any of the doctors or scientists who had examined the thirty-nine recent victims of prussic acid poisoning to provide conclusive answers, and why they hadn't called any of the toxicologists who had written the quoted texts on prussic acid poisoning. 'Instead,' he added scathingly, 'it was left to the uncertain opinions of Mr Champnes, Mr Nordblad and Mr Pickering, three very young and inexperienced men, of little practice, who never saw man, woman or child who had been poisoned by prussic acid, whose opinions did not agree with each other, and whose opinions were not derived from experience but were founded upon authoritative texts which themselves contained conflicting opinions.'

It was a powerful charge against the prosecution – and a just one.

Moreover, he continued, while science had determined the quantity of arsenic or opium that caused death, the same could not be said for prussic acid. 'Will you be the jury to first decide such a question,' he charged the jurors' alarmed faces, 'to make a ruling in the absence of positive evidence, resting solely upon the opinions of persons who had formed them from reading books, and knew no more than you might learn in half an hour by reading?'

It was another just charge, reminding the jury and the spectators, especially those in the Petit Jury gallery, of their own confusion and uncertainty as the witnesses had talked about grains, drachms, ounces, minims and the rest. Even now, they could not recall the exact conclusion of all the myriad measurements.

Kelly then discussed the evidence of the chemist, John Thomas Cooper, who had never previously examined the remains of a prussic acid victim and had admitted that his tests were incomplete. Cooper could not say how much prussic acid was found in his first few experiments and, in attempting to determine the likely volume, he had extrapolated from his final experiment, assuming that the prussic acid was equally diffused throughout the whole of the stomach contents. 'Now, seeing that Mr Cooper only spoke from recollection of the original quantity of stomach contents,' Kelly advised, 'and seeing also that he admitted in his evidence that he found very little of the acid the first time, more the next, and still more the third, thus showing that as he got nearer to the bottom of the contents he got more of the solids, those portions of the contents that would produce prussic acid, I beg you calmly to observe these things. If there was not enough prussic acid in the stomach to account for death, there is an end to the case. If you do not wish to commit murder yourself, how can you convict the prisoner?'

The barrister's sombre voice, his constant references to their fellow man now living and breathing in front of them, who they were being asked to send to the gallows based upon vague opinions and conflicting evidence, his reminder to the jury of their awful responsibility and of the irreparable consequences if they made an error, held the court in a state of breathless tension. Some of the jurymen appeared haunted, even horrified.

Kelly then referred to Cooper's experiments with the apple pips, declaring that this was also incomplete as Cooper hadn't attempted to determine how much apple was in the deceased's stomach, nor how much prussic acid he had obtained from his experiment with the pips of fifteen apples. 'I wish to impress upon you that, next to bitter almonds, there is no substance which contains more prussic acid than the pips of apples, the quantity differing according to the nature of the apple. Some descriptions of apples contain it in a great quantity and in such a form that, if swallowed whole or slightly masticated, would render its smell imperceptible.' He contrasted Cooper's results with those of Henry Thomas, who reported extracting half a grain of pure prussic acid from the pips of fifteen apples. He gently suggested that a combination of apple pips, plum cake, partly decomposed animal matter in her stomach, and saliva 'which she must have swallowed in a large quantity when masticating the apples and which is known to contain prussic acid' might have been just enough …

There was a slight shifting in the room as the audience considered this sophistry. Whoever died from eating apples?

'But of what did she die?' Kelly continued. 'It is not for me to show.' He talked further about the post-mortem examination and the lack of physical evidence of the poison's effects. He mentioned the surgeon's admission that they had not examined the coronary arteries, the spinal marrow or the bronchial tubes. He raised the possibility of an unfortunate coincidence, telling the tale of a barrister who in a moment of insanity had cut his own throat, a wound that was sewn up but burst again a few days later, a wound that was thought responsible for his death until a post-mortem examination discovered a ruptured blood vessel. He reminded the jury that the deceased had fainted and might have choked when her neighbour poured water down her throat.

A quiet snigger rippled through the room, not loud enough to incur the court officers' wrath, but enough to disconcert Kelly momentarily. The spectators were not swallowing this line of defence. He hurried on, reintroducing the subject of John's relationship with Mrs Hart and begging the jury not to prejudice him for that reason. Then he moved on to talk about the Tawells' family life.

'That he is a man of kindly disposition, his present wife could prove, but she cannot be called as a witness,' Kelly told the court. He did, however, possess the letter she wrote to her husband on the very day Tawell supposedly committed the murder, a letter already offered to the court by the prosecution. With another flourish, he picked it up and carefully opened it.

'"My only loved one,"' Kelly read in solemn tones, '"My thoughts have been with thee throughout the day, and I can't but hope thou art feeling better than when thou left us. Do, my endeared one, endeavour to keep up thy spirits for my sake."'

Kelly looked up at the jury. 'No woman could ever write in those terms to a husband past sixty years of age if he had been a cruel and hard-hearted man.'

He continued to read the chatty letter, tears running down his face as he drew the jury and spectators into the home of this beloved husband and devoted father. This was a man who would take pleasure in hearing that 'Darling Harry has been very merry all day', a caring master who would be concerned that the housemaid was poorly.

'"Farewell, under every circumstance, thy beloved wife,"' Kelly concluded before placing the letter on the table. As he wiped away his tears, he looked around the courtroom – at the judge, jury, witnesses and spectators, many brushing away tears of their own – and said, 'No man could receive such a letter as that and do an act which would make his affectionate wife a widow and his children fatherless.'

All eyes turned to John. He had stood in the dock through-out his barrister's defence, leaning with one arm on the rail facing the jury. They could see that he too was visibly moved at his wife's words, tears glistening in his eyes. Then he straightened his shoulders and continued to listen with his usual calm fortitude.

Kelly had more to discuss, including the evening of Sarah Hart's death. He reminded the jury that John believed that Mrs Hart was acting, and also that the material found in the fireplace did not match that attached to John's prussic acid bottle. 'That is a great failure in the link of evidence against the prisoner,' he reminded the jury. 'Who could tell that some bottle procured by the woman for the purpose of acting might not have been thrown in the fire by her and burnt! Not that I mean to imply that the woman poisoned herself, for I do not believe she died of poison at all but from some one of the many causes of sudden death.'

He then talked about John's actions in the aftermath. 'As to his running, why, it was a cold night!' He dismissed the side trip to Herschel House, reminding the jury that John remained in public places dressed in his distinctive attire rather than hiding away like a criminal. He admitted that John lied to the police officers in the aftermath, but justified John's lies on the grounds that he had a happy family life back in Berkhampstead and that this, coupled with the knowledge that his former felonious activities would tar him in the eyes of the authorities, had led him to deny any knowledge of the woman. Yes, John had bought prussic acid, but it was prescribed for his own medical use. Moreover, the prosecution had not proven that he still had the phial with him when he went to Slough, as he told the chemist he had broken it.

Kelly also remarked on Sarah Hart's illness a few months previously, adding that a surgeon, who had neither seen her at the time nor even seen a prussic acid victim, had sworn that her symptoms suggested prussic acid poisoning. Yet how likely was it that someone intent upon murder would use the same unsuccessful method just a few months later?

'As to the real cause of the death of the woman, that, like many other things, might perhaps ever remain a mystery,' Kelly concluded. 'If the prisoner had evaded and departed from the truth, I hope that you won't, on those grounds, conclude that he had committed murder. A man might commit an offence in early life and retrieve himself, he might under painful circumstances be guilty of subterfuge, but I rest my defence mainly upon these confident grounds, that there was neither motive nor temptation to commit so horrible a crime.

'The great and blessed principle of justice is that where there is a doubt the accused should always have the benefit of it. I again urge you to consider your responsibility if you err,' he pleaded to the jury, looking closely at each of them, one by one, 'if you undertake an act which one day you might wish, almost to the cost of your own life, that you had not committed. Looking at the nature of this case, and the doubts and uncertainties with which it is surrounded, I confidently expect a verdict of acquittal.'

⌒

The great Fitzroy Kelly indeed! What a virtuoso performance. If the looks on the jurymen's faces were anything to go by – many staring with the blank eyes of shock, clearly daunted by the magnitude of the task facing them – he had sown the seeds of reasonable doubt necessary to secure John's freedom.

After Kelly returned to his seat, his off-sider Mr Gunning stood up and announced that he would begin calling the witnesses for the defence. The audience sparked up in response. These were the men who would substantiate Kelly's claims and demolish the prosecution's case. These were the men who would prove that Sarah Hart didn't die from prussic acid poisoning, and that John Tawell was not a murderer.

'Henry Lane,' Gunning called.

The reporters started with surprise. Who was Henry Lane? What about Dr Henry Letheby, Professor of Chemistry at London Hospital, who had sat by Fitzroy Kelly offering advice during the barrister's cross-examination of the prosecution witnesses? What about the brilliant diagnostician Dr Thomas Addison, physician to Guy's Hospital, the man who had provided John's prussic acid script, a medication he continued to use on his varicose veins during his incarceration? What about the pioneering toxicologist Dr William Herapath, Professor of Chemistry and Toxicology at the Bristol Medical School, or Dr Thomas Graham, Professor of Chemistry at London's University College, or any of the other celebrated medical practitioners and chemists who had stood near the defence table throughout the trial or could be seen in the ranks of the spectators?

Henry Lane entered the witness box and placed his hand on the Bible, vowing to tell the truth, the whole truth. 'I am the rector's churchwarden at Berkhampstead,' he told the court, 'and I have known John Tawell for four years. He has borne a very good character for mildness of disposition.'

Master builder Joseph Gomme of Berkhampstead followed. 'John Tawell has a good character for kindness, charity and benevolence,' he testified. Berkhampstead coal merchant John Tomkins and currier Joseph Baldwin, Dover cashier John Richardson and retired London businessman John Gower, one-time Australian resident Abel Salter Trew, timber merchant Henry Castle, and adventurer Chevalier Peter Dillon all made their way to the stand, testifying to John's kindly disposition as well as his benevolence and good character.

Then the defence rested its case.

Baron Parke glanced around the courtroom. 'The question is, should we go on?' he mused out loud. 'Despite the aid of the candles, I fear that the darkness is too great. Or should we adjourn until tomorrow?' He thought for a moment then announced, 'The case is too important. It would be better to adjourn.'

'Oh, go on, my lord, go on,' cried a juror, having heard like everyone else that the court would remain in session until the verdict was handed down. 'We have no objection to finish. We will sit until we finish.'

'In so important a case, gentlemen,' advised the judge, 'I cannot fairly undertake to wind it up tonight. I think we had better adjourn.'

'My lord, shall we have beds?' asked another juror.

'Certainly, gentlemen. Beds! Of course!' replied the judge.

'Why, my lord, we could get no beds last night,' several of the jurors called out. Evidently, the town's innkeepers had found a more profitable use for them.

The judge ordered the sheriff to make sure the jury members had beds. The sheriff muttered an excuse, mostly inaudible, regarding the problems of the previous night.

'We would rather sit tonight, my lord, and finish,' the jurors continued to plead.

'This case, gentlemen, is too important to be pressed for a termination,' Baron Parke announced firmly, 'and I fear I could not see sufficiently well to read my notes with the requisite attention.' He then adjourned the case until eight o'clock the following morning, leaving the night hours to dissipate the impact of Fitzroy Kelly's passionate pleas.

CHAPTER 27

Fie on these dealers in poison, say I: can they not keep to the old honest way of cutting throats without introducing such abominable innovations from Italy?

Thomas de Quincey, *On Murder, Considered as One of the Fine Arts* (1827)

AFTER THE admission arrangements had worked so admirably the day before, why did the under-sheriff revert to the arrangements of the first day? Surely he didn't think that the crowds would evaporate on the third day, the dramatic climax to this epic trial, the denouement of what would be, for many, the most exciting moment in their lives, something to tell their children and grandchildren, 'I was there on the day when …'

Strangely, the under-sheriff had decided to keep the courthouse doors locked until 8 a.m., when Baron Parke took his seat on the bench. Only then did he allow the spectators to enter the courtroom, slowly, one at a time. The squeaking doors ('which asked in distinct but disagreeable tones for the application of a little oil to the hinges,' grumbled one reporter), the pattering footsteps, the mumbles of annoyance as the privileged spectators with passes pushed their way through the crowds, the to-ing and fro-ing of jury members, the sickly coughs, the unavailing cries of 'Silence!', all made it almost impossible to hear the judge begin his summing up for the jury. His important address would steer these salts-of-the-earth in deciding the fate of the prisoner who, despite his attempts at composure, was now looking decidedly careworn.

When John had entered the courtroom that morning, his famed barrister, Fitzroy Kelly, wasn't sitting at the lawyers' table or standing nearby talking to his legal team. In fact, he wasn't even in Aylesbury, having left town immediately after the previous evening's adjournment. The captain hadn't jumped ship, although it might have seemed so to curious onlookers. Instead, he had hurried off to fulfil his commitment in Maidstone. He hadn't left John alone, either; the prisoner was still attended by his other two barristers and three solicitors as well as their clerks and assistants so, physically, the gap in numbers was barely noticeable. Nevertheless, the mighty have a presence, and their presence a lingering influence. That presence was noticeably absent in the courthouse when John's trial resumed on Friday morning, as if the lights had dimmed, as if, perhaps, the beacon of victory that had shone so brightly the evening before had been doused.

~

'It is now your duty to give your deliberate consideration to the merits of this important case,' Baron Parke told the twelve grave countenances in the jury box, 'and to pronounce upon the guilt or innocence of the prisoner, who stands charged with a crime which, I might say, is unparalleled in the history of human wickedness.'

It wasn't a good start for the prisoner. The reporters watching John saw lines of anxiety etch more deeply into his face.

The judge gave the usual admonitions to dismiss everything they had read or heard outside the courtroom, and to found their judgement only upon the evidence presented in the courtroom. 'I also feel it my duty to warn you against the impressions sought to be made upon you yesterday by the able and ingenious speech of the prisoner's counsel,' he added dryly. He then proceeded to demolish John's defence, remarking firstly upon Kelly's claim that the law required positive proof that the death was caused by poison, and that a deadly quantity of poison was indeed present. 'This is not true,' Baron Parke advised the jurors. If they were satisfied by the circumstantial evidence showing that Sarah Hart's death was caused by poison, it was not necessary to actually prove so, or to prove that the precise poison so named had killed her, or to determine what quantity of that particular poison would destroy life by providing testimony from someone who had actually seen such a death, or to prove that such a deadly quantity had been found in her stomach. All that the law required, in fact, was a body – which they had – and circumstantial evidence indicating that the body had been poisoned – which it did.

That being the case, the jury's task was simply to determine if she had poisoned herself, as Tawell claimed, or if Tawell had poisoned her. 'The only allegation that she did so comes from the prisoner himself, and if you think the extraordinary story told by him is worthy of credit, then you agree with his account of her death. But if you do not believe it, then you have no other conclusion left than that he committed the crime imputed to him.'

The perspicacious courtroom attendees realised that John's ill-advised admission to the police officers had enabled Baron Parke to reduce his case to an undemanding scenario. Either he did it or she did it. You decide.

Baron Parke didn't stop there. He discussed the evidence of the witnesses, mentioning that Surgeons Champnes and Pickering had smelt prussic acid during the post-mortem examination and that the chemist had later discovered prussic acid in

Sarah Hart's stomach contents. 'This is very strong evidence to show that prussic acid could not have been produced in the stomach by the distillation of apples,' he told the jury, 'prussic acid having been smelt by the medical men beforehand.' He also reminded them that no apple pips had been found in Sarah's stomach contents, and only a small quantity of apple.

Baron Parke then remarked upon the conflicting accounts regarding any likely prussic acid odour, concluding that, while the smell of prussic acid indicated its presence, the absence of smell was not evidence of its absence. He also discussed the toxicity of the poison and the chemist's conclusions regarding the amount of prussic acid in Sarah Hart's stomach contents. 'In putting all the facts together,' he advised the jury, 'you must also look to the previous conduct of the prisoner and to the circumstance of prussic acid having been in his possession on the day of the deceased's death, and not the following day.'

The pressmen noticed that John was looking decidedly uneasy as the judge continued his summation. On a few occasions he abruptly, and seemingly with considerable annoyance, tapped the shoulder of the person in front of him, indicating that he wanted to talk to his solicitor, Mr Bevan. When he had Bevan's attention, he communicated a passionate remonstrance – but nobody could hear what he said.

Baron Parke proceeded to discuss John's movements on the afternoon and evening of Sarah Hart's death, and to remind the jury of John's lies when taken into custody. 'Whether his object in doing so was merely to keep from his wife the knowledge of his visits to Bath Place, or whether he was desirous of concealing from everyone the fact of his having gone there, is for the jury to determine,' he concluded.

He mentioned John's later revelation: that he had been to Sarah Hart's house on the evening in question and that he had seen her drink something from a phial, as if she intended to poison herself, then toss the phial into the fire. 'It is to be observed,' the judge added, 'that he mentioned nothing of this extraordinary statement until after he had been brought to Slough, and had spoken with his counsel.' He asked the jury to consider why, if the story was true, the prisoner had left the house and denied being there, rather than waiting around to see if she had taken poison and seeking medical assistance. And he reminded them that the fire in Sarah Hart's hearth was only small, without sufficient strength to melt glass, and that no traces of a phial had been found in the cinders.

The pressmen who continued to watch John noticed that he was listening to the judge's oration with his chin resting on his hand, his forefinger stretched out across his cheek. Occasionally, as fact piled upon fact, as the judge trampled on every bud of doubt that his barrister had teased open in the jury's mind, John moved his hand away from his cheek, and the reporters could see that it was trembling. Perhaps, however, he was simply shivering from the frigidity of the courtroom – so cold that a thick frost stuck fast to the windows.

Baron Parke agreed that Tawell's purchase of prussic acid on the day of Mrs Hart's death was no admission that he had poisoned her with it. Then he pointed out that the defence had not offered any medical evidence to prove that Tawell did indeed have varicose veins and required prussic acid to treat the affliction.

The reporters were again reminded of their earlier doubts about the efficacy of the expensive team gathered for John's defence. Considering the number of medical and scientific men they had retained, and considering the many unanswered questions and equivocal claims arising from the prosecution's case, issues that Kelly had himself pointed out in his opening address, one would think they could have found a respected authority to throw some reasonable doubt on the prosecution's evidence.

The judge's devastating summation continued. As to the suggestion that Sarah Hart had died from suffocation when the water was poured down her throat, or from a sudden emotion of the mind, or from the lung adhesion the surgeons noticed during the post-mortem examination, or any other cause of sudden death: 'surely the jury could not entertain such a notion while there was evidence of an agent sufficient of itself to cause sudden death.'

He next turned to the question of the prisoner's possible motivation. 'No motive could justify or palliate such a crime, nor is it necessary for the jury to discover the motive that led to its commission,' Baron Parke advised – then shrewdly offered one. He described the illicit relationship between Tawell and the deceased, Tawell's long-term financial support for the woman, and his recent pecuniary embarrassment. He admitted that the prisoner was back in funds a short time after Sarah Hart's death. 'But who could say what his feelings were on 30 September, or on 1 January, when he went to Bath Place? He might have gone there with the mixed feeling partly of being prepared to pay the money, and partly, if the opportunity occurred, to commit the crime and not pay the money.'

Finally, three-and-a-half hours later, the judge wound up his lucid account of the facts presented to the court by talking about the issues of circumstantial evidence and reasonable doubt, of duty to the prisoner and public confidence in the legal system. He concluded, 'That, gentlemen, is the whole of the case. It is now up to you to form your conscientious opinion as reasonable men holding the scales of justice evenly between the public and the prisoner. I have nothing more to say, and leave the issue with you.'

The defence was not happy. This was no even-handed summing up of the evidence. 'If you believe the extraordinary story told by the prisoner'… And, 'a crime unparalleled in the history of human wickedness'. If these weren't prejudicial statements, what was? Moreover, wasn't it up to the jury to decide if a 'crime' had been committed? Because if Mrs Hart had committed suicide or had died from natural causes then her death was not a 'crime' at all.

Baron Parke had also failed to mention the defence witnesses. 'I beg to remind your lordship,' Mr Gunning interposed, 'but you have not mentioned the evidence which has been given with reference to the prisoner's character.'

In truth, the judge had indirectly referred to John's character witnesses in an earlier allusion to the paucity of the defence's case. He had caustically observed that if the prisoner could offer nothing for the jury's consideration except his previous character and the supposition that no man could be guilty of so atrocious a crime, then it could weigh but little as they all knew that men were frequently convicted of committing atrocious acts.

Nonetheless, Baron Parke accepted the defence's rebuke, and reminded the jury that John's character witnesses all described him as a kind-hearted and benevolent man. He also observed that Tawell's counsel had been telling the truth when he declared that the offence for which Tawell had been transported was not one that would affect his character for kindness of disposition.

'May we retire, my lord?' the foreman asked. At 11.35 a.m. they left the courtroom, a dozen ruggedly dependable countrymen, no scientists or scholars among them.

John remained in the dock during the jury's absence, trying desperately to conceal his anxiety, to assume the air of tranquillity and self-possession he had so successfully borne throughout these tribulations. The judge's charge to the jury had rattled his composure, of that there was no doubt. He asked one of his lawyers what he thought of his case, but before the gentleman could prepare a tactful response, he said bleakly, 'The case, I now fear, looks decidedly black against me.'

~

John's trial had already taken more time than had been expected, and other cases remained to be heard. While his jury was out, another was sworn and a new case commenced – the trial of three men charged with burglary. The crowds remained in the courtroom, anxious not to lose their positions, determined to hear the verdict in John's case. Half an hour passed. The spectators were becoming engrossed in the new trial when an usher called for silence. 'The jury who have tried the prisoner Tawell have agreed on a verdict.'

The news created a slight predicament. The new jury already occupied the jury box and could not be ejected, so the ushers cleared a passage between the bar and the counsel's table allowing the jurymen to face the prisoner while delivering their verdict.

As the twelve good men turned their eyes to the dock, John blanched. At long last, he showed all the agitation that would be expected from someone in his position. But the agitation lasted only for a moment. Then he lifted his head and firmed his shoulders. With a resolute step, he advanced to the front of the dock.

The Clerk of the Crown called out the names of the jury members, who responded as demanded. He then asked, 'Gentlemen, are you agreed on your verdict?'

'We are,' answered the foreman.

'What say you: is the prisoner guilty or not guilty?'

The silence in the courtroom was absolute. No one moved, no one breathed as the foreman took his own deep breath. In a loud and very firm voice, he announced, 'Guilty!'

John's head drooped. His hands clenched the bar.

All around him, the courtroom erupted. Cheers. Violent clapping. The noise could be heard all the way down Walton Street.

'Order! Order!' cried the judge.

Some women dissolved into tears, perhaps in sadness for John but, more likely, as a relief-valve from the intensity of the three-day drama. Some were – wittingly or otherwise – offering a final adieu to the shadowy, almost-forgotten victim.

'Are you unanimous in your verdict, gentlemen?' demanded the judge. 'Is that the verdict of you all?'

'It is,' the foreman advised.

Those who knew courtroom procedure shifted their gaze to the clerk who began to address John: 'Prisoner, you have been indicted for the wilful murder of Sarah Hart, according to the law of your country, and you have been found guilty by the jury empanelled to try you. What have you now to say that the Court should not pass judgement upon you according to law?'

John's head continued to hang down. He offered no reply.

As another murmur of acknowledgement rushed around the courtroom, the clerk demanded silence. He then announced that judgement would be passed. All eyes turned again to the judge.

In a studied gesture of authority, Baron Parke pulled on the dreaded black cap. He had no need to clarify its meaning. 'Prisoner at the bar,' he began solemnly, 'the jury have just pronounced their unanimous and deliberate verdict against you.

It now remains for me to perform my duty, by telling you that for that horrible, base and cowardly crime of which you have been convicted upon clear and satisfactory evidence, you must die an ignominious and horrid death on the common scaffold.

'You thought to commit that crime and you thought no eye would see you except That Eye which sees all things and to which you probably paid no regard. But, happily, circumstances were discovered which have left no doubt on the minds of the jury, as they have none upon mine, nor, I will venture to say, upon the minds of any who have been listening with painful attention to the trial, that you are guilty of one of the most diabolical offences ever committed by man. We now see you, almost as if it were with our own eyes, mixing the poisonous ingredients in the cup of which she was to drink in a moment of unsuspecting confidence, supposing that you were her benefactor and protector.

'I wish that you may be brought to repent of that grievous sin, that diabolical and cruel murder, and of that course of your life which has been marked by hypocrisy, during which you assumed the garb of a virtuous, peaceful, benevolent and religious class of persons. I hope you will profit by the little time, which will be no longer than the law allows, and endeavour to repent of your crimes, prostrating yourself before the throne of God, seeking there the mercy which you cannot find below.

'It remains for me to pass on you the sentence of the Law, that you be taken to the place of your execution, there to be hanged by the neck until you are dead, and that your body be taken down and buried within the precincts of the gaol wherein you shall be confined after the passing of this sentence. May the Lord have mercy upon your miserable soul.'

Their eyes riveted upon John, the pressmen listened to the judge's verbal lashing and pronouncement of his dreadful fate, waiting for the inscrutable Quaker to show some reaction. At Baron Parke's final words, calling upon the Lord for mercy, John's face convulsed slightly – but only for a moment.

Before long, they saw him descending from the dock without the turnkey's assistance, his head disappearing as he climbed down the twenty-step ladder to the prison. He was showing no more emotion than he had shown at the conclusion of the previous days' proceedings.

After John departed, the spectators exited the courtroom, walking to their homes or conveyances, returning to the same dull lives they had left that morning or perhaps a few days before. Some were already making new plans, aware that the drama hadn't yet ended. The last act was still to be performed – unless the play was cancelled in the interim.

Those who left Aylesbury took the news of the verdict with them. Word spread across Britain faster than seemed possible – 'as if the birds of the air carried the intelligence', marvelled one newspaper.

Most of the spectators and townsfolk agreed that the verdict was just, although some received the news with surprise. The only complaints came from the gamblers, those who had punted that John would be acquitted. The *Aylesbury News* wrote disgustedly, 'We wish it had been possible for *all* these despicable speculators in the lives of their fellow creatures to have lost their money.'

Meanwhile, Sarah Hart's mother and children were waiting in a nearby inn. They had spent the last few days in Aylesbury so young Alfred could be called if any doubts were raised regarding John's identity. The visual impression would be as striking as any verbal testimony: the wee motherless boy who strongly resembled the man standing in the dock, the man accused of murdering his mother.

The boy knew why he was here. 'Mr Tawell poisoned my mother,' he said frequently, having absorbed all the talk around him. Yet when someone stuck a head through the inn door and shouted the verdict and sentence, the boy burst into tears. Despite his young age, he knew what it meant. Maybe he had felt a sense of connection, if not fondness, for the family's regular visitor. Had he known that John Tawell was his father? The records would remain silent.

Grace Hadler and her grandchildren remained in Aylesbury for the night. On the Saturday morning, just before they departed, Superintendent Perkins approached them, holding Sarah's watch. With two hands, he made a circle of the chain and lowered it over young Alfred's head, positioning it carefully on the boy's chest. The watch would remain one of the children's few mementos of the mother lost to them.

⌒

He would be restored to her that night, Sarah Tawell had convinced herself on the Thursday evening, having received word that the court would sit until the trial ended. She made preparations for John's return, drawing a hot bath and carefully laying out his linen. She had already planned a holiday, and had invited guests to join them the following evening.

Then she sat and waited. And waited.

CHAPTER 28

Depend upon it, sir, when a man knows he is to be hanged
in a fortnight, it concentrates his mind wonderfully.

James Boswell,
The Life of Samuel Johnson (1791)

JOHN'S AIR of magisterial indifference disappeared as he retreated from the reporters' scrutiny. His legs buckled beneath him and he slumped down the ladder to the ground. The turnkeys lifted him up and carried him into the 'condemned cell', the special quarters reserved for those sentenced to death. First, they entered the day room, which was about twenty feet by ten, with five doors along one wall, each leading into a sleeping cell. Then they stepped through the door of one of the sleeping cells and deposited him on the bed. The room's musty air had been partly leavened by the fire crackling in the hearth.

Although John had expected an acquittal, Mr Sherriff had anticipated otherwise. Without informing his prisoner, he had prepared the condemned cell, which had lain unused for nearly a decade. While the judge handed down the sentence, he moved John's belongings to his new quarters.

When John recovered from his breakdown and found himself in the new cell, he was astonished and angry at such high-handed treatment – or more likely at Mr Sherriff's lack of faith in his innocence. Upon reflection, however, he realised that the decision to warm the bitterly cold room was a gesture of kindness, and he thanked the gaoler for such consideration.

The gaoler had another duty to perform. 'Search him carefully,' he quietly instructed the turnkeys, who understood his concern. They patted down John's clothes and dug through his pockets, taking away even his watch key.

It was the final indignity. John's lamentations began. 'Oh dear! Oh dear!' he exclaimed in low and harried tones, starting to pace up and down his cell. 'Oh dear! Oh dear! What will become of my poor wife and children!' For hours he continued moaning and crying, rejecting his dinner, saying that he couldn't eat. At long last his grief eased and he politely asked for his meal. As he sat between the two turnkeys, eating his beef-steak, he looked around the day room and said to them, 'Oh what a dreadful thing for a man like me, who has a family and who was in such comfortable circumstances, to be placed in such a position as this!'

It was a strange comment from a man judged to be responsible for his own predicament – unless, perhaps, he was truly innocent.

⌒

The news reached Berkhampstead around 2 p.m., two hours after the jury delivered its verdict. A feverish excitement had gripped the town all week. Everyone had been demanding copies of the London daily newspapers with their reports of the previous day's proceedings. They avidly read all the details, oohing and aahing over the new revelations in addition to the well-digested evidence, mirroring the fervent interest in households across Britain.

Of course, the residents of Berkhampstead felt a special attachment to the story. They knew the man personally – or at least by sight – and they all had opinions about him. Some had continued to praise his kindness and benevolence, refusing to condemn him until the court reached its own verdict. Others had long turned against him, perhaps even before the events of that New Year's Day. Miles's Boy wasn't the only town dweller irritated by John's activities as town surveyor. The Quaker-hater's diatribes had inevitably influenced others, if not at the time then in the aftermath of John's committal. A few residents told the pressmen traipsing around with their notebooks in hand that they had long disliked the haughty and contemptuous attitude that Mr Tawell had displayed towards his neighbours. Some told tales of his unwillingness to purchase goods from the town's tradespeople, preferring to buy everything in London and persuading his friends to do the same. When he did make a purchase in Berkhampstead, he would invariably offer only two-thirds of the price asked. Yet when a Quaker opened a general store in town, he instantly became a devoted customer.

Despite the ambivalence in the locals' attitudes to John, most retained their sympathy and affection for his wife. 'The conduct of this amiable, excellent and true-hearted lady throughout the whole of this distressing and lamentable affair has been the admiration of everyone in the neighbourhood of Berkhampstead, and all sympathise most deeply with her.'

As news of the verdict reached the town, there were widespread nods of agreement with the decision. Of course, no one wished to be in the shoes of the two gentlemen from Aylesbury who, alighting from the express at 2 p.m. that Friday, sought directions to the Red House.

⸺◠⸺

Twenty hours passed before Sarah's shock and extreme distress eased. 'I will never believe he is guilty unless he makes a confession of his guilt,' she told her family and friends. 'He is incapable of so cruel an act and if he suffers for his crime, he will die a martyr!'

Some feared that Sarah would never recover from the shock, and also feared for the effects on the whole family. One newspaper wrote: 'She has one child, about eighteen months, who is about to be rendered an orphan in a way calling for the greatest sympathy and pity. Poor child! May God temper the wind to the shorn lamb!'

⟋

Hannah Chapman Backhouse was used to receiving messages from God, yet this one was particularly powerful. He advised her to visit John Tawell, then awaiting trial in Buckinghamshire. A cousin of prison campaigner Elizabeth Fry, Mrs Backhouse was a renowned Quaker minister in her own right, especially famous as a medium for God's communications. She regularly travelled the countryside, and sometimes across to America, holding public rallies and attending local meetings for worship. She was preaching in Cornwall at the time she received the divine message. After her engagements finished, she and her son-in-law travelled the two hundred miles to Aylesbury, arriving at the gaol not long after John's guilty verdict had been handed down.

Mrs Backhouse asked to see John and was advised to seek permission from a visiting magistrate, the nearest of whom resided three miles away. The magistrate arrived the following morning during their Scripture reading. He was a kind, intelligent man, deeply moved by the difficult situation, with tears flowing down his cheeks when he talked with them about the case. He went to the gaol and brought back the gaoler.

'The prisoner is in bed and in such a state that I hardly know if he is sensible,' Mr Sherriff told them. He added that he wanted Tawell to eat his breakfast before seeing them, although perhaps Mrs Backhouse's son-in-law should go in first and speak with him. The young man agreed but soon returned, asking his mother-in-law to follow him.

She could hear the dreadful moaning long before she stepped into the little cell, bare except for a bed and a chair, the only light coming from the doorway. She went up to him and laid her hand on his own and said 'John Tawell' in a voice that quietened him. Then he began to sob – dreadful gut-wrenching cries. After some time, he beseeched in a low tone, 'Pray for me.'

She stood by the bed for a while, letting God's light infuse her, then spoke the words that came to her. After a while, he calmed. She then said quietly but plainly: 'You must endure the furnace,' adding that he should not waste time in superficial work but instead focus upon the Lamb of God who takes away the sins of the world.

'Is it a question of days or hours?' John asked plaintively.

'I do not know,' she said gently, 'but I beseech you not to think about that, but to attend to your own business.'

～

Friday ended late for the editor of the *Aylesbury News* as he busied himself reporting in detail on the trial and everything related to it. 'The community's interest is intense,' he had written prior to the trial. In the aftermath, it was beyond anything he and his staff had ever experienced – or expected.

The staggering demand during the week for extra copies of their weekly Saturday issue warned them of the need for a huge print run. Requiring so many more copies in time for the country post that left at 5 p.m. on Friday evening, they pinned a notice on the front door saying that over-the-counter copies would not be available until after 6 p.m. When they at last opened their doors, customers besieged them, snatching newspapers almost faster than the pressmen could hand them over.

Alarmed at such unprecedented demand and at their customers' unruly behaviour, and with large orders still to be dispatched for the London and late posts, they locked the doors again, posting a lad outside to explain that they would reopen at 8 p.m. The lad, faced with angry buyers, eventually locked the outer iron gate as well, leaving the irate customers cursing from the roadside. At 8 p.m., the staff gave up and threw open their doors again. For more than two hours customers badgered them, clamouring for copies – not just single issues, but by the half-dozen and dozen. The staff ran the presses all night trying to print enough to satisfy the newsmen in the morning, but they were unable to meet the demand, let alone all the orders that should have gone out the previous day or to their ordinary customers in the morning. They kept printing and printing, the office a nightmare of ill temper and confusion, yet new orders kept coming in.

'Having no other power but that of human muscle, we were utterly unable to cope with the demand,' the editor later wrote. Customers scuffled and rioted, windows were broken, messengers assaulted. Eventually, exhaustion forced them to stop for the weekend, after printing five thousand copies of the tiny local newspaper in twenty-four hours. They began again on Monday, ultimately printing more than seven times the normal number and knowing they could have sold thousands more.

Customers reported their own experiences of the unprecedented demand. A Chesham vendor wrote that his shop was so busy on Friday evening that he was compelled to put up his shutters for safety. 'One man,' he reported with amusement, 'on being told that there would be some copies available on Saturday morning, left his dog to wait at the shop all night. The following morning, the faithful dog conveyed the first copy to his master.'

Among the information gathered by pressmen employed by the *Aylesbury News* was the inside word from members of the jury and others involved in the trial. Some jurymen were convinced of John's guilt immediately after hearing Mrs Ashlee's testimony. Others were persuaded after they heard the policemen's testimonies, one reciting John's denials, the other his unexpected revelation. 'As no phial was found in Sarah Hart's home, only the part of Tawell's story that told against himself was believed, and the admission that he had been present at the actual poisoning of the woman told frightfully against him.'

Conversely, Fitzroy Kelly's passionate address had swayed six of the jurymen. 'The adjournment of the court, allowing the jury to sleep over their excited feelings and bring the cool reflections of sober morning to dispel the intoxicating influence of Mr Kelly's evening eloquence, was decisive of the prisoner's fate,' the editor revealed. Yet the night's reflections hadn't moved the mind of one jury member, and his dread at sending a fellow creature to his death meant that his colleagues had difficulty persuading him to give way. The judge's clear summing up and obvious directions had left the other jurymen in no uncertainty as to what their decision should be.

The *Aylesbury News* also discovered one piece of alarming information: that their words of caution before the trial had not been heeded – in one household, at least. A local summoned for jury duty was told by his wife: 'If you come back without hanging the wretch, you will deserve to be hanged yourself and I will never regard you anymore.'

In the days that followed, word 'leaked' that John's legal team thought little of their predecessors' efforts, particularly the counselling that had led John to admit to being at Sarah Hart's that evening. 'It is considered that whoever advised or suggested that Tawell should make such a statement to the constable,' said the crafty barristers through the mouthpiece of *The Times*, 'made a most injudicious step, the more especially after the line of defence which was subsequently determined upon by his legal advisers.'

Of course, John's previous legal advisers would have valid grounds for arguing that Fitzroy Kelly and his team should have employed a different defence – if making passionate and seemingly sound arguments then calling only unimportant character witnesses could be considered any defence at all.

The *Law Magazine* offered its own sardonic opinion. While many condemned Kelly's tears as the weakest component of his speech, the editor deemed it to have been the strongest, as his tears washed down a defence that would otherwise have been difficult to swallow dry.

Kelly's defence was a hotchpotch of confusion, lacking a clear pathway that the jury could follow to reach the goalposts of reasonable doubt, if not innocence. If his team had adopted the line of defence that common sense should have suggested – that is, following and fortifying Tawell's statement to the policemen – then even Baron Parke's 'masterly' summing up might not have dispelled the doubts the jury almost certainly would have had, particularly when his character witnesses were paraded in the aftermath. In that scenario, his witnesses would have strengthened his case, rather than serving as a stark exposé of his defence's deficiencies. Instead, the members of his defence team seem to have stuck their collective heads in the sand and pretended that John had never made such a statement – unless he had unwittingly torpedoed his own case by not revealing this disclosure.

Ironically, 'Apple Pips Kelly' became Fitzroy Kelly's moniker thereafter, leading many of his contemporaries to comment upon the nickname and its foundation. One memoirist would claim that Kelly foolishly adopted the 'apple pips' defence upon the recommendation of a chemistry professor. Another more accurately observed that Kelly hadn't made the claim himself but had merely remarked upon a statement made by the Crown's witnesses. No one knows who first tossed the phrase 'Apple Pips Kelly' into the air, no doubt as an amusing throwaway line, but the name appealed to the popular consciousness and stuck like a burr.

Kelly had admitted to a companion before John's trial that he would have an uphill battle to fight. He continued to fight for his client even after the trial. In fact, he was among those petitioning the queen for mercy when new evidence surfaced regarding the medical and scientific evidence offered by the 'experts'.

CHAPTER 29

All things are poisons and nothing is without poison.

Paracelsus,
*'Third' Defence Concerning the Description
of the New Receipts* (1564)

'THERE IS nothing more perplexing to the average person than to be called to decide upon the conflicting evidence of experts,' wrote the *New York Times* in 1874 in an article titled 'The Case of John Tawell'. A similar cry would rip through the American nation, indeed the world, some 125 years later, after the historic O.J. Simpson trial. 'Experts are, in some cases, more diametrically opposed to each other than almost any other class of witnesses,' continued the *New York Times*, 'and what one set will propound as fact, another will scout as fable. Who shall decide when the doctors disagree?'

The simple answer in John Tawell's case was the judge, a man trained only in matters of the law, and the jury, the 'highly respectable' countrymen who had little or no scientific education whatsoever. When faced with diametrically opposed views on complex subjects they knew nothing about, these jurymen had little choice but to ignore the medical and scientific evidence and to decide the case upon circumstantial evidence and gut instinct. Was this acceptable when a person's life was at stake?

This raised the question as to whether the judge and jury had reached the correct verdict. Had the prosecution presented a case that was truly convincing, one that on the grounds of evidence alone would prove beyond reasonable doubt that John was guilty – or was he a scapegoat, sacrificed because other accused poisoners had failed to pay the law's price for their own infamy?

Britain was not merely suffering a 'poisoning epidemic' at this time, but a cyanide poisoning epidemic – and most of the poisoners were getting away with the crime. In the 1780s Captain Donellan was convicted of killing his brother-in-law with deadly laurel water, a distillate of cherry leaves which themselves contained cyanide, but, in the decades since, no cyanide deaths had led to murder convictions. Most cases didn't even make it to the courts. Foul play was suspected in the death of a pregnant Bromley maiden in November 1843 but the perpetrator's identity couldn't be determined. Murder seemed almost certain when the pregnant wife of Surgeon James Cockburn Belaney died from prussic acid poisoning in June 1844, yet, to the astonishment of the nation, the jury acquitted him.

'If the jury had delivered a just verdict,' the *Examiner* would thunder after John's conviction, 'we thoroughly believe that Sarah Hart would not have perished.' The article described the similarities between the Belaney and Tawell cases: the choice of poison; the pretence of medicinal use; the story that the woman had taken the poison (accidentally, according to Belaney, but for suicidal purposes according to Tawell); the many falsehoods; the reliance upon character – which, along with the claims of a loving relationship, apparently underpinned the jury's verdict in the Belaney case. 'It is probable that the jury in Belaney's case were the direct instigators of Sarah Hart's murder and that the wicked thought of the safety of the deed flashed on Tawell's mind upon reading their verdict.'

Medical and scientific professionals were also intrigued and concerned about the repercussions. Dr David Skae had taken a particular interest in the recent spate of prussic acid poisonings and, in an article published in the *Northern Journal of Medicine*, discussed the evidence in Tawell's case. First and foremost, he remarked, it was extremely important that the odour of prussic acid had been smelt at the post-mortem examination before later chemical tests confirmed it.

Baron Parke had thought similarly. By mentioning this evidence at the start of his summation, he made it clear that it was crucial in his own decision-making process. Yet, as the body of evidence clearly shows, the surgeons lied under oath. They did not smell prussic acid prior to the chemical testing. No one did. In fact, no one smelt it until after the prussic acid test produced a positive result. The surgeons lied because the medical texts declared that, if prussic acid was the cause of death, they *should* have smelt it during the post-mortem examination. They lied in order to confirm their belief that prussic acid had been present in Sarah Hart's stomach prior to the testing process and was not produced *by* the testing process. They lied in order to convince the judge and jury of their evidence and to convict John Tawell, despite knowing that the medical texts raised doubts about the accuracy of their conclusions. They lied even though they knew that if their lies were believed, Tawell would probably be hung by the neck until he was dead. 'I will keep them from harm and injustice,' the surgeons had declared when swearing the Hippocratic Oath, yet in court that day, they chose to do otherwise. They succeeded in convincing Baron Parke – and accordingly John's fate was sealed.

When Baron Parke chose to believe the surgeons' invented olfactory memories, he also chose to ignore the compelling evidence that belied these claims, the evidence of the very tests undertaken on Sarah Hart's stomach contents. John Thomas Cooper testified that the surgeons said they thought oxalic acid was responsible, not prussic acid. His statement is borne out by the fact that he first tested for the presence of oxalic acid then spent hours testing for other toxins prior to concluding that prussic acid was the only deadly acid left – as he and the other surgeons all stated under oath. If the surgeons had indeed smelt prussic acid, why wouldn't they have sped up the process by mentioning it and having Cooper test for it first?

In his article, Dr Skae also offered an acute observation: that John's description of Sarah Hart's reaction after swallowing the contents of her phial – throwing her arms about and falling to the floor in a fit – mirrored the symptoms of prussic acid poisoning before the poison was actually identified. Baron Parke was also influenced by Superintendent Samuel Perkins's testimony regarding John's alleged admission. In his summation, the judge told the jury that, courtesy of John's statement that he had been present when Sarah Hart took the poison, all they had to do was to decide whether Sarah Hart had committed suicide or John had killed her. At least one jury member admitted that John's admission was crucial in his own decision-making process.

Yet the records raise serious questions about this evidence as well. The newspaper reports reveal that Perkins did not mention John's admission when the inquest continued the following day. Perkins later testified that it wasn't until five days afterwards that he first told the coroner – without explaining the delay. The police reports also reveal that he didn't even mention it to Inspector Wiggins of the London Metropolitan Police until eleven days after John's admission.

Strangely, Inspector Wiggins also kept this information private by omitting it from his daily report. He did, however, mention it to his governor, Superintendent Hughes, who added a brief note to that effect at the bottom of Wiggins's report. Yet the note failed to explain why Perkins had remained silent for so long, nor did it explain why the Paddington police were seemingly colluding in keeping John's admission unofficial.

Significantly, by the time Perkins did reveal John's admission, he himself would have known that the chemists had discovered prussic acid in Sarah Hart's remains, and the effects of that poison on the human body.

After Perkins testified, Constable Hollman had been called to the stand. Hollman had entered Perkins's dining room just after John started talking, yet he refused to support all of Perkins's statements about the conversation. He said that he heard John say he was present when Sarah Hart drank the porter, but added: 'I did not observe the prisoner showing, by any sign or motion, what the deceased did after she drank the porter.' Seemingly, another witness had lied in an effort to influence the court into believing that Sarah Hart had died from prussic acid poisoning.

Lastly, regarding the verdict, Dr Skae proclaimed that it was 'providential' as well as being opportune and extremely instructive. Not only had a conviction resulted from circumstantial evidence, but also the judge had established significant legal precedents regarding the evidence required in such cases.

The precedent to which he was referring was Baron Parke's statement regarding the evidence necessary for a poison conviction. This was in response to Fitzroy Kelly's opening address in which he had advised the jury that, for a conviction, the prosecution had to prove to the jury's satisfaction that the deceased had died of poison, and that the poison was prussic acid taken into her stomach – a reasonable statement considering the wording of John's indictment. Yet Baron Parke in his summation declared that Kelly was incorrect. He told the jury that it was not necessary for the prosecution to prove that the death was caused by poison, or that a particular poison had caused the death, or that a deadly quantity of that particular poison had been found in the deceased's stomach, nor was it necessary for the prosecution to determine the quantity of poison needed to kill by the testimony of one who had seen such a death. All the law required was a dead body, along with circumstantial evidence indicating that the body had been poisoned.

Baron Parke's 'precedent' would have been understandable in previous centuries when it was impossible to test for poisons. In this Age of Science and Reason, however – in particular, in the new field of forensic toxicology – his charge to the jury members was astonishing. Not only was he advising them to ignore the wording of John's indictment, he was telling them to ignore the scientific evidence and rely instead upon the circumstantial: that if it appeared that the deceased had been poisoned, and if the evidence pointed to a particular culprit – the defendant – then that was good enough to send the defendant to the gallows.

What Baron Parke's 'precedent' reveals is that he was aware that the medical and scientific evidence presented by the prosecution was both inconclusive and contradictory. By directing the jury in this way, he was ensuring that these issues would not become a source of reasonable doubt – as they should have been. He was determined to get a conviction, as he made clear when he began his summation by saying that John 'stands charged with a crime which, I might say, is unparalleled in the history of human wickedness'. Not only was this an alarmingly prejudicial declaration, Baron Parke was avoiding the fact that if Sarah Hart had not been killed by prussic acid poisoning, then the prosecution had failed to provide evidence showing that John Tawell was responsible for whatever had killed her, and worse had offered no evidence to prove that a crime had been committed in the first place.

Doctor of Philosophy Gustave Louis Maurice Strauss agreed. The 'Old Bohemian' – who was also a surgeon, chemist, journalist and linguist – had done his homework, noticing the discrepancies between the surgeons' evidence regarding the prussic acid odour smelt – or not, in fact, smelt – at the post-mortem examination. 'My conviction is that prussic acid had nothing whatever to do with the poor woman's death,' he announced to an astounded public.

As Strauss revealed in his lengthy 'Remarks' published in the *Morning Advertiser*, he had personally examined the bodies of three victims of prussic acid poisoning, and his conclusion was based on the absence of pathological alterations in Sarah Hart's body. He would have expected to find the venous system, liver, brain and lungs gorged with dark violet or black blood, the oesophagus, stomach and intestines inflamed, and the eyes showing a peculiar and characteristic brilliancy. 'How is it possible that any professional man, possessed of the slightest knowledge of his art, can, in the face of these facts, come to the conclusion that the death of Sarah Hart is chargeable upon prussic acid, simply because prussic acid was obtained by distilling the contents of her stomach?' Even the celebrated father of toxicology, Mathieu Orfila, had advised that detecting prussic acid in the digestive system didn't entitle those investigating suspicious deaths to conclude that prussic acid had been administered unless the victim showed the characteristic symptoms and pathological alterations.

Strauss further commented upon the confusion regarding the amount of prussic acid likely to cause death. He argued that the French epileptics had not died from so small a dose as seven-tenths of a grain of pure acid – a miscalculation based on confusion about the strength of the Paris Pharmacopoeia brand – but from somewhere between two-and-a-quarter and six grains for every patient. If the dose had been correct, they would have received around one-and-one-third grains of pure acid. 'Could there be such a grosser blunder than this?' he cried.

He added that he himself had taken as much as two grains of pure hydrocyanic acid diluted in water without feeling much inconvenience. 'It is by such evidence and such authorities that one of the most clear-headed judges of the land has allowed himself to be completely misguided.'

Strauss challenged the scientific and medical communities to refute his statements, and ended with two questions. Would any impartial observer be bold enough to assert that Tawell had received a fair trial and had been condemned on indubitably conclusive evidence? And, considering these doubts, wouldn't Tawell's execution under such circumstances amount to legal murder?

The battle of the experts – the hired guns – that hadn't been fought in the Aylesbury courtroom found its shooting ground in the press. Strauss fired the first volley and others followed. Some were echoes from allies, horrified at the thought of a potential miscarriage of justice and an innocent man being hanged. They had also been reminded by Strauss's remarks of their other concerns regarding the trial, including the extraordinary bias in the judge's summation.

Others fired back, ridiculing Strauss's claims although not his scientific evidence. 'A foolish pamphlet has been written by a person of the name of Strauss, impugning the evidence, in not very courteous terms, of the medical gentlemen at John Tawell's trial,' came the pompous response from that personification of British respectability and conservatism, *John Bull*. 'This opinion is pronounced with infinite dogmatism founded upon a smattering of chemical knowledge. Is Mr Strauss aware that no less than eight of the most distinguished medical practitioners and operative chemists were in court, subpoenaed on behalf of the accused, and that Mr Fitzroy Kelly, in the exercise of a sound discretion, forbore to examine any one of them, so direct and conclusive was the testimony of the medical witnesses for the prosecution?'

Yet these distinguished medical practitioners and chemists were among the dozens petitioning the Crown for mercy, and they included the foreman of the jury himself.

Part 5

AGONY

We hire the hangman to preach to the world the sacredness of human life.

Punch (1849)

CHAPTER 30

A criminal under sentence of death ... becomes
immediately the town talk ... the hero of the time. The
demeanour, in his latter moments, of Sir Thomas More
– one of the wisest and most virtuous of men – was
never the theme of more engrossing interest than that
of Hocker, Tawell, Greenacre or Courvoisier.

Charles Dickens,
'Letter to the *Daily News*' (28 February 1846)

THE NOOSE! It was a contentious subject arousing passionate
feelings among many community members, Mr Dickens among
them. In his letters on capital punishment published in the years
following Sarah Hart's death, he argued that society's fascination with the murderer was fed by the likely punishment: death
by hanging. He explained that forgery was once considered a
crime of adventure and mystery, and that forgers like Quaker
Joseph Hunton were the town talk, until the crime was struck
from the Bloody Code. 'Now they are mean, degraded, miserable criminals, and nothing more.'

The frenzied appetite for murder (and murderers) wasn't the
great writer's only concern. He asked whether the 'irrevocable
doom' that could never be reversed should ever be pronounced
on a fellow creature by men of 'fallible and erring judgement'.
Such wise counsel had little chance of penetrating the minds
of those convinced that the State's retribution needed to be

visible – and terrifying – in order to deter. Among them were many, indeed too many, of the Parliamentarians who dictated the nation's laws.

The remainder of the population had little interest in the moral or philosophical questions involved. They just wanted to know the date. The magistrates made their decision: Tuesday, 25 March. John was to be executed a mere ten days after his conviction.

Aylesbury's citizens were aghast. 'We always hang on Fridays, up there, facing the Town Hall, with a scaffold we keep for the purpose,' they cried. Most had forgotten that it was eight years since the gallows had last been pulled from storage, and prior to that ... well, no one could really remember. 'We always hang on Fridays,' they persisted. Accordingly, the date of John's execution was changed to Friday, 28 March, two weeks to the day after his conviction.

There would be no appeal. Not only had the officials taken the assize court on the next leg of its legal journey through the Norfolk Circuit, appeals were not permitted in criminal cases, only in civil ones. John's sole hope of a reprieve lay with Her Majesty, Queen Victoria.

Petitions had been flooding in to Sir James Graham's Home Office in the government of Sir Robert Peel. They came from Sarah Tawell, from John's solicitor and barrister, from prominent medical practitioners and chemists, including many who had attended the trial, from Quakers at Chichester and residents of Berkhampstead, Aylesbury and Saffron Walden, and from concerned members of the public. Some refuted the medical and chemical foundations of the conviction, declaring that John Tawell hadn't received a fair trial. Some accepted his conviction but pleaded for a reprieve on humanitarian grounds, arguing that society would be equally 'protected' if his sentence was commuted to transportation – showing no concern for the protection of those who would, as a consequence, have a convicted murderer deposited on their doorstep. The Aylesbury petition, which included the jury foreman's signature, extended its plea for mercy to cover all the condemned prisoners languishing in the nation's gaols – not that there were many in gaol at any given time, most having been shoved onto Britain's scaffolds with similar unseemly haste. One petitioner reminded the Home Office of the recent execution in Ipswich of a man who, only a short time later, was determined to have been innocent.

The Tawell file at the Home Office grew larger and larger. One petition referred to Baron Parke's 'virulent, rancorous and damnatory' charge against Tawell in his directions to the jury, pointing out that the jurymen might have found him innocent if a different judge had presided at the trial. Another explained that medical jurisprudence was still a young discipline, only a recent addition to medical and legal studies, so there were few men qualified to give evidence; moreover, the medical witnesses in Tawell's case, judging from their testimonies, were 'totally unfit for so perilous a duty'. This petitioner, and two others, offered examples of miscarriages of justice founded upon similar medical ignorance to buttress their arguments.

Two petitions raised new and alarming evidence: that Sarah Hart had previously threatened suicide because of money difficulties. One was from a local bigwig, Lord Nugent, Buckinghamshire's former Member of Parliament, who was once the Governor of Jamaica and the British Army's Commander-in-Chief of India. Lord Nugent even offered a scenario that might account for the tragic events of that New Year's evening:

Tawell was in the habit, as the Doctor's prescription shows, of having prussic acid for varicose veins in his leg. Let me suppose he carries his phial with him to her house, and that she has possession of it, to put it away where no accident might happen from it. A quarrel arises. She takes it before he can prevent her and falls into convulsions before him. All the circumstances of his having bought the poison, and his being alone with her, and she in a dying state, throw him into a panic which a manly and well-regulated mind would not have admitted. He runs away in his alarm and, the day after, when apprehended, tells all sorts of falsehoods about never having been there until he is brought down to Eton in custody, when he tells what I am supposing the true story to the Constable, namely that she poisoned herself.

Lord Nugent continued by pointing out that if Tawell was planning to commit murder, his preparations were absurd – unless he was mad, which he plainly was not. Other petitioners remarked likewise that Tawell bought the poison at a shop where he was known and told staff at a coffee house beforehand that he would be away; that he overdrew his account in order to have enough money to pay Mrs Hart, indicating that he intended to give her the money; that he travelled to Slough by a public train wearing his usual distinctive attire and walked the mile or so to Sarah's house along the busy Bath Road; that her house sat among a row of houses and that he entered through the front door, which would make it likely for at least one of her neighbours to see him enter – or leave – as did indeed happen; and that he returned to the same apothecary the following day for more prussic acid, which not only would have reinforced any memory of his previous visit, but also confirmed that he did require the prussic acid for medical purposes. All posed the oft-asked question: 'How could John Tawell, under any circumstances, murdering her thus as it were in public, hope to escape detection?'

The Quakers also discussed petitioning the Crown to commute John's sentence. They were concerned that he was telling the truth, that Sarah Hart had indeed poisoned herself. There was no proof, after all, that he had given the poison to her. Some were motivated by personal distress, but most by their long-expressed humanitarian principles. However, after reading the lengthy reports, the various meetings abandoned the idea of petitioning for mercy. Baron Parke's summing up was unequivocal. It left, they said, no doubt that his own opinion on the facts mirrored the jury's verdict. Here, they failed to recognise that the jury's verdict was largely consequent upon the judge's speech, rather than the other way around – that the summing up had certainly been 'damnatory', as another petitioner declared.

Nevertheless, the Quakers continued to offer spiritual solace to their fallen Friend. They sent religious tracts, which John appreciated and studied carefully. Some even visited him, John's psychic mentor, Peter Bedford, among them. Then rumours began to spread that some of his Quaker visitors had more in their sights than the prisoner's comforts.

Shortly after his conviction, John had received a visit from the local magistrates. His respectful attitude and composure, combined with his careworn appearance and evident unhappiness, was so affecting that sympathy stirred within them. They agreed to relax the prison regulations and grant him every indulgence during his remaining days, allowing him to continue having his food provided by the White Hart. They also allowed him to abandon the required prison dress and wear his own choice of clothes, both in gaol and on the scaffold. What did he wish to wear when he met his fate? John's decision was unsurprising – to the magistrates at least.

Many Friends, though, reeled with horror. Quaker attire on the gallows? When John failed to take the hint, they petitioned the magistrates.

'The people thought Tawell's conduct a disgrace to manhood,' wrote a later Quaker memoirist, 'while the Friends looked upon it as a disgrace to their costume.' This biting comment reflected the concerns held by many Quakers that their preoccupation with the outward trappings of their faith exposed them to justifiable ridicule. As it turned out, in the following decade a radical restructuring led the sect to abandon many of its 'peculiar' customs. Some would even claim that the attention focused upon their dress in the aftermath of the Salt Hill Murder contributed to their decision to discard it.

The denigration of their costume by association wasn't the Quakers' only concern. They were also deeply troubled by the whole 'Quaker-murderer' association. The *British Friend* lamented that whenever Tawell's name cropped up, his religious profession was appended, which didn't happen with other denominations. 'Who ever heard of So-and-So the Episcopalian, Presbyterian, Baptist, Methodist, Papist murderer?' the editor asked plaintively.

The simple answer was that 'Quaker' denoted more than just a religious persuasion. It conjured up a visual image as graphic as the word 'Amish' today, with far more to this picture than a mere costume. The word evoked images of bodies quaking in the presence of God, of dreadful persecutions, of the courage of a conviction so strong that a believer would adopt a distinctive uniform rather than hide behind the fashions of the time, of a religious elite renowned for their humanity, morality, piety, peace making and also, strangely, money making.

It was the very contradiction in the terms 'Quaker' and 'murderer', the inherent paradox, that spawned the moniker. Initially, it was spoken in astonishment or confusion, or as a snigger from the scornful, like the vitriolic Miles's Boy and others determined to knock the high-and-mighty Quakers off their pious pedestal. It stuck because it was so distinctive and so distinguishing: there were no others. Although the Quakers failed to recognise it, in a twisted sort of way, it was the ultimate accolade.

In addition to receiving spiritual solace from his Quaker friends, John received regular visits from the prison chaplain. The Reverend Cox had first attended him during his hours of torment after his conviction, intent upon offering some small relief. John declined on the grounds of religious differences, all the while thanking him for such kindness and consideration. The chaplain urged him at that time to make a confession – without success. 'I am not prepared,' was John's curious response.

Did he mean that was not *ready* to do so – yet? Or did he mean that he was not *willing* to confess to something he had not done? No one was quite sure.

At no point did John boldly proclaim his innocence – or complain about his sentence, for that matter. In fact, he never alluded to Sarah Hart's death or his own conviction. His silence was considered by many a tacit admission, as revelatory as any explicit avowal. The closest he came to commenting on his sentence was his suggestive statement: 'The judge was a just judge, but a stern one.' Yet of the crime itself, he would only say: 'I can consciously acquit myself of cruelty or treachery to anyone.'

This puzzling inconsistency left the nation in a quandary. Day after day – endlessly, repetitively – the press speculated as to whether John would confess. *The Times* decided that he wouldn't: 'From the extreme coolness and strength of nerve which he has maintained throughout his lengthened incarceration, now upwards of ten weeks, and his conduct during his three days' trial in court, it is not expected that he will make any confession of the horrid crime before his untimely death.' The *Aylesbury Times* thought he would: 'It is stated on the authority of one who has been admitted to an interview with him that it is probable that the wretched man will leave behind him in writing a full account of every circumstance connected with the murder, including other incidents of his chequered life.' If only he would corroborate the jury's verdict, it would set everyone's mind at rest! Then there would be no more doubts over whether justice had been served – or perverted.

One pundit suggested that John's religious sentiments were such that he would not disclose his guilt unless some sudden impulse, some yearning of the spirit to unburden itself, prompted such a revelation. The more cynical argued that John was awake to his fate but by no means impressed with the sinfulness of his deed, and that his imminent execution was a doom he had thought to avoid and hoped yet to escape.

John's manner was also perplexing, particularly to those monitoring his every move. 'Calm', 'self-possessed', 'tranquil', 'resigned' were the words generally used; 'the air of a martyr' occasionally slipped in as well. Some asked whether a sense of hope spurred by the public support was responsible for this air of tranquillity under such trying circumstances. Others suggested that his manner must be proof of his innocence.

Most, however, had been quick to judge, quick to condemn. They were pleased to see a conviction, although not so gleeful at the thought of an execution. While only 164 Aylesbury residents signed the petition asking for John's sentence to be commuted – mainly religious dissenters opposed to capital punishment – others found themselves tugged between powerful emotions: horror at the crime and hatred of the criminal versus repugnance at the thought of judicial murder, especially in such a public and degrading manner. The editor of the *Aylesbury News* was among them: 'We can only hope that the ends of public justice will be satisfied without a public murder being perpetrated.'

A gloom descended upon the town, one that wouldn't lift until after the situation was resolved – one way or the other. The magistrates cancelled the town ball planned for the evening before the proposed execution. They were appalled at the thought of dancing on the same floor the doomed man would shuffle across a few hours later, of forcing him to listen to their hours of revelry as he counted down the hours until his death.

CHAPTER 31

It isn't what we say or think that defines us, but what we do.

Jane Austen,
Sense and Sensibility (1811)

IN THE pressmen's desperate hunt for morsels to sate their readers' appetites, rumour and speculation were added to the menu. The list of John's victims grew from one to many. 'It is suspected ...' the newspapers coyly claimed, before providing details about other likely victims: his first wife, his two sons, a Sydney partner who died suddenly leaving John all his property. There were suggestions that the runaway gig incident, when the pregnant Sarah Tawell and her friend had jumped to safety, had been an attempt by John to kill his second wife and stepdaughter, and that after telling the ostler to go inside, he had loosened the bridles and blinkers allowing them to slip off and startle the horses.

'Nothing can be more absurd and reprehensible than some of the inventions which idle gossip has promulgated,' intoned *The Times*. Out of consideration for John's distressed family, the paper published details from their letter of rebuttal: there had never been a Sydney partner, and his first wife and sons had all died of pulmonary disorders. The vitriolic Miles's Boy himself would come to John's defence regarding the runaway gig, writing that the devil was not always as black as he was painted.

Another incredible report came from Berkhampstead's Quakers themselves, disclosing an incident that had occurred at one of their meetings. They had welcomed a visitor on the morning in question, a Yorkshire preacher, and silence had reigned as usual until, all of a sudden, he jumped up and began talking. 'A distressing feeling has taken possession of my mind for which I cannot account,' he began tentatively, 'except on the supposition that there is someone present who is contemplating an act of extreme wickedness and atrocity.' The astonished worshippers listened as he talked further about the powerful feeling that had infused his mind regarding a member of the room. He exhorted the individual, whoever it might be, to reflect upon his intentions and to implore his Maker's pardon for such evil thoughts. Finally, he advised the stunned faces staring back at him: 'If my warning voice, now raised, is not heeded, the individual will never again receive a similar offer of mercy and recall.'

The meeting broke up in alarm and confusion. As the Tawells walked back to the Red House, Sarah reportedly said to John, 'What a remarkable sermon that was. Why, one would think we had a murderer among us!'

～

The Tawells' friends and family knew that John was incapable of committing a single murder, let alone many. 'It really staggers belief,' one publicly exclaimed. All spoke well of him. Indeed, many accounts surfaced of his acts of kindness and generosity both in England and Australia.

Those who first met him after his incarceration also struggled to believe in his guilt. 'But for a cast in his eye, which in a man cannot fail to give a sinister expression, nothing could be more benevolent and prepossessing than his aspect,' wrote the

Bucks Herald. 'His demeanour is kind and meek in the extreme, and he is evidently a man of some natural talent.'

The magistrates who visited the gaol after his conviction were equally impressed by him. Not only did they agree to relax the prison regulations, they told him that he wouldn't have to face a repetition of the humiliating visits he had received two months earlier, before his trial. 'Nobody will be allowed to visit but those you express a wish to see.'

'I desire to see nobody but my wife,' John replied.

As it turned out, Sarah was so distressed by John's conviction that she was initially unable to visit. This was probably fortunate, as John's own exhaustion and despair had left him indisposed in those first few days. When his accustomed air of tranquillity and self-possession returned, he still feared seeing his wife, however. 'I dread her visit more than life itself,' he told the gaoler. It would be their first encounter since the courts had branded him a murderer.

They arrived at the gaol on the Monday morning after his conviction: Sarah, her daughter Eliza and her brother-in-law, William Tawell. The governor seated them in his parlour. He ordered a turnkey to bring Tawell to the room, adding that the turnkey was not to tell him why his presence was required. When John stepped through the door, he instantly saw his wife. His face blanched and he stood still, seemingly paralysed with shock, a picture of abject misery.

He needn't have worried. His family still believed in him, despite the court's judgement. They talked and prayed together for two hours, later declaring their astonishment at how rapidly the time had passed. John and Sarah expressed great affection towards each other: 'my enamoured one', 'my dearest one', they said. After the visit, Sarah mentioned that she felt more reconciled to John's fate, while John himself appeared calmer. His brother, though, remained profoundly distressed.

During the following days, John devoted much of his time to writing and answering letters, penning notes to his brother and solicitor and a lengthy daily missive to his wife. His solicitor urged him to finalise his affairs, and he did so with an accuracy of memory that amazed his friends and legal advisers, one of the reasons, they concluded, for his business success. Yet his solicitor couldn't help noticing that John behaved as if he were leaving for an extended trip rather than 'that bourne from whence no traveller returns'.

John's failed defence and continued need for legal advice had seriously dented his finances. As it transpired, he could have supported Sarah Hart and her children for another four decades with the money he spent on his case. Although most newspapers reported that his defence cost £700, a source within his legal team revealed that the total bill was closer to £2000. John's solicitor would officially report a few years later that he was still owed £1100 in fees and other associated costs.

As John organised his affairs, he decided to allow the Quakers to use the Sydney meeting house rent free, rather than grant them the promised title. Their continued rejection and current repudiation was deeply hurtful, and, under the circumstances, it was a generous offer. Of course, it is doubtful if the Quakers would have – indeed could have – accepted the gift of the title by this time. Repudiating him on the one hand; accepting his beneficence on the other. That would be hypocrisy for sure …

But that's what they had done five years previously.

John also replied to some of the letters arriving at the gaol from across the country, a dozen or more by each morning's post. Few reached him as the gaoler vetted them first. Officious and abusive communications as well as religious tracts were all tossed into the fire (much to the *English Churchman's* alarm – about the religious tracts, that is). Those that passed the initial inspection were handed to the chaplain to make the final decision as to whether they were worthy of John's attention.

One letter, written by an Ipswich stranger, asked John: 'Can you – appealing to the omniscient Jehovah and that faithful monitor *conscience* – declare, "I am innocent of the crime for which I am about to suffer."?' This letter passed through the vetting process, with the gaoler and chaplain curious to see John's response.

John managed to sidestep mentioning Sarah Hart's death in his odd reply:

> *My dear Friend,*
>
> *In reply to so excellent an address – to so earnest an entreaty – I am compelled, on every account, to be brief – seriously conclusive – on the awfully serious importance of those subjects which that address revives and impresses – and oh! that the language so earnestly there breathed may be that of MY SOUL unto THY REPENTANCE.*
>
> *Repentance towards God and faith in our Lord Jesus Christ;*
>
> *Who came to seek and to save that which was lost.*
>
> *O may that great Sacrifice that was 'offered up once for all' be the unspeakable, the inexpressible privilege of me to partake. So GREAT, SO UNWORTHY a sinner as I can truly and justly acknowledge myself to be; and I have nothing but the unmerited mercy of my Lord and Saviour to*

rely upon; unto whom I have nothing to bring or to offer but my nakedness and my numerous transgressions.

    Farewell! Solemnly Farewell!!
    Thy deeply afflicted Friend,
                      John Tawell

I desire most gratefully to offer up my thanks for the interest felt on my behalf.

Was John admitting his guilt, or was this the confused outpouring of a disintegrating mind?

Sabbath of the second weekend dawned and slowly passed as John waited anxiously for Sarah's appearance. The rain drummed incessantly on the gaol roof and puddles formed on the floor, the heavens seeming to lament with him when she failed to arrive. The press reported that he had passed the day undisturbed in his prayers and reflections. In truth, he was quietly nursing his misery. Every day he awaited her letters and consoled himself with their affectionate and religious sentiments, but he longed to see her.

When he had told the magistrates that he desired to see nobody but his wife, they had advised him to forgo such scenes and spare her the heartache. He wouldn't listen. He declared that he must see her. He didn't explain that just the thought of seeing her again kept his spirits alive.

Much to his relief, she arrived on the Monday, again with her daughter and his brother in tow. For two hours they talked and prayed, their tones loving, their devotions earnest. 'I will come again on Wednesday,' she told him as she was escorted from his cell. Unspoken between them was the disclaimer 'unless he had been executed in the meantime'. The date had not been disclosed to either of them.

Mr Sherriff came to bid her goodbye and, as she responded, she expressed her sincere appreciation for his kindness, and most especially for ensuring that John was not subjected to anything likely to disturb his mind or interfere with his meditations. The governor silently marvelled at her self-command, and John's too, for that matter. John was no longer merely one of the riffraff who populated his gaol – of course, as a Quaker businessman, he had never really fallen into that nasty set. Instead, John was a prisoner he had grown to respect and genuinely like. He had observed the man's behaviour both before and after the trial, and he had noticed many changes since his conviction.

John's air of briskness and confidence was long gone, and his behaviour was restrained and righteous. He talked easily with the turnkeys and sometimes mentioned his past and his family, although he never referred to the murder and barely alluded to the reason for his incarceration. He continually thanked his captors for their kindnesses.

Sherriff, along with others around the gaol, had found himself referring to John as a 'wonderful man'. Indeed he could feel nothing short of admiration for John's conduct and self-command. He and the turnkeys had noticed that it was only at night, when John retreated to his cell, that despondency settled over him. But as soon as anyone entered his cell, he would firm his carriage and control his visage, regaining his dignity. The man was truly amazing.

⌐∕

Tuesday brought visits from John's brother and solicitor, along with unwelcome news. Despite all the petitions and pleas, the

Home Secretary could see no sufficient reason for interfering with John's sentence.

The *Morning Advertiser*, the newspaper that had published Dr Strauss's remarks upon the questionable medical and chemical evidence, responded scathingly. 'Now either Sir James Graham is not able to comprehend the scientific objections made by competent men to the opinions of the medical witnesses or, as is usual in less disreputable cases, he has implicitly relied upon the opinion of a judge whose summing up must be deemed a most melancholy demonstration that medical jurisprudence has yet obtained no place in the acquirements of the men on whose views the lives of their fellow creatures solely depend.'

Later in the day, the gaoler and chaplain entered John's cell and told him gently, 'You may regard the remaining interim between yourself and eternity more as hours than days.' The momentary look of horror that crossed his face revealed that he hadn't thought it would be so soon. But he didn't ask what day and, astonishingly, his self-command returned almost immediately. *The Times* reported hopefully: 'There is now an air of something like penitence as well as piety and resignation about him – a feeling which, it is hoped, will tempt him to a confession.'

John received more visitors in the evening. Mr Sherriff ushered in Buckinghamshire's Lord Nugent accompanied by some other magistrates. They talked about John's situation, asking whether he appreciated the visits from the prison chaplain. 'I like the man very much,' John assured them. 'He is a charitable good sort of man and deserving of attention, but I do not require his services as I think that a man might prepare himself to make his peace with God without the intervention of any substitute.' Even now, he continued to live by the fundamental Quaker beliefs.

The magistrates urged him to make a confession. 'I am not prepared,' John said again. Lord Nugent applied the persuasive powers of his eminence and authority as a politician and a member of the upper class, whose respect John had sought for much of his life. *The Times* reported in the aftermath: 'There is a reason for supposing that Tawell will write some kind of confession, if he has not done so already, and deliver it under seal to the chaplain, or the governor of the gaol, to whom he is very gratefully attached.'

A previous issue of *The Times* had alluded to important disclosures that would be left in writing and published in the papers after Tawell's execution, adding, 'A mysterious silence is, however, for the present being observed upon the subject.' The paper provided no clue as to the source of their information, or whether the disclosures would come from John himself or the authorities. It was seemingly content to maintain the mystery and to keep its readers guessing.

⁓

Wednesday saw the arrival of John's family again. Sarah was still unaware of the looming date as all newspapers were being kept from her. Both her family and the concerned gaoler wished to spare her as much distress as possible, and ensure that she would not learn the precise details of John's execution until afterwards, if at all.

The family talked for some time, then John handed Sarah a bundle of papers. He explained that they contained some reminders for her and a few small commissions he wished her to undertake, as well as details of a trifling debt or two. 'I owe not a penny,' he said proudly, adding that if anything further came to mind he would commit it to paper.

Although nothing was said, an air of finality and despair

hovered around them. Seventeen-year-old Eliza wept most of the time. As Sarah readied to leave, as they bade each other their usual affectionate farewells, she mentioned seeing him again, reluctant to abandon hope of a favourable response to the petitions sent to the judge and queen.

The grim-faced chaplain arrived a short time later. He advised John that he had just seen his wife for the last time. The warrant for his execution had arrived that morning.

John slept restlessly that evening, saying the next morning that it was because he wouldn't see his wife again. He ate breakfast with his usual air of tranquillity, though, remarking that he should require little else throughout the day. Concerned that the imminence of his death had not yet sunk in, Mr Sherriff softly asked, 'Are you acquainted with what will soon occur?'

'Yes,' John said. 'I suppose tomorrow is the day. I thought as much. Well, I have no complaint to make.'

He did not appear unusually cast down. In fact he added, 'I am glad that it is so close at hand, and that my family will soon be relieved from their present harassing position.'

Of course, their pain might ease but it would never end. The stain of such notoriety was not only indelible, it would outlast them.

Mr Sherriff mentioned that he intended to sit up with him through the night, and that the chaplain would join them. John thanked him again for his ceaseless compassion. For the rest of the day he maintained his usual dignity and composure. He wrote letters and read, he talked and prayed.

Meanwhile, Sarah spent a quiet Thursday in Berkhampstead. It was the day of the Quaker's Quarterly Meeting for the counties of Buckingham and Northampton, a meeting she wasn't allowed to attend because of her marriage. When the Quakers had previously convened at Berkhampstead, the Tawells had

always offered their home as an open house for the accommodation and entertainment of those attending. Not this time,
though. The meeting drew a larger crowd than normal, yet no
one visited her. At a lengthy prayer meeting after the close of
business, they submitted their prayers of mercy to the Lord for
a reprieve and, if the petitions failed, for John's soul.

⟶

Mr Sherriff kept an eye out for any official communication relating to his prisoner. John and his family were not alone in hoping
for a reprieve. Mr Sherriff had received no word in Thursday
morning's post, nor did anything arrive later in the day. John's
brother William, who came with further papers to be signed,
reported that he too had heard nothing.

By early evening the gaoler realised, with immense sadness,
that the execution would go ahead as planned at eight o'clock
the following morning.

Chapter 32

The vast numbers who go to see the writhings of the wretch slain by his fellow men do so from a feeling as completely brutalised as that which induced the half-civilised Romans of ancient days to throng to the Colosseum and gloat over the criminals torn by wild beasts, or gladiators perishing in mortal combat – for no object but the gratification of the appetite of a senseless multitude.

Dover Chronicle
(29 March 1845)

LEX TALIONIS – legal retribution. It had its origins in pre-history, a primitive form of justice, the simple, visceral balance of 'a life for a life'. The execution was the climax of the vengeance ritual, the sacrificial victim hoisted high on the altar of retribution, visible to all, a warning, a symbol. Yet the sacrifice was also a celebration, a thanksgiving, the triumph of life over death, of order over anarchy, of empowerment. Society's wrath had been unleashed on the condemned malefactor. No longer need the community live in fear.

Lex talionis. It had a romantic appeal – in principle. The reality, though, was quite different. Those who thronged to these legal slayings included many who were likely to end their own days on the gallows. The crowds – sometimes thousands, even tens of thousands strong – watched with salacious eyes. They cheered or booed or hissed when the culprit arrived, yelped with horror if the culprit died slowly and painfully, then flocked to the next execution to seek the same thrill. If delays occurred, the mob turned restive. If the culprit received a last-minute reprieve, the mob turned violent. If something went wrong and the mob panicked, the consequences could be disastrous. The Aylesbury authorities were not looking forward to Friday, 28 March 1845.

Once the news was out that John Tawell's execution would go ahead as planned, sightseers began to arrive in Aylesbury, some as early as Thursday afternoon. The late trains from Paddington, in particular, offloaded an increasing number of excited strangers. These tourists included representatives from Berkhampstead, Slough and Gravesend – Sarah Hart's home town – who all justified their attendance on the grounds that they had a personal interest in the case. As yet there was nothing to see. Although the huge blackened beams had been brought from their resting place to be dusted and examined, the gallows would not be erected until morning.

Laughing, chatting, drinking and carousing, the visitors congregated in Aylesbury's inns. The town assumed an air of festivity, much to the consternation of its good citizens who considered that such an event besmirched their town's reputation and attracted rabble to their locale.

The riffraff of British society were not alone in being drawn to the execution. The 'swell-mob' were also driving into town, the young nobs with lots of money, and their friends, the cadgers. Two such gentlemen had travelled to Aylesbury the previous week to find a suitable vantage point for the coming entertainment. They approached a respectable maiden lady who occupied a shop in the square overlooking the county hall, and offered a handsome inducement for permission to watch from her window. The *Aylesbury News* reported with great delight that their offer had been rejected. 'They not only got a point-blank refusal, but a very sharp lecture (as only maiden ladies can give) for their insolence in making a proposal so distasteful to humanity, and in supposing that she would make a trade in the blood of her fellow creatures.'

The standing patterers also stepped off the London trains, lugging bundles of pre-printed pamphlets entitled 'last dying speech and confession'. Slipping through the crowds were the well-known faces of professional pickpockets, their shifty looks spurring the local police superintendent to swear in five more special constables. Hanging as a deterrent to crime – not likely!

Every lodging house was crammed, some so full that the landlords littered straw across the floor to accommodate the overflow. Still, people came. One visitor was a short beefy man, rugged, energetic, rather like a prosperous grocer or trader. He made his way to the county hall, abiding by the regulation that he must bed down in the gaol on the night before an execution. The enthusiasts who regularly trekked around the countryside to attend the nation's most popular spectator sport – 'hanging matches' they were called – immediately recognised the man. He was William Calcraft, England's most notorious executioner. Calcraft would later be honoured as Britain's longest serving executioner, although by no means the best. He was renowned in particular for his 'short drop', which left his clients strangling to death.

Calcraft was not Mr Sherriff's initial choice. Usually the Aylesbury officials chose a fellow prisoner to undertake the repugnant task – and they never had a shortage of volunteers. In John's case, they even received a letter from a Great Marlow resident offering his services, much to the horror of his fellow townsmen who felt he had disgraced them. A disgusted newspaper editor reported that he knew the man's name and would consider publishing his infamy in the next issue.

Concerned at the community's frenzied interest, and alarmed at the thought of anything going wrong, Sherriff decided instead to employ the Old Bailey functionary. Unlike a gaol inmate, Calcraft wasn't cheap, charging £10 to £15 for a country execution. He received perquisites as well: the prisoner's clothing and any other property found on the body after the execution, items that he usually sold on to Madame Tussauds; also the rope, which could be worth up to five shillings an inch to relic-hunters, depending upon the prisoner's disrepute. The Quaker would provide a tidy bonus to be sure so Calcraft accepted the commission.

As the afternoon passed, two dozen pressmen descended on Aylesbury gaol, eager to learn the arrangements for the following day. At what time would they be allowed into the gaol to fill their notebooks with impressions of the condemned man's final moments, as was customary?

Never, Sherriff told them. 'It has been the invariable custom to allow no persons to be present but those whose official duties require them to take part in the proceedings,' he explained. Many in the town were against capital punishment, and this was one aspect of the distasteful proceedings that remained within their control.

The pressmen demanded to know who was responsible for such a preposterous decision. The gaoler handed over his instructions, a letter written by Under-Sheriff Tindal acting upon the authority of the High Sheriff of Buckinghamshire.

With glares and muttered imprecations, the pressmen retreated, but they had not given up. Over drinks at the White Hart, the representatives of the prestigious London morning newspapers decided to appeal to Tindal himself. If he wouldn't permit *all* the reporters into the gaol to witness the prisoner's last moments, would he allow just the one? The reporters also warned that the High Sheriff's decision to ban them would lead to a suspicion of favouritism. Indeed, the *Morning Chronicle* would later put it thus: 'The impression in the town appeared to be that there was a disposition on the part of the under-sheriff to favour the unfortunate prisoner and that, as he had shown a repugnance to being gazed at by strangers, Mr Tindal wished to spare his feelings from this last infliction.' Other papers speculated whether the many indulgences allowed John and his family would have been granted a poor wretch without a penny or a friend.

To the pressmen's surprise, their messenger returned saying that Under-Sheriff Tindal had 'no answer' to their letter. Believing that Tindal could never behave in such an ungentle-manly fashion – 'he is an attorney and therefore a gentleman by Act of Parliament!' – they decided that the messenger must have misheard him, and sent another note asking for his true answer. Hours later, Tindal replied that his directions to the gaoler were quite clear in his letter. Nevertheless, in the after-math of the execution, he would allow the gaoler to provide his own impressions for the benefit of the reporters and the wider public.

Repeated entreaties and remonstrances failed to change Tindal's mind. *The Times* would later bitterly editorialise that it was a common saying that Aylesbury was a hundred years behind any other town in England, and that the authorities' actions now proved it. 'Reporters do not covet the painful duty of witnessing the last moments of a murderer; but they are the representatives of the public and it is through them that the great moral lesson which such awful scenes teach is conveyed to the world at large.'

The demands to the Aylesbury authorities seemed unceasing. John's family pleaded to have his body delivered to them for burial afterwards, despite being informed that this was not the custom. Their hopes remained strong until Thursday evening when they were told, with finality, that the grave had been dug in the grounds of the county hall. The family also wanted to provide a superior coffin for his burial rather than the cheap elm box the authorities issued, but this too was denied.

Physiognomists from Nottingham and Edinburgh arrived in Aylesbury requesting permission to make casts of John's head, following a popular belief that cranial bumps and other facial features provided insights into the soul and, most especially, into the criminal mind. They were refused permission after John's family begged the authorities not to allow such a violation.

Meanwhile, a London gentleman sidled up to Executioner Calcraft and flourished wads of cash in the hope of purchasing John's clothes after the event. *Punch*'s editor, a strident opponent of the death penalty and all the hypocrisy attached to it, inked his quill:

> *Anxious not to lose 'one shred of that immortal man', the gentleman offered £25 for the black coat and trousers and silk vest which, being worn by a murderer in his death-struggle, would have, of course, 'magic in their web'. It was hinted that the clothes were required as an additional attraction for a certain public exhibition in the metropolis! We have no doubt that they would have made 'a tremendous hit'. How gentlemen and tender, delicate ladies – sensitive souls that squeal at a black beetle or the 'most monstrous*

mouse' – would have flocked to gaze on the buttonless
wonder! We would have him exhibited with a phial
in either hand; in one vessel, prussic acid; and in the
other Mr Fitzroy Kelly's tears.

The gentleman from London failed in his mission. Presumably John's family had offered the executioner more of a remuneration than Madame Tussauds' envoy.

As the word spread that the authorities had barred the pressmen from the gaol, rumours about the reason for such a decision followed. One proposed that the Quaker would be spared the ignominy of being executed on the public scaffold: 'Tawell will not live until eight o'clock tomorrow morning. He will be allowed to quietly put himself out of existence with a dose of poison – likely prussic acid.' Others speculated that he had already done so. Still others declared that he would be granted a last-minute reprieve and have his sentence commuted to transportation. The purported reason for such an indulgence? 'While in New South Wales under sentence of transportation, he was very useful as a spy for the Home Government, and furnished information respecting the conduct not only of the condemned but of official persons in that colony.'

This laughable piece of folly fuelled the frenzy of the throng carousing around town as they awaited break of dawn. It also teased more money from the betting-men, at least those who included the 'hanging matches' – in this case, that of the 'Old Quaker' – in their usual sporting sweepstakes.

～～

Aylesbury dwellers and spectators were not alone in thinking about John Tawell that night. The introspective English actor William Charles Macready lay awake for hours, wondering at

John's thoughts and actions, pondering the big questions: 'What a lottery is this world and what a miserable race of beings are crawling over it? What is our mission here? What would illness make me, or any reverse ...'

The question of capital punishment continued to torment many of England's men of letters. When dramatist Douglas Jerrold was discussing Tawell's case with friends, he made a passing comment about the absurdity of capital punishment. Historian and satirist Thomas Carlyle burst out, 'The wretch! I would have had him trampled to pieces under foot and buried him on the spot!'

'*Cui bono* [to whose benefit]?' asked Jerrold, deprecatingly. '*Cui bono?*'

CHAPTER 33

May it rain in such torrents that no crowd will be able to withstand the storm.

Aylesbury News
(March 1845)

JOHN WAS still awake and sitting in the day room when Aylesbury's clocks chimed the witching hour. It was remarkably quiet outside, a striking contrast to the usual evening revelries before a London execution. Violent winds and bucketing rain had begun a short time earlier, driving the roisterers inside.

He had a long night ahead of him. He had eaten heartily at tea-time a few hours previously. In time, he was joined by the gaoler and chaplain. He expressed no interest in retiring to his cell to sleep. Around 10 p.m. he asked to see Mr Sherriff's son; an hour later, the gaoler's wife. To both, he expressed his deepest appreciation for their kind attention during his incarceration. They later said that this touching thoughtfulness was typical of the courteous man they had come to know so well, the man they had come to like and respect.

At one point, John handed the gaoler a large packet of letters to mail. Sherriff piled them onto his desk and read them, hoping that one would offer a final statement of some kind. As it turned out, the letters related to private matters and did not even allude to Sarah Hart's death.

As the night drew on, Sherriff relieved one of the turnkeys.

The man had lent John a penknife to erase something from a letter he was writing, and had forgotten to retrieve it before he left the cell. Sidling up to the gaoler, the turnkey whispered his problem, adding that he couldn't see his knife on the table. Sherriff reprimanded the man for his carelessness, then suggested that he ask the prisoner for the knife.

'Ah, Mr Sherriff, you are quite right,' John replied, having overheard Sherriff's reply and instantly comprehended the concern. He rarely needed explanations. 'I commend your prudence,' he continued as he handed back the penknife, 'but there is no occasion, I assure you, for any such care.'

Midnight passed and the clock began ticking away the wee hours. Mr Sherriff and the chaplain remained with John as he read the Bible and prayed. Tears trickled down his face when the chaplain prayed with him for divine mercy. He listened attentively to several passages the chaplain pointed out to him, and himself selected others from the Book of Psalms, reading them out loud and commenting upon them.

Every so often he withdrew to his sleeping-cell and fell upon his knees, praying loudly and fervently, expressing heartfelt penitence. He felt nothing for himself, he told them gravely, nothing for his own suffering, only for his wife and family and friends for the terrible disgrace he had brought upon them. However, his prayers revealed concerns for his own soul's well-being too.

Post-conversion sin was another evangelical conundrum. If faith sanctified the soul, then how could a neophyte, a true believer, a genuinely sanctified soul, lapse into sin? If conversion bestowed righteousness, was a lack of righteousness evidence of unbelief? If salvation required the right kind of faith, a faith reflected in righteousness, then what was the spiritual fate of those who continued to sin? Some evangelicals soothed themselves with the concept of a 'continued recourse to the fountain', but for the intellectuals and the more introspective, the question continued to niggle. This created another anxiety, another source of psychological strain for sinners like John. If he doubted his own faith or questioned his own conversion experience, was he embracing eternal damnation?

~

At 2 a.m., John requested coffee and savoured the toast that accompanied it. An hour or two later, after continuing his prayers and Bible reading, he asked if he might be allowed to sleep a little. He looked exhausted, yet as he retired to his cell, he said to Mr Sherriff, 'If I should sleep beyond five o'clock, have the goodness to call me.' He undressed and lay down, falling asleep in a moment.

Half an hour later, the sounds of his breathing subsided. Concerned, Sherriff entered his cell and approached the bedside. His movements, though hushed, disturbed John, who turned around and greeted him. John didn't try to go back to sleep again. Instead, he rose and dressed in his black coat and trousers, black silk vest and large white neckerchief – a Quaker to the very end.

Around 5 a.m. he requested some breakfast and asked the gaoler and chaplain to join him. His manner remained the same as before: polite to his companions, calm and collected in his bearing as if resigned to his fate. This appearance of extraordinary fortitude and presence of mind was now challenged, though, by his increasingly haggard countenance.

After he had eaten, Mr Sherriff warned him that the time was drawing nigh. 'Have you any little matters I could arrange for you, or anything I could take care of for you?' he asked.

John picked up his silver spoons and some other trifles and put them into his box, giving Mr Sherriff the key. He then sat down and wrote on a couple of pieces of paper, requesting that his few remaining shillings be given to a couple of fellow prisoners. He also handed the gaoler a letter dated a few days previously:

Dear and worthy friend Mr Sherriff,

It is not less any duty than great pleasure as well as from feelings of deep and sincere gratitude that I can thus offer my poor but unqualified thanks to both thyself and poor Mrs Sherriff for the continued and marked kind attention which has been shown so uniformly to myself and my family and friends since my unfortunate confinement in this prison by allowing us all the access which urbanity and philanthropy could suggest under such circumstances. And now their deeply distressing probation is clearly concluded, I have to desire that this may be accepted as the most grateful acknowledgement both on account of myself and them. I can for myself desire that the Divine blessing may largely rest on thyself and Mrs Sherriff and your family; and my own valuable family will lastingly have to re-echo this poor but sincere benediction of thy faithful but afflicted friend, John Tawell.

Sherriff read the letter, deeply touched. Looking back at the prisoner, he told him how much he truly appreciated it. But it wasn't quite what he had been waiting for, hoping for. Gently, he asked John for a written confession.

$$\sim$$

As John was eating his final meal, four workmen had ventured out into the wet squally pre-dawn. They began erecting the

gallows above Aylesbury County Hall's main entrance, right
before its Great Window. The 'new drop' as it had been called
for the past two decades was an ideal location for an execution,
or any public entertainment. The county hall sat on low land
with a large square in front, and from there the ground rose
gradually to the market house some three hundred yards distant. The square offered ample room for an audience of eight
to ten thousand and provided all the advantages of a natural
amphitheatre.

Carpenters had already completed the necessary work inside
the hall. They had erected a temporary staircase and flooring
leading to the Great Window, which opened onto a large iron
balcony similar to those fronting many drawing-room windows.
Although the balcony had long been Aylesbury's execution site,
workmen had recently demolished the gallery and stairs leading to it, making the temporary construction necessary. The
magistrates had prematurely decided that 'the drop' would no
longer be needed as it was eight years since the last execution
and plans were underway for a new prison.

The workmen draped black canvas over the balcony railing and began hammering away. They built a square platform
to sit atop and project over the railing. Some euphemistically
called it a 'stage' although it was in fact the gallows floor. It
contained a trapdoor with an oiled bolt that could be drawn
using an attached cord. The black-screened balcony itself now
resembled a box or trap into which the malefactor would fall
when the gallows floor divided underneath him. He would drop
until his feet nearly touched the balcony floor below.

The hammering continued as they built five steps leading
up from the balcony to the gallows floor. Then they hefted the
huge black beams onto the balcony and slotted the two upright
posts into iron fastenings on either side of the square stage,

connecting them with the cross-beam above. The cross-beam was marked with three equidistant bruises in the wood, the chalk-marked indentations made by the ropes that had hung malefactors of bygone days. The deeper central indentation had been notched some decades previously when an enormous man had been executed for sheep-stealing.

Around 6 a.m. the workmen completed their odious task. A few keen sightseers had watched them from the start, but the bitter wind and another violent rainburst had kept most folk indoors.

As the rain eased to little more than an annoying drizzle, people descended upon the square. Those not accommodated in town could be seen wending their way along nearby roads: rustics in their smock frocks and 'Jim Crow' hats, sturdy tradesmen, mob-capped maidens, all coming by foot. Dashing past them in their handsome carriages were the dapper young blades and their modish ladies – or perhaps, on closer inspection, 'women' might have served better as some seemed, to the discerning eye, to be of 'questionable character'. They all planted themselves on the square, jostling for the best viewing position.

The rain ceased altogether around 7 a.m., although the wind remained gusty and the sun was hidden by clouds. By 7.30 a.m., thousands thronged the market square. Dozens of others peered through the front windows of houses and inns lining the square, or hugged balcony rails, or sat atop projecting shop windows or any other eminence the eager and agile could reach.

Aylesbury's oldest inhabitants exclaimed that they had never before seen so many people assembled for such an occasion, although the editor of the *Aylesbury News* had his wish: the foul weather deterred many, while others were discouraged by the distance from London or the belief that Tawell would be granted a last-minute reprieve. Few of Aylesbury's 'respectable' citizens could be seen among the crowds, and most of the shops remained closed in protest.

The emissaries from the less respectable London newspapers were highly visible. They plastered the walls with huge signs advertising their newspapers and could be seen strolling through the crowds passing out hand-bills. A regiment of Londoners carried colossal placards mounted on poles twelve feet high advertising one newspaper's forthcoming report of the execution – 'a disgusting piece of bad taste,' spat a rival correspondent. The peculiar nasal twang of those selling broadsides and penny sheets could be heard over the crowd's babble and over the children's gurgles as they romped under the gallows.

At 7.30 the foreman reported to the under-sheriff that the preparations were completed. The execution could begin.

CHAPTER 34

Death is a fearful thing.

William Shakespeare,
Measure for Measure

❧

A LETTER in the first morning post caught Mr Sherriff's attention. He ripped it open and read it. The letter wasn't the hoped-for reprieve, just another of the hundreds that continued to swamp the gaol, the outpourings of those who wanted their opinions heard or their rage and bitterness felt, desperate to believe that, in the vastness of humanity, their own existence somehow mattered.

Meanwhile, John had spent the two hours after breakfast in prayer and conversation, remaining extraordinarily calm and controlled yet showing traces of anxiety as the time passed ever so slowly. At 7.30, he said to the turnkeys, 'I wish it to be over as soon as possible!' He returned to his cell and was kneeling down praying when Mr Sherriff walked through the doorway and picked up his broad-brimmed hat.

John looked at his hat then up at the gaoler. He knew what it signified.

'Are you quite prepared?' Sherriff asked.

'Quite,' said John. 'I am ready to go.'

The county's under-sheriff stood nearby in the day room along with the chaplain and turnkey. With John between them, the four men left the condemned cell and began the death march, their footsteps echoing as they strode through the gaol and along the passage to the ladder, up to the dock, through the courtroom and into the Great Hall. They halted when they reached a chair near the makeshift stairs. As they stood there, John remarked in a surprisingly steady voice, 'This is a very curious time with me.'

A black-garbed man approached them and the gaoler introduced John to his executioner. With ludicrous but exceedingly British politeness, the two men shook hands. Then Calcraft told John to sit down.

John instantly understood. Looking up at the strapping executioner, he said quietly, 'Oh, I am to be pinioned, I believe, now.' Calcraft confirmed that it would be necessary for him to perform that painful duty. John replied calmly, with an air of sadness and touching bravery, a willing martyr sacrificing himself for the greater good, 'You will not find me giving you much trouble.'

The executioner pinioned his arms firmly and removed his neckerchief, tucking it neatly into John's coat pocket. Before long, it would be replaced by the 'hempen neckcloth'. Then Calcraft placed the graceless but symbolic black nightcap on top of his head and tugged it down slightly.

'Will you take the Sacrament?' Reverend Cox asked.

'I have no wish to do so,' John replied, although he added obligingly that if they requested him to do so, he would waive his objection. The chaplain didn't press the matter, instead beginning to recite some prayers. John joined in with regal self-possession. They assisted him to stand again. As readily as his pinioned elbows allowed, he shook hands with Mr Sherriff, Reverend Cox and the turnkey. He then lifted his eyes to the Great Window. It stood invitingly open, its glass doors already pushed back to allow access to the balcony.

With the black-robed chaplain in front, swinging his incense lantern and prematurely intoning the Service for the Burial of the Dead, the procession moved to the stairs and began to climb them, a bizarre parody of the angels' ascent to heaven. The chaplain fell silent as he stepped through the window onto the balcony and moved to one side. John followed him, halting for a moment before climbing the extra five stairs up to the scaffold, the lamb walking alone to the sacrificial altar.

⌒

Eight o'clock was the published hour for John's execution, the usual hour for Aylesbury executions. At 7.43 a.m. a ripple ran through the crowd. 'He is coming.' A sudden, intense silence followed.

A slight figure dressed in black with an incongruous night-cap on his head stumbled onto the scaffold, with the beefy executioner and turnkey behind him. So suddenly and unceremoniously did he appear that a moment elapsed before many among the assembled multitude realised that the ritual had actually commenced.

On the gallows itself, John stared at the sea of faces with a look of startled surprise as if he were an unprepared actor dragged from his dressing room and thrust onto the stage of a gala performance. Quickly regaining his usual aplomb, he inclined his nightcapped head respectfully towards the crowd. Directly in front of him, he could see a huge placard announcing that the next issue of the *Weekly Dispatch* would contain 'A Final Account of the Last Moments of Tawell'. With this blunt reminder, his eyes were drawn inexorably upwards towards the great black beam, stark against the ashen sky.

He stared at it for a moment then began to tremble. His legs buckled underneath him. He sank to his knees, clasping his hands together as if about to pray, but the turnkey lifted him up. Again he sank down. Again the turnkey lifted him up, and Calcraft used the opportunity to pull the nightcap over his eyes. The executioner then slipped the coarse rope over his head and was adjusting it around his neck when John turned his head towards him and said, 'Allow me to kneel down for a minute to pray.'

'It is not necessary,' said one of the officials, evidently forgetting that visible repentance was a desired part of the ritual, of the atonement of a death for a death. The turnkey tried to hold John erect but again he fell to his knees. With his face turned away from the crowd, he began to pray.

'I have sinned before God and trust in his mercy alone for forgiveness,' he cried, before pleading repeatedly, 'Sweet Jesus, receive my spirit!' He then fell silent and lifted his face towards the heavens.

The crowds could see John's hands clasped tightly in prayer and his lips moving as if begging for mercy. They were eager for a confession, scaffold speeches being another part of the desired atonement ritual, the completion of the cycle. It was also part of the excitement of the day, allowing the spectators to boast afterwards that they heard it first from the culprit's own lips!

But the contrast between the slight figure – meek, submissive, penitent – kneeling beneath the hulking executioner with his blasphemous white kid gloves, stirred new feelings among the crowd. The silence continued but the mood began to turn from anticipation to pity.

While John prayed, Calcraft, with his usual unhurried patience, adjusted the rope around his neck and threw the other end over the cross-beam. It took an unusually long time to attach the rope to the beam as there was no chain Calcraft could tie it to. Eventually, he tossed it over the beam a couple of times, knotting it with what the sailors called 'three half hitches'.

John remained kneeling. He made no attempt to rise until the executioner took hold of his right arm and lifted him up, turning him so that he again faced the crowd. At that point, his extraordinary fortitude deserted him. 'Oh dear! Oh dear!' he cried, the words echoing through the silence. 'Oh dear! Oh dear!'

Having completed the preparations, an endless few minutes after John had first stepped onto the scaffold, Calcraft and the turnkey withdrew to the balcony. John stood there alone. His face was partly covered by the black nightcap. Behind his head, the deadly cord ran up to the menacing black beam above. His hands remained clasped and his body visibly trembled. The cries continued to spill from his lips: 'Oh dear! Oh dear! ...'

'Now! Now!' murmured the eager spectators.

With a loud clunk, the drop opened. John's body fell through the opening. The destiny he had eluded thirty years before had at last caught up with him.

~

That should have been it. John's weight and the force of gravity combined with the carefully positioned rope should have instantly broken his neck. But John was only a slight man, and the executioner, renowned for his short drops at the best of times, had used more rope than normal in securing the noose to the cross-beam. Long drops of two yards or more, with length determined through a careful calculation of height and weight (too long a drop mimicked the results of a guillotine), and brass eyelet holes that allowed the rope to tighten smoothly, were not customary for another half a century.

John's body quivered and quaked. His arms and legs writhed, jerking upwards and downwards as if the puppeteer pulling his strings had become enraged. His tightly clenched hands remained locked in prayer as if his mind was still directed towards heaven despite his physical suffering. He was alive and in agony.

No cheers or cries or even ribald observations came from the crowd during John's death throes. As his body continued to convulse, some began to shout, 'He is not dead! The rope must have been misplaced!'

Others recognised the truth. They knew Calcraft's reputation. It took unending minutes for John to strangle to death.

Some women fainted; a man as well. Many exclaimed, 'This is dreadful!' All seemed shocked at the absence of the scaffold rituals –the speeches and ceremonies that usually dignified these occasions and helped build tension until the final dramatic conclusion.

For an hour John's body dangled in the strong gusts, twisting one way then the other, becoming grotesque with swollen veins and lividity. Below, the more eager spectators handed over their pennies to purchase the 'full, true and particular account' of his execution, with its woodcut illustration, as a souvenir. Avidly, they began to read the broadside report that, surprisingly, showed marked differences to the event they had just witnessed.

Above them, the sun burst from behind the clouds with unusual brilliancy.

~~~

'Judicial butchery!' the *Manchester Guardian* blasted.

'They turned him off like a dog!' exclaimed the spectators, more in sorrow and disgust than anger.

'A just observation,' railed *The Times* correspondent, still bitter at being refused admission to the gaol. 'It was truly a hang-dog affair.' He continued his diatribe, declaring that there was nothing about the ceremony to serve as an example to the badly disposed (although surely, under capital punishment's guiding principles, such a horrible demise was the ultimate deterrent). He denounced the event as being badly organised, adding that it shouldn't have taken place before the scheduled time, that it lacked the appropriate air of authority because only the executioner and turnkey could be seen on the scaffold, and that there was no solemnity to the proceeding. In truth, the crowd bestowed their own air of solemnity through their quietness and horror at John's death struggle.

The thousands of spectators who watched the hanging were soon joined by more, those who hadn't expected the entertainment to commence until 8 a.m. All they saw was John's body swinging in the breeze. Others who arrived even later – having thought midday was the appointed hour – saw nothing more than the gallows being taken away. They too grabbed copies of the 'full, true and particular account' of the execution as consolation.

The authorities had decided in advance that John's body would remain on the gallows for only an hour. They wanted to dispel the public excitement and disperse the crowds as speedily as possible. Accordingly, at 8.45 a.m., his body was taken down.

'The removal of the body was quite consistent with the rest of the resulting exhibition,' the disgusted *Times* correspondent reported, 'for it was not cut down. Instead the turnkey held up the legs while the executioner untied the rope, which was certainly a new one and probably considered worth saving for some purpose or other.'

Calcraft tied a handkerchief around John's head and face and the two men laid his remains in the cheap elm coffin. Before the clock chimed a quarter past nine, John's coffin had been lowered into a grave at the back of the courthouse, near the large gates opening onto Walton Street. Only the chaplain, officials and turnkeys were there to farewell him.

After John's body disappeared, the spectators began to disperse. Within a short time, the square looked little different to a standard market day, except for the public houses and beer shops filled to overflowing. A large booth was erected near the station for dancing; fights broke out; a publican was robbed; life went on as normal.

As trains carried the spectators out of town over the course of the day, voices from the platforms at the stations along their route called out to inquire if the passengers had come from 'the doings' at Aylesbury. 'How did he die? How did he die?' they demanded to know.

'He died hard!' the passengers yelled back, to the satisfaction of all.

As the guards slammed the doors, those waiting on the platform called out one last question: 'Did he confess?'

CHAPTER 35

A respectable garb, sedate demeanour and outward
benevolence have seldom concealed a more wicked and
unprincipled heart.

Annual Register
(1845)

MR SHERRIFF was a man of his word. The previous day, when
rebuffing the angry pressmen demanding access to the prisoner,
he had assured them he would provide his own recollections and
impressions afterwards. Later on the Friday morning, after he
had attended the burial and dealt with the essential paperwork,
he called a meeting of the press.

As the reporters gathered around, Sherriff hesitated, overcome with emotion for the moment. For three months he had
walked beside John Tawell, coming to know him, to genuinely
care for him. Two hours ago he had watched him die a brutal
death. When he could collect himself, he began to recount the
events of the previous evening and early morning.

Around midnight, after determining that the letters John had
given him to post did not include a statement of any kind,
Sherriff returned to the 'condemned cell' to speak with John.
He began by reminding him that he had assured Lord Nugent
he would make a statement.

'Do I stand engaged to leave something of the kind behind?' John responded reluctantly.

His friend Sherriff told him that he had given his promise. 'Truth and justice and society demand such a disclosure.'

'Well, then, I will. I will do it,' John said. Sometime later, he sat down at the table and wrote a letter. He sealed it and kept it in his side pocket, pulling it out every so often and glancing at it with trepidation as though hesitant to hand it over, then tucking it away again.

Sherriff had thought John would include this letter in the final batch he handed over after breakfast. After skimming through them, however, he realised that it was not among them.

'Mr Tawell,' he urged, 'I think there was some promise made me of a statement you intended leaving.'

John had been hoping to avoid such a late request. He replied, grudgingly: 'If I promised, I will do so.' He pulled out the letter written earlier in the evening and read it over. Then he copied it out again and tossed the old version into the fireplace. Warily, he walked over to Sherriff and handed it to him, stating as he did so that he was entrusting it into the chaplain's care.

Sherriff passed the letter to Reverend Cox who was still in attendance. Cox opened the envelope and slid out the sheet of paper, the statement the nation had been waiting for. It was short. As he scanned the lines, he realised that this was not the denial of an innocent and unjustly treated man. Nor was it the exculpation of one who had found himself in an acrimonious situation and had lashed out rashly and fatally.

By this time, John was sitting by the fire leaning his head against the mantle-piece. He could hold in the words no longer. 'Yes, I am guilty of the crime,' he admitted at last. 'I put the prussic acid into the porter, and I also attempted the crime in September last, not by prussic acid, but by morphia.'

He then made a strange request, one that would have unexpected long-term consequences. He asked the chaplain to keep his confession private, neither reading out the words nor making any copy of it. He added, however, that he had no objection to the purport of his confession being communicated to the public.

———

'John Tawell made a full and ample confession of his guilt, although it is in rather brief terms,' Mr Sherriff told the pressmen. They besieged him with questions. One stood out among all the others: 'Why?'

Tawell said that it wasn't for financial reasons, the gaoler explained. He said that he didn't begrudge Sarah Hart her allowance. Instead he lived in constant dread that his wife would find out about her.

The reporters demanded to see the confession for themselves. That's when the trouble began. Sherriff explained that Tawell had given his statement to the chaplain, obtaining his promise that neither the confession itself nor a copy would be released to the public. All eyes turned towards the chaplain. The pressmen implored, the under-sheriff insisted, the Buckinghamshire magistrates ordered.

'I really cannot enter into it. I can say nothing about it – anything at all,' cried the beleaguered chaplain, claiming that it was his duty to comply with John's dying request and to refuse all demands, official or otherwise.

'Reverend Cox's silence is likely to be limited,' reported *The Sunday Times* complacently. 'When he is at liberty to make a disclosure he will do so. Tawell would not otherwise have written the memorandum merely for the perusal of one man, to whom a verbal confession would have been in that case as conclusive of his guilt.'

But John had demanded the word of a man of God, and Reverend Cox had given it. The issue became the subject of furious debate in the papers, particularly in the religious press, and also at the Aylesbury quarter sessions. Eventually it was raised in the House of Lords. Should the chaplain as an officer employed by the magistracy be obliged to hand over a confession offered to him while serving in that role? The divide between church and state, the rule of canon law, even the importance of confession within the Episcopal doctrine, were in play.

Then the magistrates learnt that Reverend Cox had transmitted copies of the confession to the Home Secretary Sir James Graham and to Judge Baron Parke, thereby breaching his sacred promise. They appealed to the Home Office, still without success. After raising the matter at every quarter session for another fifteen months, they at last left the chaplain in peace.

⁀

Britain felt widespread relief that John had confessed. The pressmen could not recollect any other case in which the nation was so anxious for a confession to remove all doubt.

Then conspiracy theories surfaced, claiming that the mysterious statement was a complete fabrication intended to quieten the public's doubts, and that by refusing to hand it over there was little risk of exposure as the handwriting couldn't be compared with John's own. 'Looking at the character of Tawell and his demeanour from first to last, it requires no depth of penetration to discern that he was the last man to make *a confession* of his guilt,' wrote the *Railway Bell*, showing a marked distrust of authority, whether church or state, or a desire to drum up more business. 'That Tawell's life was justly forfeited, there can be no rational doubt. As to his confession – *Credat Judaeus.*'

That John Tawell did confess in his last hours, there can be no doubt. The substance of his confession, however, was a truly contentious issue. Two decades afterwards, his defence barrister, Fitzroy Kelly, raised the subject at a Parliamentary Commission into capital punishment. When asked if cases of poisoning offered a particular danger of wrongful conviction, Kelly blithely told the commissioners, 'There was a most remarkable proof of it in the case of John Tawell, who was undoubtedly guilty but who was convicted, sentenced to death and afterwards executed upon evidence from medical men and chemists regarding the way in which the woman had taken the poison which turned out to be wholly erroneous. Only a little while before his death, he told the whole truth to Lord Nugent and some other Buckinghamshire magistrates. Though he freely admitted that he had poisoned the woman, he told them, and proved to them, that it was in a totally different way, so that the evidence of these people, the whole system of evidence upon which the man was convicted, was absolutely incorrect from beginning to end.'

This wasn't the first time such a claim had surfaced. Kelly had made a similar comment in a letter to British toxicologist Dr William Herapath, an attendee at John's trial. The letter was quoted in the *American Law Register* in 1857. The journal's editor remarked that although this extraordinary version of the murder had leaked out, they had no authority to cite regarding the actual details.

It was a startling revelation. Was it true: that John had not only verbally confessed to the magistrates, he had also claimed – indeed, proved – that he had administered the poison in some other manner? Evidently he had disclosed something to Lord Nugent and the other magistrates on that Tuesday evening before his execution because, later that night, he wrote to

Quaker minister Hannah Chapman Backhouse to advise that he had made a 'full confession'. What had he told them?

Correspondence half-a-century later in *Notes and Queries* offered a few clues. After bracketing Tawell's name with that of another criminal, the editor explained, for those unfamiliar with his story, that he 'slew a woman under circumstances of such revolting cruelty as to defy description'.

Although not intended to be provocative, the throwaway line generated responses from across the nation, most quoting the contemporary newspaper accounts and ridiculing this sensationalist claim. However one correspondent, Edward Peacock, confirmed that the circumstances of Sarah Hart's death were indeed of revolting cruelty, that he had heard so from a most trustworthy source but couldn't bear to put the details into writing.

The editor latched onto Peacock's statement, declaring that the full particulars were never divulged in print as the newspapers hadn't dared provide them. 'Not even in the "decent obscurity of a dead language", and certainly not in written or spoken English, could we convey what we know,' he wrote, adding pompously that readers should take these assertions on trust and not seek to obtain further information.

That was simply too patronising and evasive for the distinguished public prosecutor Henry B. Poland, a man widely respected and later knighted for his work in major criminal cases. He mentioned having heard the rumour himself a short time after the trial although, like most others, he had dismissed it and long forgotten it. 'It is clear that not a tittle of trustworthy evidence has been produced to prove that Tawell ever wrote or said anything to justify the positive assertion of yourself and Mr Peacock,' he declared, before asking snidely if the editor's 'trustworthy' source was the same as Mr Peacock's.

The editor snapped that his information was from a different source – an eminent Fellow of the Royal Society, in fact! – and refused to disclose anything more. The topic died away, along with those who 'knew' the sordid details.

Neither John's confession nor the two known copies have surfaced since his execution. The truth about the events of 1 January 1845 will probably never be known.

~

Was John even the man who died the horrible death on the Aylesbury gallows? Many had their doubts. A police officer appearing before a House of Lords Select Committee in 1856 to answer questions about public executions expressed his concern that if executions were no longer public, the community would wonder if deceptions were practised and criminals allowed to escape. 'Even up to the present day,' he said, by way of example, 'many persons do not believe that John Tawell was executed.'

And what about the 'extraordinary disclosure relating to the murder' that some newspapers hinted at even before John's meeting with the magistrates? Despite promises to elaborate on this topic after the execution, no further information was published – unless Miles's Boy was alluding to the same subject.

The vitriolic Miles's Boy didn't allow John's death to silence him. A few weeks after the hanging, he wrote another letter to the *Bucks Gazette*, this time reporting that he had journeyed to Aldeby to question its inhabitants about a certain rumour that he had heard: 'the first piece of capital villainy committed by the fiery-headed scoundrel – viz. the murder of the poor little boy'. He had limited success, he admitted, as the Aldeby folk maintained an 'imperturbable silence'. From the information he did gather, he could supply the press with a weekly epistle about John Tawell for the next year if he wanted to, he claimed. Of course, he didn't.

It wasn't scandal-mongering alone that kept John's name in the public notice. Concerns about funding for criminal trials, capital punishment, public versus private executions, botched executions, the distinction between premeditated murder and manslaughter, and the inequalities between rich and poor in retaining counsel brought his name to Parliament's attention over and over again. Lawyers used his case as a legal precedent. The courts and press mentioned it when other cases relied upon circumstantial evidence or hinged upon the testimony of scientific witnesses. Medical and pharmaceutical books and journals continued the debate about the effects of prussic acid for decades. The press raised parallels whenever men killed their mistresses to save themselves money, or killed their mistresses with poison, or used poison to kill anybody at all. They also gleefully reminded their readers of Fitzroy Kelly's 'blubbering' when another barrister tried similar theatrics, or ridiculed the 'apple pips' defence when another tried something equally unlikely. A minor author, John Cleveland, drew upon John's story when forming the experiences of his protagonist in *The Children of Silence*. One of John's statements even passed into common parlance for a time, with wags admonishing friends who accosted them: 'Thou must be mistaken in thine identity!'

Some issues were mere trivialities, others of grave importance. Immediately after John's execution, the people of Aylesbury united to fight capital punishment, with Lord Nugent leading the charge. At a public rally, Lord Nugent told the assembled multitude:

> *About a month ago, John Tawell stood in that dock,*
> *righteously, I think, convicted on strong evidence of a*
> *murder as black, as deliberate, as cruel as the human*
> *mind can contemplate. From that dock he was ordered*
> *to the scaffold to be publicly deprived of the life that*
> *God gave him, for example's sake. What was the*
> *example? The space below was crowded by the curi-*
> *ous but the feeling was deep horror of the spectacle*
> *and the suffering. What was the result? Before the*
> *sun had set, the public-houses were echoing with the*
> *sounds of revelry. The streets were thronged with*
> *drunken quarrels and ruffianly fights. A publican*
> *was robbed. So much for the example!*

But it wasn't only the efficacy of the example that concerned Lord Nugent. It was the deeper public perception:

> *On that scaffold stood two men: the one a murderer;*
> *the other the law's executioner. I ask you which of*
> *these two, the murderer and the hangman, was the*
> *object of sympathy and which of disgust and repul-*
> *sion? Why is he who carries out the law's sentence to*
> *be a 'man forbid', the object of repulsion and disgust?*
> *Why? Because public opinion, the natural feelings of*
> *man, are against the law.*

Loud cheering greeted Nugent at the conclusion of his speech. He was returned to Parliament at the next election, riding the crest of Buckinghamshire's abhorrence of the death sentence. Two decades later, legislation against public hangings was passed. It took another century for an enlightened Government to abolish executions altogether.

Chapter 36

No man morally sane could have been guilty of that crime upon so pitiful a provocation.

Robert Louis Stevenson, *The Strange Case of Dr Jekyll and Mister Hyde* (1886)

❧

BACK IN Berkhampstead, Sarah Tawell was waiting to hear that her beloved husband had been martyred for a crime he did not commit. When the messenger arrived with the dreaded tidings, she greeted him calmly and listened to the news with fortitude. Then the messenger reported that her husband had confessed.

It took a long time for her to recover from the shock and heartbreak – if she ever truly did. How does one live with the knowledge of having married such a man, fathered a child by such a man, loved and trusted one who could not only commit such a heinous deed but could look at her afterwards and ask her to continue loving and believing in him because he was innocent. And not just innocent of one attempt at murder, but two – which meant that, after the first time, he had come back to their home, come back to their bed, and carried on as if nothing had happened, all the time believing that he had committed the perfect murder.

When had he realised that the woman had survived the first attempt? Had he purchased the local newspapers, poring over every column to see if there was any mention of a tragic death in Salt Hill? Had he travelled to the village on that Monday evening

before Christmas to find out for himself if she was dead? Did
he spend Christmas Day plotting his next attempt at murder?
Who was this man she had loved so dearly?

⤙⤙

The words of John's brief confession, secondhand though they
were, offered profound insights into his troubled mind, not only
in their contents but in their essence. He admitted attempting to
kill Sarah Hart twice, so his actions were coldly premeditated.
He also claimed that he killed her not for the money but for
fear that his wife would learn of her existence.

But his wife already knew about her, according to a
Berkhampstead friend. Sarah Tawell had reportedly found a
letter from the woman in John's pocket, a request for money
on the grounds that she hadn't received her allowance and
was suffering difficulties. When John arrived home, she had
confronted him with the letter. 'Why, what claim, John Tawell,
can any woman living have on thee?' John had replied evasively,
so she knew there was more to the matter than he was willing
to explain.

That pleading letter, no doubt, sealed Sarah Hart's fate.
While she remained hidden away, a dutiful servant to his needs
and manipulations, he accepted her existence and willingly
supported her and her children. When she wrote to him complaining of her financial difficulties, when she found her voice
and demanded to be heard, she upset the rules of his game. In
doing so, she promoted herself from pawn to queen, suddenly
powerful and dangerous and, what was worse, unpredictable.
Like many courtiers in days gone by, John decided that the best
way to control the errant queen was to lop off her head.

Yet why resort to such a drastic step? The explanation can
be found in John's emotional longings. He craved respect and

acceptance above all else, not only from the broader community and the Quakers, but from his second wife. To John, this intelligent and exceedingly capable gentlewoman was his soulmate, Victoria to his Albert. When everything else was disintegrating around him, she remained his staunch ally, adoring and supporting him. To lose her respect at such a dreadful time of his life would be simply too much to bear.

Nevertheless, to resort to murder merely to maintain his wife's respect was an extreme step, particularly for one who had tried for nearly half-a-century to live by the code of a deeply religious body. Was he truly religious or, as Britain's press would conclude, 'a hypocrite unparalleled in the criminal annals of any country'?

For instance, what did he think he would gain by his decision to confess? Confessing to such a crime would destroy his reputation in the eyes of the whole world – not just the eyes of his wife. Of course, by this time John's horizon had shifted. He was looking beyond the temporal world to the spiritual. To confess – that is, to prove that he truly acknowledged and repented his sins – would offer him a passage to heaven, gaining him eternal 'respect' in God's kingdom, his earthly sins forgiven by his benevolent maker. To not confess, however, was a one-way ticket to hell.

John was a true believer, as well as a determined strategist. He knew that he had to confess to save his soul, although he chose the coward's way out, confessing at the last moment so that he didn't have to face his wife in the aftermath. If he had admitted his sins beforehand, the chance of a reprieve based upon the medical and scientific uncertainties would also have slipped away from him.

Cunning ran side by side with cowardice, traits embedded in his criminality itself. In the hierarchy of brutality, poisoning and forgery were cowardly offences. They were non-confrontational crimes, evasive yet insidious toxins that crept through businesses and bodies with the deadly effects of a gun or a knife, but with more fright attached to them, somehow, because the victims could not see the threat coming.

John's own victims suffered because he saw them – and others – as a means to achieving his own ends. He used Sarah Hart for sexual gratification, discarding her when she no longer suited him and making her vanish, first metaphorically and later physically, to protect his own reputation. He cared little for his illegitimate children. He was even selfish in his pursuit of Sarah Cutforth, knowing that her decision to marry him would lead to her expulsion from the Quakers and the loss of her way of life. And his selfishness continued. One newspaper mused that, to save his wife's feelings, John had committed a deed that plunged her into the deepest misery. In truth, it wasn't his wife's feelings that drove him to commit the murder, only his own. It all came down to *his* fear and *his* suffering if she learnt the truth and viewed him differently. Confessing was the ultimate sign of his selfishness. In so doing, he might have secured himself a place in 'heaven', but he succeeded in destroying his wife.

Yet while John was deeply flawed, he had positive qualities as well. His kindness could be seen in his personal generosity and his charity work, particularly his efforts in establishing schools for the poor. Moreover, John had the love of three worthy women, the friendship of many pious Quakers (including the discriminating missionaries James Backhouse and George Washington Walker), and the respect of the shrewd Sydney business community.

Surely the *desire* to do good, to be good, to be thought good, reflected some innate worth within the man. Which leads to the obvious question: was John Tawell a true Jekyll-and-Hyde character, a riven soul – perhaps even an unconscious model for Robert Louis Stevenson's seminal protagonist?

If John at an early age had recognised an ugliness within and wanted to control it, he might have seen Quakerism as a vehicle for achieving mastery over his dark impulses. Not only were the Quakers a wealthy and respected sect wearing a garb that seemed to make them incorruptible, their creed was founded upon a belief in a personal relationship with an omnipotent deity and the infusion of divine wisdom. Their God offered spiritual guidance, a providential helping hand.

But Quakerism was an unsuitable faith for one such as John. Its standards were too high and its reactions to major sins and minor regulatory breaches were equally harsh. Moreover, there is an inherent danger in any 'faith' that believes a supernatural being guides personal choices – not the least because of the difficulty in determining if one's impulses stem from 'spiritual guidance' or personal desire? Some might argue that the scriptures provide the framework, in the same way that the law sets boundaries to distinguish acceptable from criminal behaviour. But the law changes all the time as society's moral compass shifts: what was once acceptable (slavery and wife-beating, for example) is now criminal; what was once criminal (contraception, homosexuality) is now acceptable. Laws vary from country to country and from state to state. There is no simple right and wrong. The same is true of Biblical injunctions and 'divinely-inspired' behaviour. The decision to choose missionary work, for example – or historically, to participate in a Crusade – may be considered praiseworthy among those with a particular religious affiliation, little realising that religious bigotry, arrogance and intolerance can destroy cultures and lead to war.

If there is no simple right or wrong, legally or spiritually, the fall-back position has to be an individual's moral code. Yet if a religious devotee's moral compass is misaligned, then a faith that believes in divine inspiration is particularly dangerous. Perhaps this off-kilter moral compass underlies some of John's paradoxical behaviour, the Dr Jekyll receiving one 'message' while Mr Hyde received another. Nor would his experiences in the New South Wales penal settlement have helped a man struggling to set definitive moral boundaries. He saw the poor being hanged for theft and the rich getting away with murder, and his own punishment for wrong-doing gained him almost everything he had wished for. It was the wrong message for someone fighting personal demons.

John tried hard to fight them. In the final months of 1844, he visited Quaker psychic Peter Bedford twice, and also wrote to his missionary friend James Backhouse. Neither provided the inspiration or the warning he needed to triumph over adversity. He was a deeply troubled man when he left his Berkhampstead home on the morning of 1 January 1845, never to return.

Backhouse wasn't among the Quakers who visited John at Aylesbury. He lashed out at John in a letter written to his friend George Washington Walker some time afterwards: 'Thou art so well aware of the evil that has often shown itself in his character that I conclude no fresh development of moral turpitude on his part would greatly surprise thee!' This from the man who had entrusted New South Wales Quakerism into his care, who had only ever referred to John and his wife in his letters and diaries as our 'dear friends'. Had Backhouse and Walker truly sensed 'evil' lurking within John, as Peter Bedford had, or was it simply a matter of hindsight? The Quaker committees that rejected his applications for readmission had perceived serious flaws in John's character. It is not surprising. In the lay terminology of today, John Tawell would be branded a psychopath.

John's mask slipped enough times to expose his inner soul. He was the devotee who sat through Quaker meetings plotting to rob his brethren. He was the aspirant who assured a Quaker committee that he truly believed in their moral and religious codes and the beau who vowed love for a Quaker woman, while illicitly fathering children with his housekeeper. He was the ex-lover who left justificatory Bible verses while plotting against her. He was the gentleman who wore his virtuous Quaker garb while murdering the mother of his children.

John Tawell was a devil dressed up as a saint, one of the kindly, charming, generous, pious breed who fool almost everyone – including, in John's case, his wife.

⟶

Sarah Tawell and her two children remained in the Red House at Berkhampstead for the following four years, struggling to support themselves for much of that time. John's pre-emptive deed assigning his estate to trustees was invalidated upon his conviction and execution, and his estate automatically escheated to the Crown. Sarah had to battle not only for a provision for herself and her children, but to have her own money released as well. In the end, the Crown reached a settlement with John's trustees, handing most of his assets back to his surviving family.

Early in 1849, Sarah and her two children moved to Essex to reside near John's brother, William Tawell, who had provided so much emotional and financial support during the troubles. The family circled their wagons, with Sarah's daughter Eliza marrying William's son Samuel in 1851. Sarah purchased a wheat farm in nearby Wakes Colne and around 1860 established her then seventeen-year-old son as farmer.

'Henry Augustus Tawell, who knew nothing of farming, would have preferred almost any other kind of business, but no one questioned Grandma's judgement – or authority!' wrote Henry's son in later years. 'So he had to make the best of it.' The indomitable widow built a new and successful life for herself and her offspring, eventually dying at Earls Colne on 16 October 1884. She never remarried.

Nor did Sarah abandon John's orphaned children. She included their claim in her own petition for the release of John's escheated estate and, in the meantime, provided funds for their continued support. The children remained in Gravesend with their grandmother, Grace, who decided to have them baptised with the surname Lawrence in the Wesleyan Chapel their own mother had once attended. Little Sarah didn't require much financial support as she died within the following two years. Grace joined her granddaughter in the Wesleyan cemetery in 1850. Alfred Lawrence was still residing with his newly remarried step-grandfather in 1851 but disappears from the records thereafter. Perhaps he saw opportunities in distant lands, setting sail for Australia or America or one of the other countries eager for young, willing, hard-working men and women.

While the Crown's financial settlement helped the Tawell family's funds, the consequent ripples grew into a tidal wave by the time they lapped Australian shores. Having released John's Antipodean properties to his trustees, the Crown's law officers advised their colonial counterparts to determine the lands' title and, if necessary, prepare the appropriate grants. Crown Solicitor George Cooper Turner was among those employed by John's lawyers to undertake the process. Turner authorised an auction without obtaining the necessary Crown grants – unwise but not illegal. After the purchasers handed over the money, however, he handed some to John's agents and decamped with the rest.

Aghast, John's trustees petitioned the Crown, whose legal officers decided that the sale was in fact illegal and agreed to another under the governor's grant but without refunding any of the purchasers' money. The purchasers fought back, supported by the colonial authorities, all arguing that the trustees' agents were at fault, so they were the ones who should bear the resulting financial loss. Dozens of letters sailed back and forth until eventually, in 1860, Britain ordered the New South Wales Governor-General Sir William Denison to grant the properties to John's trustees under the colony's Great Seal. Obligingly, Denison sent the duly prepared grant to the New South Wales Premier Charles Cowper to have the Great Seal affixed. Cowper bluntly refused and offered his resignation.

John Tawell had just acquired another 'first'. The financial affairs of the wealthy ex-convict murderer had precipitated the first constitutional crisis under responsible government in New South Wales. It left the press asking how much ministerial authority had truly been granted to the government under the much-vaunted constitution legislated only a few years beforehand.

The first constitutional crisis in New South Wales, the first Quaker meeting house in New South Wales, the first retail pharmacy in Australia, perhaps even the first veterinary service in the country: John Tawell's colonial blue ribbons alone would have bestowed upon him a minor celebrity status in their respective history books. His international blue ribbons, though, were of much more significance. He was the first British murderer convicted of using prussic acid – cyanide – as a weapon of destruction; today, this poison remains a favourite in the shadowy world of espionage, both real and imagined. He was one of the first murderers to use the railway as his getaway vehicle. Most importantly, he was the first murderer caught by the revolutionary electric telegraph.

The telegraph's subsequent nickname, the electric constable, conjures up images of policemen fighting crime with the most potent weapon of them all, the physical and moral power of 'God's lightning'. *Punch* would write: 'God's lightning is become a true and active thing. The inexorable lightning – the electric pulse – thrills in the wires. The murderer, who would not be swayed by the thought of heavenly lightning, may pause, awed by the thought of lightning ready – the unerring telegraph.' Within the decade, the electric constable's leading role in apprehending the infamous 'Quaker Murderer' was used as an argument for extending the telegraph across the whole of Britain – and, within a generation, for nationalising the system. But John Tawell's apprehension had even more extraordinary consequences – both nationally and internationally.

EPILOGUE

The telegraph even to this point was very little known to the great mass of the public, and might have continued for some time longer in obscurity but for its remarkable agency in causing the arrest of the Quaker Tawell. This event, which took place on [1 January] 1845, placed it before the world as the prominent instrument in a terrible drama, and at once drew universal attention to its capabilities.

Andrew Wynter, 'The Electric Telegraph',
Quarterly Review (1854)

SOME MONTHS after John's execution, Sir Francis Bond Head, late Lieutenant-Governor of Upper Canada, was travelling from London towards Slough in a crowded railway carriage. 'For nearly fifteen miles, no one had uttered a single word,' he would later write, 'until a short-bodied, short-necked, short-nosed, exceedingly respectable-looking man in the corner fixed his eyes on the apparently fleeting posts and rails of the electric telegraph, then nodded significantly to us all as he muttered aloud, "Them's the cords that hung John Tawell!"'

No longer were the telegraph wires invisible and unnoticed. The glare of public interest in the murder had illuminated them, the beam focusing in particular upon the electric telegraph machine itself. No longer was it merely a toy or an instrument of pleasure, but an agency for inflicting pain – a mortal wound, in Tawell's case. The consequences, in terms of the success of the electric telegraph, were profound.

For an innovative technology to succeed – indeed for any business to thrive – it requires, in the words of Malcolm Gladwell, a 'tipping point', a moment of critical mass when something happens that might seem small at the time, something that spreads knowledge of the product through the community with the speed of an epidemic. It can take only a single person and a single message to trigger such a tipping point, as Gladwell displays with the story of Paul Revere and the message that sparked the 'American Revolution' (as the British called it) – but it requires the right person and the right message at the right time, and the message itself needs to be powerful enough to stick in people's minds.

That's what happened with the electric telegraph. By Christmas 1844 the telegraph had survived its teething problems, and its list of clients was building. Interest, though, was growing slowly – for understandable reasons. The general populace knew little or nothing about the technology because publicity had been minimal. Between 1837 and 1844, Britain's major newspaper, *The Times*, included references to the electric telegraph in only a handful of articles each year – and, in some years, no references at all. Many regional newspapers never mentioned it. Consequently, when Cooke and Wheatstone – and Samuel Morse in America – attempted to sell the technology to potential clients or investors, they were often starting from a foundation of unfamiliarity, not just of electricity and the electric telegraph but, in these days before mass education, sometimes of general scientific principles in themselves. To convince each client of the electric telegraph's value for their business required a drawn out, costly, difficult selling cycle. Their own businesses would not expand with the rapidity needed to ensure success until something happened that gave the electric telegraph mass publicity, something that provided their potential clients and investors with a foundation of knowledge – preferably positive – about the telegraph and its worth as a vehicle for rapid communication. Something they couldn't forget.

Then this man in the peculiar garb was caught by 'the wires'. Not only was the means of his capture remarkable and memorable, so was Tawell himself. His intriguing life story, his exotic religious customs, the bewildering paradox of his character, the uncertainties and complexities of his case: all presented a mystery that unfolded in the weeks of the investigation and trial with the pace of a Dickens serialisation. Tawell's story captured the nation's attention. It was reported in city and regional newspapers, in railway, religious, scientific, medical and legal journals. Such broad coverage spread his story across Britain like an epidemic. It also planted knowledge of the once little-known electric telegraph in the popular consciousness of the nation, then the world's leading empire with a reach far beyond its borders. But Tawell's story not only intrigued Britain, it angered the nation – so this knowledge settled not just in the reasoning, logical brain but in the amygdala, the ancient part of the brain that deals with emotions. And that made his story and, by extension, the electric telegraph unforgettable.

Tawell's apprehension provided the necessary foundation of knowledge about the electric telegraph for potential business clients and investors as well as the broader public. Moreover, Tawell's subsequent execution meant that the electric telegraph now insisted on being taken very seriously indeed – not only by business but as a potential crime-fighting weapon in the police force's arsenal. Such a public exhibition of its power was crucial in opening the financial floodgates. The Electric Telegraph Company was formed later in 1845 – and thrived.

The message that afforded Tawell's capture was the tipping point for the electric telegraph and the start of the Communication Revolution that would follow in its wake.

Within four years of Tawell's apprehension, 'the wires' carried messages to more than two hundred telegraph offices in England alone, nodes along the arteries radiating from the telegraph's dynamic heart in London. Visitors wandering along Lothbury opposite London's Bank of England saw the forefinger of a black hand pointing down an alley. At the bottom of a small cul-de-sac stood the office of the Central Telegraph Station, its tall, narrow facade boldly emblazoned with a clock-face above its arched doorway. Stepping inside, they found themselves in a handsome reception hall forty-five feet high with tiers of galleries cascading down its sides, all illuminated by a magnificent skylight. Lining one side of the ground floor was a long counter with green curtains partitioning it into six private desks. Hunched over the desks were human forms of all shapes and sizes painstakingly writing expensive words onto pre-printed forms.

When completed, the forms were pushed through a glass window into the Booking Office, where they were checked and annotated then slipped into a box that flew up through a chimney to the Instrument Office in the 'attic'. There, nimble-fingered youths manned eight compact instruments inscribed with the station names along their particular artery. Ringing a telegraphic bell, they alerted all the operators along their line, then indicated which station was to receive the message. A moment later they began transmitting, each hand holding a brass handle attached to a dial, each wrist twisting and turning the dial to communicate the relevant letters of the telegraphic alphabet. The quivering movements of the dials at the receiving station were deciphered by their counterparts, who forwarded the message to their own Booking Office to be dispatched to the intended recipient.

The Central Telegraph Office also contained an Intelligence Department. It condensed important and interesting snippets from the London morning newspapers and forwarded them by 8 a.m. to the central telegraph stations in the major country towns, where the local press eagerly took in the details. Prices of shares and funds, shipping arrivals and departures, losses at sea, Parliamentary and general news of the day: information that in the past would not have reached Manchester until mid-afternoon, or Glasgow until late at night, was available around breakfast time. Information itself had become a commodity that people were willing to pay substantial sums to receive.

Twenty years on, submarine cables carried telegraph lines across some of the world's major oceans. Another two decades later, standard time zones were established to divide up the globe. The world's nations had begun the journey towards a global community, connected in a manner previously imagined only by visionaries. And the once slowly spinning cycle of supply and demand began to spin ever faster, a petulantly unceasing demand for more information and speedier access *now*.

The electric telegraph would be the harbinger of peace, according to Britain's press and literary journals, allowing the free exchange of ideas and the clear communication of perspectives, eliminating the power of demagogues and despots, creating a global community, a united world, utopia. A utopia with British traditions, of course. The electric constable would keep a stern eye on all and sundry.

What of the spiritual world? If the mysteries of electricity allowed instantaneous communication with distant family and friends, why not with departed family and friends, a link between heaven and earth? The Victorian séance-goers were intrigued by the possibilities; the Ouija board had a competitor. Perhaps the electric constable could patrol both this life and the hereafter?

As it turned out, like every new invention the electric telegraph had its downside, becoming a vehicle for crime, particularly gambling on the horses or stock exchange, as well as a means for political control and repression. Yet, similarly to the Internet today, the benefits far outweighed any disadvantages. Although the hidebound initially ridiculed the technology and dismissed its potential, and the religious shouted apocalyptic warnings, they could no more halt the life-changing effects of this new form of communication than they could control lightning itself.

As the first commercial use of electricity, the electric telegraph also proved that this remarkable power source could be harnessed and exploited with limitless possibilities. Today, electricity drives our world: our homes and businesses, our trains, cars, boats and planes; indeed, the widespread destruction of the world's electricity grids would be catastrophic, destroying life as we know it. It also spawned our current telecommunications systems – telephone, television, radio and the Internet. With the advent of the electric telegraph came the beginning of the information age, and the world that we inhabit today.

As the sun rose on the information age it set on John Tawell's life, yet his twilight still hasn't ended. A broad range of disciplines have embraced his story and used it for literal or metaphorical purposes of their own: in the fields of communications and transportation, in electricity, engineering and physics, in pharmacy, medicine, chemistry and toxicology, in forensic science, criminology and criminal psychology, in media studies and popular culture, and, of particular interest today, the Internet. Tawell's story is more than simply the intriguing tale of a peculiar man pursued by the electric constable at the dawn of the information age. It continues to resonate beyond its origins, challenging not just the intellect, but the imagination.

Indeed, there is a delicious irony in his story, as if a Greek dramatist had deliberately crafted his tale of hubristic downfall. The arrogant man who believed in his own cleverness and invincibility, who had long hidden his demons behind a mask of piety, was unmasked by the mask itself. If Tawell hadn't worn his Quaker garb, the historic message would not have been sent, and he would, quite literally, have got away with murder. Yet it was the vehicle of his destruction that lifts his story from that of a simple morality tale to an epic, a tale for all time. He mocked the gods and broke their rules and they wreaked their vengeance through 'God's lightning' itself. Hubris writ large.

AUTHOR'S NOTE

Each time historians like myself begin to research a new topic, we start with a shadowy outline, as if the past is a jigsaw puzzle laid out in front of us with only a superficial picture and some scattered pieces positioned on the board as a guide. To find the remaining pieces and determine where they fit in, we must become historical detectives who are driven by the thrill of the hunt and by our stubborn determination to find even the most tiny, seemingly inconsequential piece of information, because we know that the best details and the best stories are found in the most unexpected places.

I first came across John Tawell's name when writing a history of my First Fleet ancestors' family. My resulting one-sentence reference to Tawell – he was robbed by someone connected with the family – led a reader to ask if I knew that he was later executed in England for murder. His name cropped up again and again in the following years – as so often happens – and it was only after I had become a professional writer that I discovered the details of his astounding story. This historical detective was hooked.

Naturally, I returned to the original historical records to research his life story. I soon realised that previous treatments had mostly been brief and superficial – and often error-ridden. He proved to be a more multi-layered individual and his story one of greater importance than others had realised.

So how does one communicate such a story? Many historians draw out the facts and write the story as an ongoing narrative from the perspective of an omniscient narrator, as if they had watched the events unfold through time-warp binoculars and are recounting what they saw – with the addition of exposition and analysis as required. The truth is: there are no time-warp binoculars. Historical records rarely provide an overarching narrative. Instead, they document fragments of information from a moment in time – a birth record or a census entry, for example – and accounts provided by individuals. Much of the information relating to Tawell's story comes from the inquest and trial testimonies of those caught up in the drama. But when the details drawn from these testimonies are combined to produce a single stream of narrative, viewed through the lens of an omniscient narrator the drama and immediacy of the individuals' experiences are lost. History can seem dry as a result.

Initially, though, any story has to be built up as a simple narrative, brick by brick, through exhaustive research. Among other records, I examined over a hundred British newspapers for the four-month period from January to April 1845, not only searching for the important facts (court records and half-a-dozen newspapers were enough to provide those) but for the little details that added to the visual picture. One newspaper mentioned that a bottle and two glasses were sitting on a table in Sarah Hart's house, another that the glasses were tumblers, another that the bottle was dark, another that it had a Guinness label, and so on. Each detail was added to the narrative until eventually the rows of bricks formed a three-dimensional house.

Once it is time to structure and layer the story, my approach is to get closer to the roots of the individuals' experiences. The witnesses and others involved in the drama stood in the witness box and recounted their personal experiences: 'I saw', 'I heard', 'I thought', 'I felt', 'I said', 'I did'. Their testimonies provided a graphic account of their own part in the drama. Not only do we hear what they said, we hear what others replied – including the protagonist. So, to offer readers the immediacy of fiction without fictionalising the narrative, I let these individuals live their own stories. When they 'enter stage left', they effectively become the narrator. It is their point of view we hear as recounted by them in their own descriptions of their involvement. For dramatic effect, however, rather than repeating everything they said in the relevant courtroom scene in the narrative, I put the exact words of the recounted conversations into their own mouths at the time of the events they are describing. The immediacy of the resulting drama, action and dialogue reflects history written in the active-voice narrative, rather than the usual passive-voice narrative. It helps bring history to life and offers the immediacy of fiction, without fictionalising the narrative.

To clarify: the dialogue in this book is not made up. Imagined historical conversations often reflect how a writer thinks historical characters would have spoken – and, more importantly, reflect what is considered acceptable among today's publishers and readers. I quote people's words as they said them. Accordingly, the dialogue may sometimes seem stilted and unnatural, a consequence of the differences between the language of 1845 and the language of today.

In bringing such a story to life, it is also important to read between the lines and to consider the subtext. What is not said can be even more important than what is said. It is necessary to have empathy, to close one's eyes and put oneself in a character's shoes and consider what he or she would be thinking and feeling at the time. When Mrs Mary Ann Ashlee stood at Sarah Hart's door hearing her moans, she looked back at the Quaker fleeing down the road and thought she saw him looking back at her. She reported that she had shivered. It was a cold winter's night. Was she shivering from cold – or fear? Empathy provides the answer. And that can be communicated using the many tools of fiction that narrative non-fiction can draw upon: stream-of-consciousness, metaphor, simile, personification and so on, again without the need to fictionalise the narrative.

Many people expect history to be written only in the passive voice and fiction in the active voice, failing to recognise that factualness and style are separate tools in the writer's toolkit. Bringing history to life, making it vivid and exciting, is a function of how it is written. History has the best stories. I hope you all enjoy my rendition of this fascinating tale.

⁓

John Tawell's story involved background research into a number of different topics and disciplines: the electric telegraph, the railways, Quakerism, pharmacy, chemistry, toxicology, criminal psychology and many more. While a writer must necessarily go back to the original records in investigating the protagonist and the events in question, it is impossible to start from scratch in every other discipline. I had several experts and outside readers assist me with some of the critical areas that were outside my range of knowledge. However, I take full responsibility if I have made any errors despite that assistance.

John Liffen, Curator of London's Science Museum where the electric telegraph that apprehended John Tawell is held, was of great assistance with details of the electric telegraph technology of the time. He sent me an article he wrote, 'The Introduction of the Electric Telegraph in Britain, a Reappraisal of the Work of Cooke and Wheatstone' (2010), which made it clear that errors had been made in the original attribution of some of the instruments, and even errors in comments made in later years by the inventors themselves regarding the equipment they used. These errors led to mistakes being made in many publications discussing the electric telegraph. Accordingly, I relied on John Liffen's conclusions in my publication and I thank him for his assistance.

I also wish to thank my other readers: Keith Johnson, my erstwhile mentor and employer, and long-time friend; Kate Wingrove, who continues to be 'always right'; Mike Elliott, a Stoke Pogis resident who has long been fascinated by and gathered information about John Tawell, and has not only been of great assistance to me, but has become a friend; Jeffrey Bloomfield, a US crime writer who has also taken a great interest in John Tawell and wanted to write a book about him – until I pipped him to the post (sorry about that); Nicholas Evens, a descendant of John Tawell, who by the most incredible coincidence visited the Library of the Society of Friends in London on the day I popped in for a final quick visit before catching a plane back to Australia, his wife Hilary, who has become immersed in researching John's second wife, Sarah Appleby/Cutforth/ Tawell, and their niece Bryony Evens; writer John Porter, who read the manuscript and provided some useful editorial suggestions; and also Anne Hare, and the late Ben Dwyer.

My very great thanks to my literary agent, Tara Wynne, for her wonderful support over many years as well as her valuable suggestions for the Tawell manuscript, and also to Pippa Masson and Annabel Blay for helping when Tara was on leave; to my publisher at Oneworld, Robin Dennis, for jumping at the opportunity to publish John Tawell's story internationally and for her exhaustive and helpful edit; and to Holly Roberts and Ruth Deary for their involvement as copy-editor and editor. I also wish to thank my publisher at Allen & Unwin, Rebecca Kaiser, for eight years of much-appreciated support and friendship through thick and thin.

Also my grateful thanks to Trevor Allen, who kindly drove me long distances to places of interest when I was visiting the Slough district; Dr Kathryn Watson, a crime specialist with a particular interest in poisonings; Associate Professor Christopher Keep, University of Western Ontario; Professor Donald W. Black, University of Iowa College of Medicine; Dr Michael Stone, Professor of Clinical Psychiatry at Columbia and a true-crime specialist; Dr Tom Perera, Professor Emeritus of Psychology at Montclair State University; Garey Barrell, Edward Rankins and Steven Roberts, who have a particular interest in the electric telegraph; Michael Palmer, Archivist of the Zoological Society of London; Dr Michael Green, Emeritus Professor of Forensic Pathology at the University of Sheffield; Dr Dick Roe, veterinary historian; Michael Neaylon, for alerting me to Malcolm Gladwell's *The Tipping Point*; Sarah Charlton and Rachel Simon, Centre for Buckinghamshire Studies; Zoe Gray, Gravesend Library; Eve McClure, Norfolk Heritage Centre; Jennifer Milligan and the staff at the Library of the Society of Friends, London; Wendy E. Chmielewski, Curator of the Swarthmore College Peace Collection and Christopher Densmore, Curator of the Friends Historical Library at Swarthmore College, Pennsylvania; Gwyn Jones, Local Studies Librarian at Hillingdon, Greater London; Jenny Sherwood of the Berkhamsted Local History & Museum Society; Sara Mihajlovic of the British Library and the other staff at the library itself and at the then newspaper library at Colindale; the staff and librarians at the National Archives at Kew, Aylesbury Library and the Centre for Buckinghamshire Studies, Bank of England Archives, Bedfordshire Record Office, the Steam Museum of the Great Western Railway, Guinness Archives, Norfolk Record Office, Society of Genealogists, London, Mitchell

Library, Sydney, and State Records of New South Wales; and also Sam Bellringer, David Lea, Randall McGowen, Ian Middleton and Fay Richardson.

Finally, to my very precious family who always complain that I leave them until last. That's because they are the most special and appreciated of them all: my beloved husband, Allan Ashmore, and offspring, Camillie and Jaiden, and mother, Jill Baxter. Thank you for always being there for me – even when you get bored listening to me talking about my latest 'friends'!

BIBLIOGRAPHY

The bibliography provides a list of the major primary and secondary sources examined. More detailed information is found on the book's website, including an extensive annotated timeline documenting information found for John Tawell and his two wives and mistress, newspaper dates and page references, information about collateral connections (relatives, friends and others mentioned in the book), and a more extensive secondary-source bibliography organised by subject. For these more detailed source references, please visit: www.johntawell.com

PRIMARY SOURCES – AUSTRALIA

AUSTRALIAN RECORD REPOSITORIES

Mitchell Library, Sydney, New South Wales

Articles re John Tawell from *Truth* magazine found in Newspaper Cuttings [ML ref: Q991.1/N; Reel FM4/7955]

Backhouse, J. and Walker, G.W. 'Reports &c: Letter to Colonial Secretary', 13 May 1836 [ML ref: B706 Vol. 1, p.347; Reel CY 1736]

Bonwick Transcripts: William Redfern to John Thomas Bigge [ML ref: BT Box 26 pp.6215–19]

Colonial Office Miscellaneous letters re NSW, 1832: Case of John Stephen Jnr. [ML ref: A 2146 p.394; CY 1011]

Convict Return 1816: John Tawell [ML ref: HO 10/3 fol.254; PRO Reel 60]; & 1817 [ML ref: HO 10/8 fol.268; PRO Reel 61]; & 1818 [ML ref: HO 10/10 fol.334; PRO Reel 63]; & 1819 [ML ref: HO 10/1 fol.168; PRO Reel 60]; & 1820 [ML ref: HO 10/13 fol.217; PRO Reel 64]; & 1821 [ML ref: HO 10/16 fol.165; PRO Reel 65]

Diary of James Backhouse [ML ref: B731; Reel CY1698]

Journal of George Washington Walker, 23 Jul 1835 [ML ref: B713–B717; Reel CY 464]

List of applicants for their wives and families to be sent to this colony at the expense of the Crown, 12 Feb 1822: John Tawell [ML ref: A1198 p.226 No.49; CY Reel 519]

NSW Calendar & Post Office Directory 1832, 1835, 1836 & 1837

State Records of New South Wales, Kingswood, New South Wales

Colonial Secretary In-Letters – Letter: John Tawell, 24 Feb 1836 [SRNSW ref: 4/2323.3 No. 36/1834]

Colonial Secretary In-Letters – Petitions: John Tawell, 7 Dec 1818 [SRNSW ref: 4/1856 p.265; Fiche 3190]; & 1 Jan 1820 [SRNSW ref: 4/1861 p.81; Fiche 3204]; & 7 Oct 1825 [SRNSW ref: 4/1875 p.225; Fiche 3252]

Colonial Secretary In-Letters 'Proceedings of a Medical Board held at the General Hospital, Sydney, by order of Governor Macquarie to enquire into the state of disease in the colony commenced on 2 and ended 9 June 1820' [SRNSW ref: 4/1744 p.75; Reel 6049]

Colonial Secretary In-Letters re Land: John Tawell, 24 Dec 1827 [SRNSW ref: 2/7985 No.27/11789; Reel 1188]; 19 & 20 Dec 1828 [SRNSW ref: 2/7985 Nos.28/10186 & 28/10187; Reel 1188]; 30 Aug 1831 [SRNSW ref: 2/7985 No.31/6778; Reel 1188]; 24 Feb 1836 [SRNSW ref: 4/2323.3 No. 36/1834]

Colonial Secretary Out-letters: to John Tawell, 10 Nov 1825 [SRNSW ref: 4/3515 p.573; Reel 6015]

Colonial Secretary Out-letters: to Newcastle Commandant, 16 Dec 1815 [SRNSW ref: 4/3494 p.286; Reel 6004]

Colonial Secretary Out-letters: to Principal Supt of Convicts Office, 20 May 1831 [SRNSW ref: 4/3670 pp.500–1 No. 31/417; Reel 2649]

Convict Indent – *Marquis of Wellington* 1815: John Tawell [SRNSW ref: 4/4005 p.32; Reel 393; Fiche 635]

Conditional Pardon: John Tawell, 1820 [SRNSW ref: 4/4430 p.146; Reel 774]

Escheated lands of the late John Tawell: Indenture signed by John Tawell, 31 Jan 1845 [SRNSW ref: 4/3478 No.62/4647 pp.21–24 Enclosure No. 1 in 32]

Surveyor General: John Tawell to Surveyor-General Oxley, 18 Mar 1826 [SRNSW ref: 2/1711]

Land and Property Information, Sydney, New South Wales

Old System Land Records

Newspapers

For complete bibliographic details, including article titles and dates, please visit the notes associated with the timeline of events at www.johntawell.com

Atlas

Australian

Colonist

Commercial Journal and Advertiser

Courier (Hobart)

Maitland Mercury

Monitor

Parramatta Chronicle

Sentinel

Star & Working Man's Guardian

Sydney Gazette

Sydney Herald

Weekly Register of Politics, Facts and General Literature

PRIMARY SOURCES – BRITAIN

BRITISH RECORD REPOSITORIES

Bank of England

Committee for Lawsuits: John Tawell, 2 Feb 1814 [BE ref: M5/314 p.91]
Freshfield Papers: Forged and Other Imitation Bank Notes – 1814 Bank
  Notes: John Tawell [BE ref: F2/107]

Bedfordshire Record Office, Bedford

Society of Friends: Albans Monthly Meeting – Friends Removal Certificate
  from Peel Monthly Meeting: Sarah and Eliza Sarah Cutforth, 23 Dec
  1829 [BLARS ref: FR 2/7/5/79]
Society of Friends: Albans Monthly Women's Meeting (1830–33): Sarah
  and Eliza Sarah Cutforth, 8 Jan & 12 Feb 1830 [BLARS ref: FR
  2/2/2/5]; also Sarah Cutforth, 1 Oct & 10 Dec 1830, 8 Apr, 10 Jun,

8 Jul, 17 Aug, 11 Nov 1831, 13 Jan, 14 Dec 1832 [BLARS ref: FR 2/2/2/5]; and (1833–40): Sarah Cutforth, 10 May, 13 Sep, 8 Nov, 13 Dec 1833, 14 Mar, 3 Oct & 14 Nov 1834 [BLARS ref: FR 2/2/2/6]

Society of Friends: Albans Monthly Meeting: List of members: Sarah and Eliza Sarah Cutforth [BLARS ref: FR 2/7/1/2] Society of Friends: Albans Monthly Men's Meeting: Sarah Cutforth, 14 Nov & 12 Dec 1834 [BLARS ref: FR 2/1/1/6]

Society of Friends: Hogstyend Monthly Meeting Minutes, 1825: William Cutforth to Peel [BLARS ref: FR 4/1/1/6]

Society of Friends: Removal Certificate – Wellingboro Monthly Meeting to Hogstyend Monthly Meeting: William Cutforth, 1812 [BLARS ref: FR 4/7/5/112]

Centre for Buckinghamshire Studies, Aylesbury

Church Registers: Farnham Royal Baptism Register: Charles Howard, 7 Apr 1844 [BKS ref: PR 74/1/4]; and Burial Register: Sarah Hart (surname later changed to Laurence), 9 Jan 1845 [BKS ref: PR/74/1/20]

Society of Friends: Upperside Monthly Women's Meeting (1807–35): Sarah Cutforth, 4 Dec 1834, 1 Jan 1835 & 23 Sep 1835 [BKS ref: NQ/2/3/3]; also 29 Sep 1836, 27 Sep 1837, 1 Mar 1838, 5 Sep 1839, 5 Mar 1840, 3 Dec 1840, 7 Jan & 4 Feb 1841, 4 Mar & 1 Apr 1841 [BKS ref: NQ/2/3/4] Society of Friends: Upperside Monthly Men's Meeting: re Sarah Cutforth, 4 Mar & 1 Apr 1841 [BKS ref: NQ/2/1/8]

Society of Friends: Upperside Monthly Women's Meeting: Eliza Sarah Cutforth, 5 Apr, 3 May, 7 Jun & 5 Jul 1849 [BKS ref: NQ/2/3/4]

General Register Office, London

Birth Certificate: Henry Augustus Tawell, 1843 [GRO ref: Sep Qtr 1843 – Berkhampstead, Hertfordshire, Vol. 6, p.461]

Death Certificate: John Tawell, 1845 [GRO ref: Jun Qtr 1845: Aylesbury, Buckinghamshire, Vol. 6, p.225]

Death Certificate: John Downing Tawell, 1843 [GRO ref: Jun Qtr 1843 – Islington, Middlesex, Vol. 3, p.173]

Death Certificate: Mary Tawell, 1838 [GRO ref: Dec Qtr 1838 – Marylebone, Middlesex, Vol. I, p.164]

Death Certificate: Sarah Hart, 1845 [GRO ref: Mar Qtr 1845 – Eton, Buckinghamshire, Vol. 6, p.225]

Death Certificate: Sarah Tawell, 1884 [GRO ref: Dec Qtr 1884 – Halstead, Essex, Vol. 4a, p.298]

Death Certificate: William Tawell, 1876 [GRO ref: Mar Qtr 1876 – Halstead, Essex, Vol. 4a, p.271]

Death Certificate: Ann Lawrence (unable to find)

Death Index: Grace Hadler [GRO ref: Mar Qtr 1850 – Gravesend, Kent: Vol. 5, p.129]

Death Index: Thomas Hadler [GRO ref: Sep Qtr 1856 – Gravesend, Kent: Vol. 2a, p.139]

Marriage Certificate: John Tawell and Sarah Cutforth, 1841 [GRO ref: Mar Qtr 1841 – Berkhampstead, Hertfordshire, Vol. 6, No.558A]

Hertfordshire Local Studies, Hertford

Queen's Warrant granting messuage formerly called Boxwells with three acres and a messuage in High Street, the property of John Tawell, convicted murderer, to trustees for benefit of family, 1847 [HLS ref: D/EX 177/21]

Humanities Research Institute, Sheffield

The Proceedings of the Old Bailey: John Tawell 1814 [http://www.oldbaileyonline.org/html_units/1810s/t18140216-58.html & -59.html]

Library of the Society of Friends, London

Account book of James Backhouse and G.W. Walker 1831–41 [LSF ref: MS Vol. S 355]

Devonshire House: Monthly Meeting: re John Tawell – Vol. 14 (1802–10) [LSF ref: 11 b 2 p.426 No. 11; p.453 No. 27; p.516 No. 6; p.521 No. 10; p.529 No. 7; p.535 No. 11]; Vol. 17 (1831–43) [LSF ref: 11 b 2 p.424 No.3; pp.433–4 No.11]; Vol. 18 (1843–44) [LSF ref: 11 b 2 p.26 No.15; p.31 No.12; pp.32–3 No.9] Devonshire House: Monthly Meeting: Register of Members (1788–1830) – John Tawell; William and Sarah Cutforth [LSF ref: 11 b 2]

Devonshire House: Six Week Meeting: Vol. 18: re John Tawell [LSF ref: 11 a 2 p.236]

Devonshire House: Meeting For Sufferings: re John Tawell, 3 April 1840 [LSF ref: MFS/M/45 p.22 No.8]

Digest Register of Deaths, 1838–1961, Surnames S–Z: Mary Tawell, 1838; and John Downing Tawell, 1843 [LSF ref: Reel 381]

Friend's Meeting for Sufferings: Letter from John Tawell, 4 Dec 1839 [LSF ref: MSS Portfolio Vol. 17, pp.115–6]

Letter: James Backhouse Letters (1837–41): to Abraham Davy & Robert Andrew Mather, 4 Jul 1838 [Ref: MS Vol. S69, p.51]

Letter: James Backhouse to John Tawell, 16 Nov 1844 [LSF ref: MS Vol.58]

Letter: Aunt G. Edmonds to Priscilla Rutter, 8 Feb 1845 [LSF ref: MS Portfolio B No.79]

Letter: John Tawell to Hannah Chapman Backhouse, 25 Mar 1845 [LSF ref: MSS 337 pp.135–6]

Obituary for William Henry Tawell in *Annual Monitor* 1834 pp.32–3; and for Mary Tawell in 1840 p.36; and for Sarah Tawell in 1885 p.192 [LSF]

Quaker Dictionary of Biography: Henry Augustus Tawell, John Tawell and Mary Tawell [LSF]

Extracts from the Journal and Letters of Hannah Chapman Backhouse, unpublished, 1863, pp.270–1 [LSF]

Peel Monthly Meeting Minutes: William Cutforth and Sarah Appleby, 24 Aug 1825 No. 2, 21 Sep 1825 No.5, & 5 Oct 1825 [LSF ref: 11 b 5]

Peel Monthly Meeting Minutes: re William Cutforth, 23 Nov & 21 Dec 1825, 18 Jan 1826 [LSF ref: 11 b 5 pp.414, 420, 425 & 427 No.8]

Peel Monthly Meeting – Register of Members, Vol. 18 (1816–25): William and Sarah Cutforth [LSF ref: 11 b 5]; Vol.19 (1826–37): William Cutforth, Sarah Cutforth and Eliza Sarah Cutforth [LSF ref: 11 b 5]

The National Archives, Kew, Surrey

Assizes: Norfolk Circuit, Buckinghamshire, Lent Assizes, 1845: J. Tawell, Murder Depositions [TNA ref: ASSI 36/5]; Gaol Book [TNA ref: ASSI 33/14]; Indictment Files [TNA ref: ASSI 94/2448]

Chancery: Draft Special Commission to enquire into and seize the effects and lands of felons: John Tawell, 1847 [TNA ref: C 217/160]

Chancery: Petty Bag Office: Special Commissions of Inquiry – Murder and Felonies: John Tawell, 24 Apr 1847 [TNA ref: C 205/16/13]

Bankruptcy Commission Files: Phillips, F. and Cutforth, W., 1825 [TNA ref: B 3/3993]

Home Office: Criminal Registers, Buckinghamshire, 1845: John Tawell [TNA ref: HO 27/75; ML ref: PRO Reel 2816]

Home Office: Criminal Registers, Middlesex, 1814: John Tawell [TNA ref: HO 26/20 f. 112; ML ref: PRO Reel 2735]

Home Office and Prison Commission: Prison Records – Newgate, London: List of Felons 1814 – Common Side: John Tawell [TNA ref: PCOM 2/187]; and Master's Side [TNA ref: PCOM 2/188]

Home Office: Criminal Petitions, Series II: Petitions regarding John Tawell, Mar 1845 [TNA ref: HO 18/153/49]

Metropolitan Police: Murder of Sarah Hart [TNA ref: MEPO 3/49]

Great Western Railway Collection – Letter: Thomas Home to Great Western Railway, 2 Mar 1887 [TNA ref: RAIL 1014/17]

Society of Friends: Durham: Newcastle Monthly Meeting – Register of Births: Sarah Appleby, 14 Apr 1802 [TNA ref: RG 6/404 p.7]

Society of Friends: London and Middlesex Quarterly Meeting – Register of Births: Eliza Sarah Cutforth, 1828 [TNA ref: RG 6/952 p.164]; Register of Marriages: William Cutforth and Sarah Appleby, 1825 [TNA ref: RG 6/1158 p.3]; Register of Burials: William Cutforth, 1827 [TNA ref: RG 6/1047 p.224] and William Henry Tawell, 1833 [TNA ref: RG 6/1126 p.38]

Treasury Solicitor and HM Procurator General: Law Officers' and Counsel's Opinions – John Tawell: The disposal of escheated and forfeited property, 17 Aug 1847 [TNA ref: TS 25/320]

Treasury Solicitor and HM Procurator General: Law Officers' and Counsel's Opinions: Escheated property – The grant of escheated property in New South Wales: John Tawell, 31 Aug 1853 [TNA ref: TS 25/708]

Treasury Solicitor and HM Procurator General: Royal Warrant assigning back to Sarah Tawell the escheated property of John Tawell, 30 Dec 1847 [TNA ref: TS 25/858]

Treasury Solicitor and HM Procurator General: Bona Vacantia, Administration of Estates Papers – Letters of Administration: John Tawell, 1847 [TNA ref: TS 17/940]

Census Returns of England

Electronic scans accessed via Ancestry.co.uk; original documents held by the National Archives, Kew, Surrey

Census, 1841: Stoke Newington, Middlesex: Eliza Cutforth [TNA ref: HO 107/669 Book 5, Enumeration District 3, folio 16, p.25; GSU roll 438784]

Census, 1841: St Marylebone, Middlesex: Sarah Hart and family [TNA ref: HO 107/679, Book 7, Enumeration district 9, folio 14, p.21; GSU Roll 438795]

Census, 1841: Gravesend parish, Kent: Thomas and Grace Hadler [TNA ref: HO 107/458, Book 8, Enumeration District 3, folio 9, p.12; GSU roll 306852]

Census, 1851: Feering, Essex: Sarah Tawell and family [TNA ref: HO 107/1783, folio 407, p.29; GSU roll 207432]; also Earls Colne, Essex: William Tawell (brother) and family [TNA ref: HO 107/1784, folio 9, p.10; GSU roll 207433]

Census, 1851: Gravesend parish, Kent: Thomas Hadler and Alfred Lawrance [TNA ref: HO 107/1608, folio 64, p.15; GSU roll 193508]

Census, 1861: Earls Colne, Essex: Sarah Tawell and family [TNA ref: RG 9/1111, folio 19, p.32; GSU roll 542755]

Census, 1871: Earls Colne, Essex: Sarah Tawell [TNA ref: RG 10/1698, folio 25, p.11; GSU roll 830745]; also Wakes Colne, Essex: Henry A. Tawell and family [TNA ref: RG 10/1692, folio 8, p.10; GSU roll 829971]

Census, 1881: Earls Colne, Essex: Sarah Tawell [TNA ref: RG 11/1802, folio 91, p.12; GSU roll 1341435]; also Wakes Colne, Essex: Henry A. Tawell and family [TNA ref: RG 11/1799, folio 130, p.8; GSU roll 1341434]

Norfolk Record Office, Norwich

Bastardy Bond – Thomas Tawell, 1779 [NRO ref: PD 713/45/13; Reel MF/RO/535/3]

Church Registers: Aldeby Parish [NRO ref: PD 676; Reel MF/RO 14B] and Horsham St Faith [NRO ref: Reel MF/RO 529/8]

Church Wardens Accounts: Aldeby Parish [NRO ref: PD 676; Reel MF/RO 14B]

NCC Probate Records – Administration Bond: James Downing 1782 No. 2 [NRO ref: Reel MF 142]

Society of Genealogists, London

Vicar General Marriage Allegations: John Downing Tawell and Isabella Bethia Blyth, 6 Nov 1833 [SG ref: Reel FC 64]

Directories

Holden's Triennial Directory, 1809–11: J. Tarvel (between Tavistock and Tax)
Pigot & Co.'s London Directory, 1828: William Cutforth
Pigot & Co.'s Directory – London and Provincial, 1832: Kent – Gravesend – Thomas Hadler

Pigot & Co.'s Royal National and Commercial Directory and Topography of Counties of Essex, Herts and Middlesex, 1839: Hertfordshire – Sarah Cutforth, p.97

Post Office Directory for Cambridgeshire, Norfolk, Suffolk, Essex, Hertfordshire, Kent, Middlesex, Surrey, Sussex, 1846: Hertfordshire – John Tawell, p.1075; Essex – William Tawell, pp.58, 995 & 988

Newspapers *(coverage of the 1814 crime)*

For complete bibliographic details, including a full listing of article titles and dates, please visit the notes associated with the timeline of events at www.johntawell.com

Aylesbury News (1845)

Morning Chronicle (1814)

Morning Post (1814)

Observer (1845)

Railway Bell (1845)

The Sunday Times (1845)

The Times (1845)

Newspapers *(coverage of the 1845 crime and trial)*

For complete bibliographic details, including a full listing of article titles and dates, please visit the notes associated with the timeline of events at www.johntawell.com

Aberdeen Journal

Age and Argus

Atlas

Aylesbury News

Bell's Weekly Messenger

Berkshire Chronicle

Birmingham Journal

Bristol Mercury

Britannia

British Friend

Bucks Gazette (1844 and 1845)

Bucks Herald

Bury and Suffolk Herald and Yarmouth Chronicle

Caledonian Mercury

Churchman's Family Newspaper

County Chronicle, Surrey Herald and Weekly Advertiser
Derby Mercury
Dover Chronicle and Kent and Sussex Advertiser
English Churchman
Era
Evening Mail
Examiner
Freeman's Journal
Globe
Go-a-head
Hampshire Telegraph and Sussex Chronicle
Hertford Mercury and Hertford and Bedford Reformer
Historical Register
Hull Packet and East Riding Times
Illustrated London News
Inquirer
Ipswich Express
Ipswich Journal
Jackson's Oxford Journal
John Bull
Kentish Mercury, Gravesend Journal and Greenwich Gazette
League
Leeds Mercury
Liverpool Mercury
Lloyds Weekly London Paper
London Journal
Magnet
Manchester Guardian
Manchester Times and Gazette
Monthly Times
Morning Advertiser
Morning Chronicle
Morning Herald
Morning Post
Newcastle Chronicle
Newcastle Courant
Newcastle Journal
News of the World
Norfolk Chronicle

Norfolk News
Norwich Mercury
Nonconformist
Northern Star and Northern Trades Journal
Observer
Patriot
Pictorial Times
Pioneer Newspaper and Oddfellows Journal
Preston Guardian
Punch, or the London Charivari
Railway Bell and Illustrated London Advertiser
Reading Mercury, Oxford Gazette, Newbury Herald and Berkshire County Paper
St James Chronicle
Sentinel
Spectator
Standard
Suffolk Chronicle
Sun
The Sunday Times
Sussex Advertiser
The Times
Trewman's Exeter Flying Post or Plymouth and Exeter Advertiser
Watchman
Weekly Chronicle
Weekly Dispatch
Wesleyan and Christian Record
West Kent Guardian, Rochester and Chatham Standard, and Gravesend and Milton Express
Windsor and Eton Express
Young England

PRIMARY SOURCES – OTHER

Church of Jesus Christ of Latter Day Saints, Salt Lake City, Utah, USA – Microfilms of Original Records

Church Registers: Chatham Parish Records: Baptisms: Sarah Lawrence, 1805 [LDS ref: Reel 1473647] and Marriages: Thomas Hadler and Grace Lawrence, 1814 [LDS ref: Reel 1469318]

Church Registers: St James, Westminster: Marriage – John Tawell and Mary Freeman (1808 No. 378) [LDS ref: Reel 1042318]

Church Registers: Wesleyan Records for Ebenezer Chapel, Milton next Gravesend, Kent: Baptisms – Hadler family (1815–27) [LDS ref: Reel 1482375 Item 15]

SECONDARY SOURCES

Abbott, G. and Little, G. *The Respectable Sydney Merchant: A.B. Spark of Tempe*. Sydney, Sydney University Press, 1976

Account of the New Universal Hall of Commerce in Threadneedle Street. London, Pelham Richardson, 1843

Adam, Hargrave L. *Old Days at the Old Bailey*. London, Sampson Low, 1932

Adam, Hargrave L. *The Police Encyclopaedia*, Vol. 5. London, Waverley Book Company, 1920, pp.69–77

Altick, R.D. *Punch: The Lively Youth of a British Institution, 1845–51*. Columbus, Ohio State University Press, 1997

'Ambrose Foss and John Tawell' in Newspaper Cuttings Vol 116 (no page) [ML ref: F991.1/N; Reel FM4/2277]

'Anecdotes from a Blue Book' in *Eclectic Magazine*, New Series, Vol. 3 (1866), p.685

Appleby, Pauline *A Force on the Move: The Story of the British Transport Police 1825–1995*. Malvern Wells (Worcestershire), Images, 1995

Backhouse, James *Extracts from the letters of James Backhouse now engaged in a religious visit to Van Diemen's Land and New South Wales accompanied by George Washington Walker*. London, Harvey and Darton, 1838

Ballantine, William *Some Experiences of a Barrister's Life*. London, Richard Bentley and Son, 1882 [pp.124–6]

Bank of England [http://www.bankofengland.co.uk/about/index.htm]

Bateson, Charles *The Convict Ships 1787–1868*. Sydney, Library of Australian History, 2004

Beatty, Bill *Tales of Old Australia*. Sydney, Ure Smith, 1966

Becker, Bernard H. *Scientific London*. London, Frank Cass and Co., 1968

Beddard, Frank Evers *Animal Coloration: An Account of the Principal Facts and Theories Relating to the Colours and Markings of Animals*. London, Swan Sonnenschein, 1892

'Berkhampstead St Peter: Introduction, honour, manor and castle',

A History of the County of Hertford: Volume 2 (1908), pp.162–71.
[http://www.british-history.ac.uk/report.aspx?compid=43265]

'Berkhamsted link with murder trial' in *Berkhamsted Gazette* 9 Jan 1970 p.4

Bertie, C.H. and others 'A remarkable criminal – The strange career of John Tawell' in *Peeps at the Past: Early Australian History*. Sydney, James R Tyrrell, 1914 [ML ref: Q990.1/B pp.59–60]

Birks, G. Fred 'An Early Australian Chemist and Druggist' in *The Australasian Journal of Pharmacy* 20 Sep 1921 pp.550–3

Birtchnell, Percy C. *Bygone Berkhamsted*. Luton, White Crescent Press, 1975

Birtchnell, Percy C. *Short History of Berkhamsted*. Berkhamsted, P.C. Birtchnell, 1972

Blythe, Richard *Danger Ahead: The Dramatic Story of Railway Signalling*. London, Newman Neame, 1951

Boast, Mary *The Story of the Borough*. London Borough of Southwark, 1997

Boddy-Evans, Marion *Artist's Pigments: The Accidental Discovery of Prussian Blue* [http://painting.about.com/cs/colourtheory/a/prussianblue.htm]

Booker, Frank *The Great Western Railway: a new history*. London, David and Charles, 1977

Borowitz, Albert *The Woman Who Murdered Black Satin: The Bermondsey Horror*. Columbus, Ohio State University Press, 1981

Boulton, W.H. *The Railways of Britain: Their History, Construction and Working*. London, Sampson Low, 1950

Bourne, J.C. *The History and Description of the Great Western Railway*. London, David Bogue, 1846

Bowden, Richard *Marylebone & Paddington*. Stroud, Alan Sutton Publishing, 1995

Bowen-Rowlands, E. *Seventy-two Years at the Bar: A Memoir*. London, Macmillan and Co., 1924

Bowers, Brian *Sir Charles Wheatstone FRS: 1802–75*. London, The Institution of Electrical Engineers, 2001

Braithwaite, W.C. *The Beginnings of Quakerism*. Cambridge, Cambridge University Press, 1955

Briggs, C.F. and Maverick, A. *The Story of the Telegraph and a History of the Great Atlantic Cable*. New York, Rudd & Carleton, 1858

'British Penal Discipline' in *The Journal of Prison Discipline and Philanthropy*. Pennsylvania Prison Society, Vol. 3 (July 1848), p.141

Broadbent, J. and Hughes, J. *The Age of Macquarie*. Melbourne, Melbourne University Press, 1992

Brodsky, Isadore *Heart of the Rocks of Old Sydney*. Neutral Bay, Old Sydney Free Press, 1965

Brodsky, Isadore *The Streets of Sydney*. Sydney, Halstead, 1962

Brophy, John *The Meaning of Murder*. New York, Thomas Y. Crowell, 1966

Browne, G.L. and Stewart, C.G. *Reports of Trials for Murder by Poisoning*. London, Stevens and Sons, 1883

Buckland, Jill *Mort's Cottage 1838–1988*. Sydney, Kangaroo Press, 1988

Bunce, N. and Hunt, J. *The Science Corner: History of Cyanide* [http://www.physics.uoguelph.ca/summer/scor/articles/scor176.htm]

Burgon, J. W. 'Martin Joseph Routh' in *Lives of Twelve Good Men*. London, John Murray, 1888

Burney, Ian *Poison, Detection and the Victorian Imagination*. Manchester, Manchester University Press, 2006

Butler, David M. *The Quaker Meeting Houses of Britain*. London, Friends Historical Society, 1999

Byrne, Richard *Prisons and Punishments of London*. London, Harrap, 1989

Calcraft, William *The Groans of the Gallows*. London, E. Hancock, c.1846 [British Library]

Calcraft, William *The Life and Recollections of William Calcraft, the Hangman* [British Library]

Campbell, W.S. 'Tawell, the Chemist' in *RAHS* Vol.13 (1927), pp.201–2

Centre for Buckinghamshire Studies: Victorian Crime – Aylesbury Gaol [http://www.buckscc.gov.uk/archives/education/victorian_crime/prison.htm]

Centre for Buckinghamshire Studies: Victorian Crime – Death by Hanging and other Punishments [http://www.buckscc.gov.uk/archives/education/victorian_crime/Victorians_Teaching_Pack.pdf]

Chancellor, E. B. *Life in Regency and Early Victorian Times: An Account of the Days of Brummell and D'Orsay, 1800–50*. London, B.T. Batsford, 1927

Chant, Christopher *The Golden Age of Steam*. Rochester (Kent), Grange Books, 2000

Christison, Robert 'Notice of a Case Illustrative of the Treatment and Fatal Dose in Poisoning with Hydrocyanic Acid' in *Monthly Journal of Medical Science*, Vol. 10 (1850), pp.97–9

Clarke, John *Touched by the Devil: Inside the Mind of the Australian Psychopath*. Roseville NSW, Simon & Schuster, 2001

Clarkson, Thomas *A Portraiture of Quakerism* (1806). Teddington (Middlesex), reprinted Echo Library, 2006

Clegg, Brian *The God Effect: Quantum Entanglement, Science's Strangest Phenomenon*. New York, St Martin's Press, 2006

Clune, Frank *Saga of Sydney: The Birth, Growth and Maturity of the Mother City of Australia*. Sydney, Halstead Press, 1961

Coghlan, T.A. and Ewing, T.T. *The Progress of Australasia in the Nineteenth Century*. Toronto, Linscott, 1903

Cook, John 'The Berkhamsted Institute' in *Berkhamsted Review*, May 1993 p.5

Cook, John 'The Institute Goes' in *Berkhamsted Review*, 1 Aug 2001 pp.5–7

Cook, Robert *Around Aylesbury*. Stroud, Alan Sutton Publishing, 1995

Cooke, Thomas Fothergill *Authorship of the Practical Telegraph*, 1867 (pamphlet)

Cozens-Hardy, B. and Kent, E. *The Mayors of Norwich 1403–1835*. Norwich, Jarrold, 1938

'Crimes and Criminals' in *Old Times*, June 1903 p.232 [ML ref: Q991/O]

Crowell, Eugene, *The Identity of Primitive Christianity and Modern Spirituality*. New York, Eugene Crowell, 1875

Crowley, Frank *A Documentary History of Australia Vol. 1: Colonial Australia 1788–1840*. Melbourne, Nelson, 1980

Cumpston, J.S. *Shipping Arrivals & Departures, Sydney, 1788–1825*. Canberra, Roebuck, 1977

Cunningham, Peter A *Hand-Book for London, past and present*. London, J. Murray, 1849

Cunningham, Peter *Two Years in New South Wales*. Sydney, Angus and Robertson, 1827

Currey C.H. 'The Great Seal Case' in *RAHS* Vol.15 (1929), pp.267–82

Davidson, Jenny '"The Electric Constable": Telegraphic Language and the Capture of John Tawell, 1845–54' in *Nineteenth Century Prose*, Vol. 24 (Spring 1997), No.1, pp.7–11

'Decline' in *Slough Observer* 23 Feb 1895 p.3 [re tuberculosis]

Dickens, Charles *The Uncommercial Traveller*. Boston, Ticknor and Fields, 1867

Dilnot, George *The Story of Scotland Yard*. London, Bles, 1926

Disraeli, Benjamin *Selected Speeches of the Late Right Honourable the Earl of Beaconsfield*. London, Longmans, 1882

Dixon, Hepworth *The London Prisons*. New York, Garland Publishing, 1985

'Dr Christison on Poisons' in *The British and Foreign Medical Review*, 1845, pp.319–22

Dumas, Alexander 'Celebrated Crimes' in *The Eclectic Review*, Jan–Jun 1947, p.248

Elam, Charles *A Physician's Problem*. London, Macmillan, 1869

Ellis, Hamilton *Four Main Lines*. London, George Allen and Unwin, 1950

Engel, Beverly *The Jekyll and Hyde Syndrome*. Hoboken, New Jersey, John Wiley and Sons, 2007

Engravers and Engravings – Processes: Copper Plate Engraving in *Edinphoto* [http://www.edinphoto.org.uk/1_EDIN_V/1_engraving_and_engravers_processes.htm#copper]

Evans, David Morier *The City, Or, The Physiology of London Business*. London, Baily Brothers, 1845

Fahie, J. J. *A History of Electric Telegraphy to the Year 1837*. London, E. and F.N. Spon, 1884

Fang, Irving *Alphabet to Internet: Mediated Communication in Our Lives*. St Paul, Minnesota, Rada Press, 2008

Fleming, J.A. *Fifty Years of Electricity: The Memories of an Electrical Engineer*. London, Wireless Press, 1921

Fletcher, M. and Taylor, J. *Railways: The Pioneer Years*. London, Studio Editions, 1990

Forde, J.M. (Old Chum) 'John Tawell and the Society of Friends' in *Truth* 7, 14, 21 & 28 Feb 1926 and 7 Mar 1926 in Newspaper Cuttings Vol. D pp.182–6; 'John Tawell: Sydney's First Apothecary' in *Truth* 3 May 1908 in Vol. A pp.1[NN]-1[O]; 'John Tawell's Gift to the Quakers' in *Truth* 8 & 22 Mar 1925 in Newspaper Cuttings Vol. B pp.128–31; etc (see indices) [ML ref: Q991.1/27A1–4; Reel FM4/7710]

Fowler, J.K. *Echoes of Old Country Life*. London, Edward Arnold, 1892

Fox, C., Pym, H.N. and Mill, J.S. *Memories of Old Friends, Being Extracts from the Journals and Letters of Caroline Fox, of Penjerrick, Cornwall, from 1835 to 1871*. London, Smith Elder, 1882

Francis, John *A History of the English Railway, its Social Relations and Revelations: 1820–45*. Newton Abbot, David and Charles, 1851

Fraser, Maxwell *Companion into Buckinghamshire*. London, Methuen and Co., 1950

Fraser, Maxwell *History of Slough*. Slough, Slough Corporation, 1973

Freeman, M. and Aldcroft, D. *The Atlas of British Railway History*. London, Croom Helm, 1985

Gibbs, Robert *A History of Aylesbury*. Aylesbury, Robert Gibbs, 1885

Gibbs, Robert *Buckinghamshire: A Record of Local Occurrences and General Events*. Aylesbury, Robert Gibbs, 1882

Gladwell, Malcolm *The Tipping Point: How Little Things Can Make a Big Difference*. London, Abacus, 2000

Gordon, Kevin 'The murder of Sarah Hart 1845' in *British Transport Police* [http://www.btp.police.uk/History%20Society/Publications/History%20Society/Crime%20on%20line/Murder%20of%20Sarah%20HART%201845.htm]

Gourvish, T.R. *Railways and the British Economy: 1830–1914*. London, Macmillan, 1968

Great Yarmouth's History [http://web.ukonline.co.uk/members/g.woodcock/gyarm/history/history.htm]

Greer, Sarah D (Mrs J.R.). *Quakerism: Or, The Story of My Life*. London, R.B. and G. Seeley, Whittaker and Co., 1852

Haines, Gregory *The grains and threepenn'orths of pharmacy*. Kilmore (VIC), Lowden, 1976

Halliday, Stephen *Newgate: London's Prototype of Hell*. Stroud, Sutton Publishing, 2006

Harper, Charles G. *The Bath Road: History, Fashion and Frivolity on an Old Highway*. London, Cecil Palmer, 1923

Hayward, Arthur L. *The Days of Dickens: A Glance at Some Aspects of Early Victorian Life in London*. London, George Routledge and Sons, 1926

Head, Sir Francis Bond *Stokers and Pokers, or, The London and North-Western Railway, the Electric Telegraph, and the Railway Clearinghouse*. London, J. Murray, 1849

Henson, G *History of J. Tawell with his life, trial, confession and execution*. Northampton, G. Henson, c.1845

Holden's Annual Directory, 1814 and 1815: Country Banks – Uxbridge

Holder, R.R. *Bank of New South Wales: A History*. Sydney, Angus and Robertson, 1970

Howell, S. and K.*Norwich City Freemen, 1752–1981* (unpublished manuscript), 1999 [NRO]

Hubbard, Geoffrey *Cooke and Wheatstone and the Invention of the Electric Telegraph*. London, Routledge and Kegan Paul, 1965

Hubbard, Geoffrey *Quaker by Convincement*. Harmondsworth, Penguin, 1974

Hull, Gillian 'From Convicts to Founding Fathers – Three Notable Sydney Doctors' in *Journal of the Royal Society of Medicine*, Vol. 94 (July 2001), pp.359–61)

Humphrey, Stephen *Southwark, Bermondsey and Rotherhithe*. Stroud, Alan Sutton Publishing, 1995

Hunter, J. and Thompson, I. *Slough: A Pictorial History*. Chichester, Phillimore, 1991

Isichei, Elizabeth *Victorian Quakers*. London, Oxford University Press, 1970

Jeans, W.T. *Lives of the Electricians: Professors Tyndall, Wheatstone and Morse*. London, Whittaker and Co., 1887

Jerrold, Walter *Douglas Jerrold, dramatist and wit*. London, Hodder and Stoughton, 1914

Jose, Arthur 'John Tawell' in *RAHS* Vol.18 (1932) pp.31–43

Jose, A.W. and Carter, H.J. *Australian Encyclopaedia* Vol. 2 (Tawell). Sydney, Angus and Robertson, 1926

Keep, Christopher '*Hung upon wires': Telegraphy, Murder and the Discourse Network of Victorian Britain*, speech at North American Victorian Studies Association Conference, 2003

Kendall, Revs. C. and H. *Strange Footstep: or Thoughts on the Providence of God; Illustrated by Incidents New and Old*. London, George Lamb, 1871

Kieve, Jeffrey *The Electric Telegraph: A Social and Economic History*. Newton Abbot, David and Charles, 1973

Kirby, Maurice W. *The Origins of Railway Enterprise: the Stockton and Darlington Railway, 1821–63*. Cambridge, Cambridge University Press, 1993

Koehler, Christopher *Consumption: the great killer* [http://pubs.acs.org/subscribe/journals/mdd/v05/i02/html/02timeline.html]

Lambert, Anthony J. *Nineteenth Century Railway History Through The Illustrated London News*. Newton Abbot, David and Charles, 1984

Langtry, Emilie Charlotte (re Cornwall Lodge) [http://www.manuscripts.co.uk/stock/20621.HTM]

Lardner, Dionysius [revised and rewritten by E.B. Bright] *The Electric Telegraph*. London, James Walton, 1867

Lardner, Dionysius *The Electric Telegraph*. London, Walton and Maberly, 1855

Laurence, John *A History of Capital Punishment*. London, Sampson Low Marston and Co., 1932

Le Strange, Hamon *Norfolk Official Lists*. Norwich, 1890 [NHC]

Lewin, H.G. *The Railway Mania and its Aftermath: 1845–52*, first published 1936, republished: Newton Abbot, David and Charles, 1968

Liffen, John 'The Introduction of the Electric Telegraph in Britain, a Reappraisal of the Work of Cooke and Wheatstone' in *International*

Journal for the History of Engineering and Technology, Vol. 80 No. 2, Jul 2010, pp.268–99

Lillywhite, Bryant *London Coffee House*. London, George Allen and Unwin, 1963

MacDermot, E.T. *History of the Great Western Railway: Volume 1 1833–63*, first published 1927, republished: London, Ian Allan, 1964

Mackerell, Benjamin *History of the City of Norwich, Both Ancient and Modern*, unpublished manuscript, 1737 [NHC]

Mackie, Charles *Norfolk Annals: A Chronological Record of Remarkable Events in the Nineteenth Century: 1801–50 (Volume 1)*. Norfolk, 1901

Maclean, J.L. *British Railway System*. London, McCorquodale and Co., 1883

Mansion House [http://en.wikipedia.org/wiki/Mansion_House,_London]

Marland, E.A. *Early Electrical Communication*. London, Abelard-Schuman, 1964

Matthews, P.W. *History of Barclays Bank Limited*. London, Blades, East and Blades, 1926

Mayhew, H. *The Criminal Prisons of London and Scenes of Prison Life*. London, Charles Griffin and Co., 1862

McLaughlin, Terence *Coward's Weapon*. London, Robert Hale, 1980

Mercer, David *The Telephone: The Life Story of a Technology*. Westport, Greenwood, 2006

Merrish, Gerry 'The Mechanics Institute' in *Berkhamsted Review*, Feb 2004 p.16–17

Miller, Geoff 'Famous Murderer Caught by the Wire' in *Pharmaceutical Journal* (Vol.269) 21/28 December 2002, pp.905–7 [http://pjonline.com/pdf/xmas2002/pj_20021221_bythewire.pdf]

Millican, Percy *The Freemen of Norwich, 1714–52*. Norwich, Norfolk Record Society Publications, Vol. 23, 1952

Milligan, E.H. *Biographical Dictionary of British Quakers in Industry and Commerce*. York, Sessions Book Trust, 2007

Milligan, E.H. *Quakers and Railways*. York, Sessions Book Trust, 1992

Mitchell, C. A. *Science and the Criminal*. London, Sir Isaac Pitman and Sons, 1911

Morgan, Chris *An Introduction to the Science of Graphology: Handwriting Analysis*. Eastbourne, Quintet, 1995

Morland, Lucy F. 'James Backhouse and After' in *The Centenary of Australian Quakerism 1832–1932*. Hobart, 1933

Moseley, Malcolm J. (ed) *Social Issues in Rural Norfolk*. Norwich, Centre of East Anglian Studies, 1978

Mourot, Suzanne *This Was Sydney: A Pictorial History from 1788 to the Present Time*. Sydney, Ure Smith, 1969

'Mr Taylor on Poisons' in *British and Foreign Medico-chirurgical Review*, Vol. 2 (1848), pp.364–6

Murray, James *Sydney: An Illustrated History*. Melbourne, Lansdowne, 1974

Nash, Henry *Reminiscences of Berkhamsted*. Berkhamsted, Cooper and Nephews, 1890

Nicholson, Ian H. *Shipping Arrivals and Departures, Sydney, 1826–40*. Canberra, Roebuck, 1964

Noakes, Richard J. 'Telegraph is an Occult Art: Cromwell Fleetwood Varley and the Diffusion of Electricity to the Other World' in *British Journal for the History of Science*, 1999, 32, pp.421–49

Oats, M. and W. *A Biographical Index of Quakers in Australia before 1862*, Hobart, M. and W. Oats, 1982 [ML ref: Ref 1/Q289.60922/1]

Oats, W.N. *Backhouse and Walker: A Quaker View of the Australian Colonies 1832–38*, Blubber Head Press in association with the Australian Yearly Meeting of the Religious Society of Friends, 1981

'On the Duty of the Chaplain of a Prison with regard to Confessions made to him in his Official Capacity' in *Jurist*, Vol. 9, No. 436 (17 May 1845), pp.138–9

Ouellette, Jennifer *Black Bodies and Quantum Cats: Tales from the Annals of Physics*. New York, Penguin, 2005

'Patients Poisoned by Prussic Acid' in *Annual Register, or a View of the History, Politics and Literature of the Year 1828*. London, Baldwin and Craddock, 1829

Perkin, Harold *The Age of the Railway*. Newton Abbot, David and Charles, 1970

Pharmaceutical Society of Australia: A scandalously short introduction to the history of pharmacy – Chapter 7: The Australian Scene [http://www.psa.org.au/site.php?id=777]

Pike, Richard *Remarkable Religious Anecdotes*. London, Hamilton, Adams and Co., 1882

Pitman, E.R. *Elizabeth Fry*. London, W.H. Allen and Co., 1994

Pollock, Frederick Macready's *Reminiscences and Selections from his Diaries and Letters*. London, Macmillan and Co., 1875

Potter, Harry *Hanging in Judgment: Religion and the Death Penalty in England from the Bloody Code to Abolition*. London, SCM Press, 1993

Prescott, George Bartlett *History, Theory, and Practice of the Electric Telegraph*. Boston, Ticknor and Fields, 1866

Presnail, James *Chatham: The Story of a Dockyard Town and the Birthplace of the British Navy*. Chatham, Corporation of Chatham, 1952

Quinn, Stephen *Convergent Journalism: The Fundamentals of Multimedia Reporting*. New York, P. Lang, 2005

Reaney, P.H. *A Dictionary of British Surnames*. London, Routledge and Kegan Paul, 1970

Review of 'Remarks and Comments on the Medical and Chemical Evidence Adduced at the trial of John Tawell' by G.L. Strauss in *London Medical Gazette* 4 Apr 1845, pp.860–6

Robbins, Michael *The Railway Age*. Harmondsworth, Penguin, 1965

Roberts, Steven *Distant Writing: A History of the Telegraph Companies in Britain between 1838 and 1868* [http://distantwriting.co.uk/default.aspx]

Robinson, Gwennah *The Book of Hemel Hempstead and Berkhamsted*. Chesham, Barracuda Books, 1975

Robinson, Henry Morton *Science Versus Crime*. London, G. Bell and Sons, 1937

Roe, Michael *Quest for Authority in Eastern Australia, 1835–51*. Melbourne, Melbourne University Press, 1965

Rose, June *Elizabeth Fry: A Biography*. London, Macmillan, 1980

Ryan, Frank *Tuberculosis: The Greatest Story Never Told*. Bromsgrove (Worcestershire), Swift, 1992

Rye, Walter *A History of Norfolk*. London, Elliot Stock, 1885

Rye, Walter *Norfolk Families*. Norwich, Goose and Son, 1911–13

Sabine, Robert *The Electric Telegraph*. London, Virtue Brothers and Co., 1867

Sclater, P.L.(ed.) *A Record of the Progress of the Zoological Society of London during the Nineteenth Century*. London, William Clowes and Sons, 1901

Scott, G.R. *The History of Capital Punishment*. London, Torchstream Books, 1950

Seddon, Peter J. *The Law's Strangest Cases: Extraordinary But True Incidents from Over Five Centuries of Legal History*. London, Robson Books, 2001

'Sensational Murder Recalled' – Newspaper cutting (c1910) in *Garish Collection 16: Biography* [HLS]

Simmons, J. and Biddle, G. (eds.) 'Telegraph' in *Oxford Companion to British Railway History: from 1603 to the 1990s*. Oxford, Oxford University Press, 1997, p.502

Simmons, Jack *The Victorian Railway*. London, Thames and Hudson, 1995

Skae, David *Trial of John Tawell for the Murder of Sarah Hart with Prussic Acid.* 1845 (self-published pamphlet – see Google books – previously published as article in *Northern Journal of Medicine*)

Slater Ian, *Friends Meeting House, Great Yarmouth: A Brief History* (monograph). 1994

Some transactions of the Belfast Clinical and Pathological Society, 1856–7: Opening of the Fourth Session [http://www.users.zetnet.co.uk/jil/ums/bcps/tbcps_s4.pdf]

Squier, G.O. *Telling the World.* Baltimore, Williams and Wilkins Co., 1933

Standage, Tom *The Victorian Internet: The Remarkable Story of the Telegraph and the Nineteenth Century's On-line Pioneers.* London, Weidenfeld and Nicolson, 1998

Stephenson, P.R. *The History and Description of Sydney Harbour.* Adelaide, Rigby, 1966

Stevenson, Charles *With Unhurried Pace: A Brief History of Quakers in Australia*, Religious Society of Friends (Quakers) in Australia, Toorak, 1974

Stoke Newington Quakers – Early History [http://www.stokenewington-quakers.org.uk/nbhist1.html]

Strauss, G.L.M. *Reminiscences of an Old Bohemian.* London, Tinsley Brothers, 1883

Sutherland, L.B. 'More about the Uxbridge Old Bank' in *Uxbridge Record*, No. 27 (September 1977)

Sweeney, Christopher *Transported in Place of Death.* Melbourne, Macmillan, 1981

Sylvanus 'The Bye-lanes and Downs of England, with turf scenes and characters' in *Bentley's Miscellany*, Vol. 25 (1849), p.603

Tallack, William *Peter Bedford, The Spitalfields Philanthropist.* London, S.W. Partridge, 1865

'Tawell, John (1784–1845)' in *Quaker Dictionary of Biography* [LSF manuscript]

'Tawell, the Convict Chemist' in Newspaper Cuttings Vol. 116 (no page) [ML ref: F991.1/N; FM4/2277]

Tawell, Thomas E. 'Life has been great' (unpublished memoir), 1953 [provided by descendants]

Taylor, Alfred Swaine, *On Poisons in Relation to Medical Jurisprudence and Medicine.* Philadelphia, Blanchard and Lea, 1859

Tegg, William *Posts and Telegraphs: Past and Present.* London, William Tegg and Co., 1878

Ternant, A.L. *The Telegraph*. London, George Routledge and Sons, 1895

'The Evidence in Palmer's case' in *The American Law Register* Vol.5 (1856–7), pp.43–4

'The Late Murders' (originally published in the *Law Magazine*) in *Littell's Living Age*, No. 57 (14 Jun 1845), pp.515–19

The Annual Register, or a View of the History and Politics of the Year 1845. London, F. and J. Rivington, 1846

The Great Western Railway in *The Times* 2 Jun 1838 p.6 & 5 Jun 1838 p.5

'The London Coffee House' in *British Muslim Heritage* [http://www.masud.co.uk/ISLAM/bmh/BMH-IRO-coffee_houses.htm]

The Norfolk Churches site: Aldeby [http://www.norfolkchurches.co.uk/aldeby/aldeby.htm]

Timbs, John *Club Life of London*. London, Richard Bentley, 1866

'Toxicology: The Trial of John Tawell for the Murder of Sarah Hart with Hydrocyanic Acid' in *Pharmaceutical Journal: A Weekly Record of Pharmacy and Allied Sciences*, Pharmaceutical Society of Great Britain, Vol. 4 (1844–45), pp.456–61

Townsend, William Charles, *Modern State Trials: Revised and Illustrated with Essays and Notes*. London, Longman, Brown, Green and Longmans, 1850

Travers, Robert 'The Apothecary' in *Rogues' March: A Chronicle of Colonial Crime in Australia*. Melbourne, Hutchinson, 1973

Turnbull, Lucy Hughes *Sydney: Biography of a City*. Sydney, Random House, 1999

Tutton, Michael *Paddington Station 1833–54*. Clwyd, Railway and Canal Historical Society, 1999

Verge, W.G. *John Verge: Early Australian Architect – His Ledger and His Clients*. Sydney, Wentworth Books, 1962

Victorian London Buildings, Monuments and Museums: Hall of Commerce [http://www.victorianlondon.org/buildings/hallofcommerce.htm]

Walvin, James *The Quakers: Money and Morals*. London, John Murray, 1997

Watson, Katherine D. 'Criminal Poisoning in England and the Origins of the Marsh Test for Arsenic' in Bertomeu-Sanchez, J.R. and Nieto-Galan, A. *Chemistry, Medicine and Crime*. Sagamore Beach (USA), Science History Publications, 2006

Watson, Katherine D. 'Medical and Chemical Expertise in English Trials for Criminal Poisoning, 1750–1914' in *Medical History* 50 (3) 1 Jul 2006 pp.373–90

Watson, Katherine D. *Poisoned Lives: English Poisoners and Their Victims.* London, Hambledon and London, 2004

Whatling, John *The Royal Navy at Chatham: 1900-2000.* Liskeard, Maritime Books, 2003

White, Jerry *London in the Nineteenth Century.* London, Jonathan Cape, 2007

Whitney, Janet *Elizabeth Fry: Quaker Heroine.* London, George G. Harrap and Co., 1937

Whorton, James *The Arsenic Century: How Victorian Britain was Poisoned at Home, Work and Play.* Oxford, Oxford University Press, 2010

Wiener, Martin J. *Men of Blood: Violence, Manliness and Criminal Justice in Victorian England.* Cambridge, Cambridge University Press, 2004

Wiener, Martin J. *Reconstructing the Criminal: Culture, Law and Policy in England, 1830–1914.* Cambridge, Cambridge University Press, 1990

Williams, Archibald, *The Romance of Modern Invention.* London, C. Arthur Pearson, 1903

Wilson, C. and Pitman, P. 'John Tawell' in *Encyclopaedia of Murder.* London, Arthur Barker, 1961

Wilson, Colin *Written in Blood: A History of Forensic Detection.* Wellingborough, Equation, 1989

Windsor, David Burns *The Quaker Enterprise: Friends in Business.* London, Frederick Muller, 1980

Wohl, Anthony S. *Endangered Lives: Public Health in Victorian Britain.* Cambridge, Harvard University Press, 1983

Woodall, W.O. *A Collection of Reports of Celebrated Trials, Civil and Criminal.* London, Shaw and Sons, 1873

Woodley, Len 'Dressed in the Garb of a Kwaker' in *Deadly Deeds! A Compilation of Buckinghamshire Murder Cases.* Dunstable, The Book Castle, 2003

INDEX

ABOUT THE AUTHOR

Carol Baxter is the prize-winning author of three popular histories with a criminal bent – *An Irresistible Temptation, Breaking the Bank* and *Captain Thunderbolt and His Lady* – all of which have been published to critical acclaim in her native Australia. Previously, she was General Editor of the Biographical Database of Australia and, before that, Project Officer of the Australian Biographical and Genealogical Record, in which roles she edited many records relating to convicts transported to Australia to serve out their sentences. These helped her to discover the subjects for her tales of true crime. She is a Fellow of the Society of Australian Genealogists and an adjunct lecturer at the University of New England (NSW). A full-time writer and speaker, she lives in Sydney.